THE ARCHITECT'S SECRET

ALSO BY J. MORDAUNT CROOK

The British Museum (*Penguin*)

The Greek Revival (*John Murray*)

The History of the King's Works
Volumes V and VI 1660–1851
CO-AUTHOR (HMSO)

C.L. Eastlake's
History of the Gothic Revival
EDITOR (*Leicester University Press*)

William Burges and the High Victorian Dream
(*John Murray*)

Alex Haig and the Victorian
Vision of the Middle Ages
CO-AUTHOR (*Allen and Unwin*)

The Dilemma of Style:
Architectural Ideas from the
Picturesque to the Post-Modern
(*John Murray*)

John Carter and the Mind
of the Gothic Revival
(*Society of Antiquaries*)

The Rise of the *Nouveaux Riches*: Style
and Status in Victorian and Edwardian Architecture
(*John Murray*)

THE ARCHITECT'S SECRET

*Victorian Critics
and the
Image of Gravity*

J. MORDAUNT CROOK

Joe Mordaunt Crook

JOHN MURRAY
Albemarle Street, London

First published in 2003
by John Murray (Publishers) Ltd,
50 Albemarle Street, London W1S 4BD

The moral right of the author has been asserted

A catalogue record for this book is available from the British Library

ISBN 0-7195-6057 8

Typeset in Monotype Garamond by Servis Filmsetting Ltd

Printed and bound in Great Britain by
Clays Ltd, St Ives plc

Contents

Illustrations

Introduction

WHAT IS THE secret of beauty in architecture? Critics have puzzled over that conundrum for centuries, not least the architectural writers of the Victorian period. This short book focuses on four influential Victorian critics – George Aitchison, Benjamin Webb, Beresford Hope and Coventry Patmore – and charts their responses to one of the eternal problems of art: the enigma of architectural form. None of these critics has been studied before in any detail, so this is a book which breaks a good deal of new ground. Each chapter began as a lecture delivered to a sophisticated but non-specialist audience; and each retains, I hope, the flavour of an academic entertainment.

Lecturing is an ephemeral art. More than most forms of communication it depends for its effect on accidents of time and place. In the field of architectural history its greatest practitioners – Harry Goodhart-Rendel (1887–1959) and Sir John Summerson (1904–92) – managed to combine impeccable preparation with an actor's instinct for timing and tone. Both claimed to doubt the wisdom of publishing lectures as essays, and both seem to have overcome that particular doubt fairly easily,

Goodhart-Rendel with *Vitruvian Nights* (1932), Summerson with *Heavenly Mansions* (1949). As academics, both achieved their greatest success as Slade Professor at Oxford, and both eventually published their Oxford lectures; Goodhart-Rendel as *English Architecture Since the Regency* (1953), Summerson in a variety of learned journals. Although both men were architects by avocation – Goodhart-Rendel had a sizeable architectural practice[1] – both seem to have found their greatest satisfaction in the delivery of lectures to a live audience. But when a lecture is expanded for publication, dressed up with references and appendices, it changes its very nature. It ceases to be a lecture and adopts the format of a study. So the four lectures presented here, thematically subtitled 'The Image of Gravity', appear in the guise of academic studies: performances re-fashioned in tranquillity. Their starting point has to be one of Summerson's slimmer volumes, *Victorian Architecture: Four Studies in Evaluation* (Columbia UP, 1970).

Summerson's *Four Studies* began life as the Bampton Lectures, delivered in 1968 at Columbia University, New York, and repeated several times at various locations in London. For my own generation of scholars, they explored for the first time the intellectual climate within which Victorian architecture flourished: a climate of discovery and doubt, eclecticism and evolution. Summerson pursued this theme by means of a series of analyses: two Victorian railway stations, King's Cross and St Pancras; two London churches, by E.B. Lamb and G.E. Street; and one Victorian architectural competition, for the Royal Courts of Justice in the Strand. By 1968 Summerson himself was well on the way to becoming an historical document, a link between the Gothic Revival and the Modern Movement. In the 1920s, as an apprentice architect, he sat at the feet of Sir Giles Gilbert Scott. In the 1930s, as a fledgling journalist, he commented month by month on the new-built icons of modernism. In the 1940s, he trailed the streets of London, picking his way through wartime debris, photographing what was left. And in succeeding decades, as Curator of Sir John Soane's Museum, he lived to do battle with brutalists and post-modernists, conservationists and cranks. His career became a living commentary on twentieth-century architectural thinking.[2]

Even before his Bampton Lectures, Summerson had begun to project his own doubts – the anxieties of a sceptical modernist – further and further back, to illuminate the psyche of his Victorian predecessors. 'Every Victorian building of any consequence', he explained, 'is a statement of stylistic belief . . . Nowhere is there any escaping this question of style . . . [Even so, this] interest in choice of style is to us something totally unreal.'[3] That was surely a voice from his own past, the voice of an architect still clinging to the verities of the Modern Movement. A generation later, we know rather better – or worse. As the 1970s gave way to the 1980s, that coalition of uncertainties which we learned to call post-modern dissolved one after another the cherished assumptions of the early modernists. Choice returned to the studio drawing-board. Just as High Victorian architecture seemed doomed to look in vain for an acceptable rationale of its own processes of design, so post-modern thinking seemed to separate itself for ever from the comfort of theoretical consensus. Choice – with all its attendant dilemmas – emerged as the correlative of plurality. It was the historical implications of this stylistic plurality – we might call it the aesthetics of abundance – which I decided to explore in my own lectures at Oxford, the Slade and Waynflete Lectures of 1979–80 and 1985–6. These were eventually published as *The Dilemma of Style: Architectural Ideas from the Picturesque to the Post-Modern* (John Murray, 1987).

Summerson himself was well aware in the 1980s that architectural theory seemed to be sinking into intellectual quicksand. But so much confusion made for fruitful debate. It was a good time to be an architectural critic; a rather less easy time to be a practising architect. After nearly fifty years of intellectual consensus, a whole register of Victorian uncertainties had returned. This 'multiplication of stylistic attitudes', Summerson noted in 1970, 'represents the bedevilment of architectural conviction.'[4] The old mantras of form and function had apparently been relativised out of existence. One solution – as I tried to explain in *The Dilemma of Style* – was to think of architecture not just as structure but as an image of the structural process; in effect, as an inevitable statement of style: a way of building codified in imagistic form. By the time of his articles on James Stirling in the mid 1980s, Summerson had himself developed a not dissimilar position, based on linguistic analogies.[5] But by then he was no longer lecturing. His presence at the podium – elegant, astringent, allusive – had become a memory, a magically potent memory for any scholar cutting his critical teeth in the 1960s and 1970s.

Summerson's greatest gift as a lecturer lay in his genius for exposition. 'You are not the modern Ruskin,' John Betjeman told him in 1946; 'you are the modern Fergusson.' In other words, the rational in his makeup was stronger than the romantic. But that did not mean there was no room for cakes and ale. 'You have a wonderful acid style,' Betjeman added; but 'I keep seeing you in my mind's eye with that curled lip and sudden laughter.'[6] Summerson's lectures and broadcasts, notably a radio series entitled *The Classical Language of Architecture* (1963) – yes, a radio series: his words needed no illustration – were invariably models of lucidity. No plan was too complex, no precedent too arcane. He could disentangle the structural imperatives – the sty-

word about design: William Butterfield. Our third critic, A.J.B. Beresford Hope, was the recognised leader of the Gothic party in the Victorian Battle of the Styles. But he was also the man who popularised the notion of Progressive Eclecticism, an evolutionary approach to design which ultimately destroyed the medieval idiom which both he and Webb had done so much to re-create. Finally, Coventry Patmore – better known, of course, as a poet – is here revealed as an architectural critic of extraordinary perception. Patmore, in fact, turns out to be the only man of his generation who saw through the fog of eclectic forms to the eternal principle which underlies great architecture at all times and in all places: the expression of gravitational thrust.

Summerson's *Four Studies* opened up the whole question of 'failure' in Victorian architecture. I can see him now, lecturing in London on that very subject – with Sir Nikolaus Pevsner in the chair – facing down a hostile audience in formal suit and Harrovian tie. Betjeman loved his 'cool Harrovian prose'. But Summerson preferred to explore a variety of questions rather than commit himself to any particular answer; and in examining the 'failure' of nineteenth-century architecture he somehow blurred the distinction between 'failure' and 'a sense of failure'. The Victorians – as I try to explain in these four studies – judged themselves too harshly. As children of the post-modern revolution, we can now see this more clearly than Summerson felt able to do. Where the Victorians saw failure – and Summerson perceived a sense of failure – we see instead a plethora of achievement. Where they saw unrelieved chaos, we see today the rich, productive chaos of an age of eclecticism. The great Victorian debate turned out in the end to be a laboratory of critical theory. And from it emerged at least two keys to the mystery of architectural form, one labelled 'image' and one labelled 'expression': the image of the structural process and the expression of gravitational thrust.

Finally, what is the evidence on which these studies are based? Victorian culture was above all a culture of the word. The explosion of literacy, the mechanisation of printing techniques, the globalisation of publishing: each contributed to an extraordinary outpouring of serial publications throughout the nineteenth century. Newspapers, journals and periodicals multiplied endlessly at local, national and international level. The range and depth of material available to the historian is almost overwhelming. And the problem of scale is compounded by the problem of anonymity. The bulk of Victorian periodical literature was consciously, self-consciously, anonymous. So any historian of the Victorian press – even with the *Wellesley Index* at his elbow – must constantly play the part of detective, ransacking diaries and correspondence in pursuit of clues to attribution. Not least in the field of architecture. As architectural practice achieved higher professional status – demarcated from mere building or engineering – so the architectural press expanded exponentially. And the ramifications of architectural debate can be traced far beyond the professional press, through innumerable non-professional journals, political, religious, artistic, literary. As an appendix to these studies I have therefore included four bibliographies, mostly consisting of articles in periodicals, many attributed for the first time. Of our four critics, Aitchison signed most of his writings, and subsequent scholarship has identified most of Patmore's. But Benjamin Webb and Beresford Hope have remained until now most obstinately anonymous. This is particularly tantalising, since their pronouncements – sometimes, no doubt, conjoined – are peculiarly various. In tone their articles are trenchant, even vicious: Lord Derby christened the *Saturday Review* the *Saturday Scorpion*; John Bright called it the *Saturday Reviler*.[7] The theme of nearly all their writings, of course, is architecture; but their readership must have been extraordinarily diverse. For architecture is a social art; and the social context of Victorian design traverses the entire spectrum of Victorian thinking. In these four studies – each based on a close reading of Victorian periodical literature – I have therefore had to narrow the territory of debate. I have concentrated on the writings of one particular group of writers, within one particular generation. And within that generation, within that group, I have singled out one particular topic – but a topic whose implications remain perennially resonant: the Victorian concept of style.

So now, at last, to business. Victorian architecture is treated here as a focus of Victorian attitudes rather than simply as an archaeological puzzle. There are four chapters, and four writers. Each chapter stands on its own; but each, I hope, contributes to a central theme. Each of my chosen writers struggled endlessly with the nature of architectural language. George Aitchison dreamed of grafting new technology onto an older system of visual values. Benjamin Webb set out to explain – among many other things – the making of a private vision: Butterfield's aesthetic of reality. A.J.B. Beresford Hope – strutting a bigger political stage – contrived to propagate something more elusive still: the virtues of eclecticism in a world of cultural imperialism. And, finally, Coventry Patmore – poet and critic – came near to achieving the impossible. He managed to distil the whole conspectus of architectural theory into a single arresting theme: the imagery of gravitational control, imagery which, through signals of stability and strength, tends to order – and will always order – our perception of architectural form. In this he hit upon a simple truth which becomes obvious only when it is repeated. A blank wall tells us nothing about the dynamics of construction; its negativity is illegible; it sends out no signals of tectonic control. But through pattern and symbol, through intelligible signs, through moulding and massing, that same blank wall can become an instrument of information, an ordered construct, part of an endless dialogue between the architect and his audience: strength plus the perception of strength. That is where architecture and engineering meet. Hence the central relevance of Patmore's thesis: the imagistic power of gravity.

Reading these four studies may require a little perseverance, but not I hope too much. It is the historian's duty to re-create the past in words intelligible to the present. I have tried to catch the temper of Victorian debate, remembering where I can the advice of one wise historian: keep on reading until you hear people talking.[8] And there, I suppose, we might leave it. But an architectural historian has to do something more: he must look as well as listen; he must open his eyes to the language of tectonic form. Hence the insertion in the text of explanatory photographs; sometimes independently chosen, but illustrating wherever possible a single controlling theme. For architecture has its own voice, speaking to the eye; its own vocabulary, speaking to the mind.[9] And these four Victorian critics understood at least a little of its mystery. So take them on their own terms; be gentle with their verbosity; try looking at architecture through their eyes; and keep on reading until you see buildings speak.

1. George Atchison (1825–1910):
'Architecture has fallen upon evil times'

Groping in the Dark:

George Aitchison and the Burden of History

'Architecture has fallen upon evil times.'

George Aitchison, 1883

IN A CHARACTERISTIC essay G.M. Young set out to find 'the greatest Victorian': not *Victorianum maximus* ('greatest of the Victorians') but *Victorianum maxime* ('most Victorian of the Victorians'). After some deliberation he chose Walter Bagehot.[1] Using the same criterion – not genius, but representativeness – we might look for the most Victorian architect, and choose not Butterfield or Burges, nor even Gilbert Scott, but George Aitchison. Not for his buildings, which are few, though full of interest, but more for his attitudes, his anxieties, his preoccupations, his priorities. Especially if we choose, as our point of perspective, Queen Victoria's Jubilee of 1897. For in 1898 George Aitchison became, uniquely, President of the RIBA, Royal Gold Medallist, and Professor of Architecture at the Royal Academy – simultaneously.

As an architect and designer, Aitchison was seldom short of work. His list of commissions runs to at least fifty items. And two of his buildings – Leighton House, Kensington (1864–6; 1877–89) and a warehouse in Mark Lane, London (1864) – feature in nearly every survey of Victorian architecture, the first for its polychromy, the second for its cast iron. But he had another career as well. As a lecturer and public speaker he was hugely prolific. The texts of some 120 performances – and his lectures *were* performances – have survived. That means more than half a million words, and probably scores of diagrams and models, hundreds of photographs and thousands of lantern slides, now lost. Polychromy, cast iron, marble and mosaic, stained glass, staircases, mouldings; doorways, windows and balustrades; architectural education; architectural sculpture; Greek architecture, Roman architecture, Byzantine architecture, Islamic architecture, Romanesque architecture, Gothic architecture, Renaissance architecture; above all, Progressive architecture – these were the themes of his lectures and speeches, in particular at the RIBA and at the Royal Academy. For Aitchison performed most publicly as President of the RIBA from 1896 to 1899 and as Lecturer (from 1881 onwards) and Professor of Architecture at the Royal Academy from 1887 to 1905. His style was literary, discursive, occasionally repetitious, sometimes eloquent, always erudite and genial. He had travelled Europe extensively; he was expert in constructional technique; he had a marvellous eye for colour; and he could draw beautifully.[2] His portrait by Alma-Tadema suggests a scholarly, gregarious, rather garrulous bachelor.[3] His photograph makes him look placid, almost smug. And yet, throughout these lectures, over a period of half a century, from the 1850s to the 1900s, there is a manifest sense of doubt, of uncertainty, even of despair.

Why? Because, like Victorian architects of all kinds – from T.L. Donaldson to William Burges, from Sydney Smirke to T.G. Jackson, from J.T. Emmett and Robert Kerr to Gilbert Scott and James Fergusson – Aitchison suffered from a burden both intoxicating and asphyxiating, the inexorable burden of history. For an architect that meant the burden of archaeology, with all the attendant dilemmas of eclecticism.[4] In a world of ideas domin-ated by two conceptual constants – the evolutionary sense and the historicist sensibility – how could architects produce a visual language appropriate to their own age, an age which looked backwards and forwards at the same time? How could they square art and science, past and present, utility and beauty? How could they combine static notions of aesthetic excellence with the progressive imperatives of technology? How, in short, could they serve two masters, History and Progress?

Aitchison's lectures over this half-century are a tantalising commentary on a very tangled story. Their subject, nominally, is History; but their substance, their thematic pulse, is Progress.

How can we 'become good architects'? Aitchison's reply is traditional: 'by studying architecture historically'.[5] No artist – and here he takes his cue from Sir Joshua Reynolds – can ever 'exclude all imitation of others . . . He who resolves never to ransack any mind but his own, will soon . . . be obliged to imitate himself.' Better go back for inspiration to the Ancients. After all, 'poets practise this kind of borrowing without reserve'.[6] To this well-worn linguistic analogy, Aitchison then adds an evolution-ary gloss. 'All the progressive arts – and Pascal says architecture is one of them – progress by the improvement of what has gone before: Art, literature, science, and architecture itself, are like . . . coral islands: each tiny insect adds its mite to the [mass of the mightier] work.'[7]

Now, Aitchison's notion of architectural progress was cer-tainly not original. It owes something to the man he calls that 'great architectural ethnographer', James Fergusson.[8] It owes more to a group of contemporary French theorists, Louis-Joseph Duc, Paul Sédille, César Daly and – most of all – Auguste Choisy.[9] But its lineage stretches back – via the Darwinian hypothesis – to the comparative taxonomy of Cuvier and

Linnaeus.[10] 'The study of comparative architecture', Aitchison explains, 'is as useful to the architect . . . as the study of comparative anatomy is to the physiologist.'[11] For therein lie the secrets of architectural evolution. One day it will be possible to reconstruct the culture of an epoch from the fragments of its architectural monuments, just as 'Cuvier could construct the effigies of extinct animals from one of their bones or talons'.[12] 'We cannot have the icthyosaurus nor the pleisiosaurus [today]; if one were to be created it would [surely] die . . . , for the conditions of its living do not exist. We can have an artificial [specimen] at a pantomime with a man behind the scenes to pull a string and make the wings flap. It is the same with architecture . . . pantomime Greek, or Gothic, or Renaissance [is no more viable today – that is, in 1894 – than] . . . an icthyosaurus, a mastodon or a sabre-toothed tiger.'[13]

So Aitchison's lectures had one overriding aim: to get 'our future architecture . . . out of the slough of antiquarianism in which it is sunk'.[14] Just as Machiavelli 'extracted the art of government' from fragments of Roman history, so we have to distil the art of architecture – that is, the art of making buildings 'joyous . . . stately, terrible or sublime' – from the archaeology of the past. 'Antiquarianism pure and simple is the death warrant of architecture.' We have to use 'the current architectural language of the day'. Just what that language should be, Aitchison never discovered. What he did know was that the function of architects as mere 'costumiers' was 'not a dignified position'.[15]

The lessons of history seemed to Aitchison quite clear. Byzantine architecture had progressed, from a novel method of arcuated and domical construction, through consequential systems of indicative moulding and ornamental form, to a new and distinct architectural style.[16] Similarly Romanesque. Those Romanesque builders, he tells us, were 'the inventors of modern architecture'.[17] How so? Because they got the method right. From pulverised fragments of the Antique they had forged a new structural system of 'titanic grandeur'.[18] Architecture, he repeats, 'involves the creating of organisms'; it is not 'merely the altering of outward forms to please the whim of the day'.[19] Alas, 'the genius of the nineteenth century is mainly devoted to forgery'.[20] Multiplied choice has merely produced multiple plagiarism.[21] 'Modern Gothic', for example, 'is generally as much like the real thing as the Book of Mammon is like the Bible; but even supposing the forgery were so excellent that it would deceive an architect from the Elysian Fields, what then?'[22] It belongs to another age, another people, another Faith. 'We do not want to build in that style now.'[23]

The root of the trouble lay in the changing nature of technology. 'This century', Aitchison announced in 1888, 'differs more from the age preceding it, than that [era] differed from the stone age.' In travel, transport and communication, 'we have almost annihilated time and space'. We have invented explosives which rival the 'power . . . of the earthquake'. Goods can now be produced with a speed once imaginable only in 'fairy stories'. Population and wealth have increased 'in a marvellous degree'. But not without cost. All this machinery has blunted our aesthetic sense with 'every form of exquisite ugliness'.[24] 'Thousands of our fellow-countrymen' have been reduced to 'a lifelong misery' so awful that 'negro slavery appears by comparison to be a paradise'; although in global terms 'nothing analogous to this vast accession of wealth has occurred since the Roman Republic'. It is time 'to pause in the race, to survey [these] heaps of gold, to [examine] the disorganisation of society, and to ask . . . how [it] can be reorganised.'[25]

Meanwhile, architecture alone of the sciences – for it is science as well as art – has compromised its integrity. If the fatal principle of copyism had been employed in other technical fields, 'we should [still] have [catapults] instead of cannon; triremes instead of steam-driven ironclads . . . wick lamps or torches . . . instead of gas or electricity . . . Would Argand ever have made his lamp if he had believed the Romans were unsurpassable? Should we have the steam-engine? Should we know the earth went round the sun? Would the law of gravitation have been found out? It should be as contemptible to copy an old building as [to copy] an old book.'[26] 'I cannot believe that the nation that has given us the steam-engine, the railway, the telegraph, the steamboat, and all the triumphs of iron; that has given us Darwin, Tyndall, Huxley and Herbert Spencer; Parkes, Simpson and Lister; Turner, Leighton and Millais; Wordsworth, Browning, Tennyson, and Swinburne, can have sunk so much below the standard of our semi-barbarous forefathers of the thirteenth century as to be incapable of developing [its own] architecture . . . No, . . . we have got into a wrong groove, and we must get out of it before architecture ever again becomes a progressive art.'[27]

That 'wrong groove' was the principle of revival, what art historians have come to call the historicist process.[28] Within this carapace of history, Aitchison believed, lurked a real architecture, struggling to get out. But how? 'We . . . want an architecture of our own time, a new architecture; that is a good wish,' he tells his students in 1897. 'But we must know how a new architecture is found. Let us see how it was found in the Middle Ages.'[29] It grew, he implies, by means of a reciprocal evolution: structural expression emerging as symbolic representation. Why not in the nineteenth century? It was all a question of cultural norms. 'The embodying . . . in building . . . of any great idea came as naturally to the people of the Middle Ages as sending a letter to the papers comes now.'[30] In other words, theirs was an age of imagery, ours is an age of language. Today we have poetry in plenty, but no poetry of form. 'Does society desire to have its aspirations embodied in buildings? No, it wants its highest aspirations embodied in an Act of Parliament.'[31]

Aitchison's very first public lectures – at the Architectural Museum in 1856, and at the RIBA in 1857 – set out to draw lessons from the polychromy of ancient and medieval buildings. Brickwork in particular struck him as full of potential: 'warehouses, . . . shot-towers . . . railway chimneys' – all these could be transformed by the use of brick and terracotta. Ordinary buildings could become extraordinary: 'we may [even] hand down to posterity not a lifeless copy . . . but a new system of coloured decoration' in keeping with a world of technological change. Even at this early stage, he declined to engage in any battle of styles. In all past styles, he believed, there were lessons for the present. But 'I am waiting', he reminds his audience, 'like the rest of the world for the new style that is to come.'[32] Seven years later it had yet to appear. But he could still berate his contemporaries – living in an age of iron – for failing to use the new material. 'What is the cause of this?' he asks; 'how can we account for this strange supineness?' The answer lies in 'our education and our want of education'. We are very good at handing down traditional techniques 'from one generation to another'. But with iron we are all 'in the dark'. 'Sooner or later . . . it will come . . . into general use'; better to use it ourselves than leave it to the engineers.[33]

Now, Aitchison came from a background which was as much concerned with engineering as with architecture. Four major architects – T.L. Donaldson, C.R. Cockerell, Sir Charles Barry and T.H. Wyatt – were close family friends.[34] But his degree course at University College, London included structural science

2. Sir J. Hawkshaw, Lockwood Viaduct, Yorkshire (1846–8).
Gravity distributed: the engineering aesthetic

as well as the arts of design. And like his early travelling companion William Burges, he grew up under the shadow of a father much involved with civil engineering. In fact, George Aitchison Senior was reputed to have designed London's 'first incombustible building of iron and brick' – Irongate Wharf, on the Thames (*c.* 1845).[35] As a partner in his father's firm in 1859–61, young Aitchison 'saw a great deal of work of an engineering character on the Chester and Holyhead Railway'.[36] In practice in his own right, from 1861, he was responsible for a number of wharves, warehouses and offices along the Thames, notably Messrs Hubbock's depository and the tobacco warehouse for Victoria Dock. But whereas Burges sublimated his engineering instincts in a riot of medieval forms, Aitchison continued all his life to wrestle with the aesthetic consequences of iron. He saw that the Victorians had equalled the best in literature; they were supreme in science and technology; but their awareness of deficiencies in art and architecture increased as the century wore on. Looking around him, he saw 'everything . . . beautiful and picturesque . . . gradually . . . being extinguished' by the spread of industrialisation.[37]

So was there any hope? In 1864 he saw a glimmer of opportunity in the very plainness and economy of this new age of utility. 'I think', he told his doubting audience, that 'a purity of outline and elegance of proportion, with an almost total absence of ornament might gradually be made to pervade everything, from our buildings to our teaspoons.' Meanwhile, he added, there is no future in 'paraphrases' of the past; in fact they are 'sublimely ridiculous'. Copyism 'cuts at the very root of architecture'; 'it has crippled the natural powers of the architect . . . it has disgusted the bulk of people, who take the same interest in it that they do in heraldry.' What then can be done? We cannot just 'put ugly construction into an ornamental box'; we have somehow to 'make the thing itself graceful [and] elegant'.[38] Then comes his peroration, to an RIBA audience clearly becoming a little restive:

'Has . . . the human mind deteriorated, and are we incapable of making our new constructions beautiful or picturesque? Is the saying of Victor Hugo true, that printing has killed architecture? I trust not . . . I fervently hope that . . . it is only through a sort of infatuated perversity that we are now so wanting in artistic invention. The conservatism of mankind is so great that it is only at certain periods of intellectual convulsion that men will dare to doubt and think . . . The happy invention of Palladio has given us a dispensation from thinking . . . From that time architecture has been blighted by a servile desire of imitation; we have tried Egyptian, Greek, Roman, Byzantine, Romanesque, Gothic of all periods, Italian and French Renaissance . . . Arabic, Chinese . . . Let us now throw [them all] aside . . . let us hold [them] in abomination.'[39]

That was 1864. In that year he designed his most *avant-garde* building, a warehouse at 59–61 Mark Lane, in the City of London. Its façade consisted of three tiers of Byzantine–Gothic arcading decorated with bands of inlaid black mastic. Behind, and independent of, the whole façade is an autonomous fireproof structure of cast iron.[40] The principle of the Chicago skyscraper – Ruskin's wall-veil, adapted to new materials – had here been foreshadowed in miniature. And around the same time Aitchison began his most ambitious design of all: a house and studio in Holland Park, Kensington, for his friend and colleague Frederic Leighton.[41] It started off modestly, with three simple brick bays to the front and a first-floor studio overlooking the garden. Then in 1877–9 came the Arab Hall, a framework for Leighton's glorious collection of iridescent tiles. There is glass from Damascus, and metal from

3. George Aitchison, 59–61 Mark Lane, London (1864).
Gravity transposed: ornament as metaphor

4. George Aitchison, Leighton House, Kensington, London (1864–6; 1877–9): 'A Moorish dream . . . projected from a nineteenth-century mind'

Cairo; there are bronzes from China and silver from Turkey; there are Persian rugs and statuettes from Renaissance Italy, as well as Isnik and Syrian ware; there are marble columns from Caserta, and tiles from, it seems, half the countries of the Middle East: from Damascus, from Rhodes and Egypt, from the tomb of Sakhar on the Indus. There is mosaic by Walter Crane, and alabaster by Boehm; there are birds designed by Caldecott, and still more tiles from the workshop of de Morgan. There is furniture inlaid with ivory; there is black lacquered woodwork touched with gold; there are marble fireplaces set with brass, and a fountain shimmering with reflected light; there is Venetian glass and Nankeen china; there is even a cast of the Parthenon frieze. Leighton House was a bravura display of High Victorian eclecticism. Vernon Lee thought it almost as good as Ravenna: 'Quite the eighth wonder of the world.'[42] And yet, as Leighton reminded his father in 1864, 'architecture and much *ornament* are not inseparable'.[43] Despite the addition of yet another studio, supported on plain iron columns, Aitchison cannot himself have been content with his creation. Mrs Haweis's description – 'a Moorish dream . . . projected from a nineteenth-century mind' – must have seemed a little too close for comfort.[44] His doubts remained, and his lectures continued to belabour the architectural deficiencies of his own age.

During the 1870s Aitchison had less to say publicly: a wise course for any practising architect. But he had in effect already turned from architecture to interior decoration – the polychrome rooms he designed for 15 Berkeley Square, for example;[45] or the dining room at 52 Princes Gate, designed for Mrs Eustace Smith, with a painted frieze by Leighton. Both were virtuoso performances. Aitchison was at his best as a colourist: his decorated ceiling at Goldsmiths' Hall (1871) must be one of the finest in London. And in 1878–89, at 1–2 South Audley Street, he even indulged in a minor riot of Flemish Renaissance ornament. But by the 1880s he had clearly become disenchanted with the whole business of architectural practice. 'Architecture', he announced in 1883, 'has fallen upon evil times.' In part the cause of the decline had been social: architects had come to think of themselves as gentlemen rather than bricklayers. 'Architects must free themselves from this nonsense,' he announces; 'and strive to be great constructors, doing what they can to impart character to . . . buildings.' 'Architects are before everything constructors, and paper architects are a mere burlesque.' All true, no doubt; all true. But there was also a deeper cause. Generally speaking, architecture is two things: it is science and it is art. 'The scientific mind with no art, and the artful mind with no science,' he explains, 'are . . . like two horses pulling in opposite directions.' For example, 'there is a wonderful scope for ingenuity in trying to make a girder sightly'.[46] 'I believe we could [even] make a steam-engine beautiful, or one of the hideous abortions of the engineer, if [only] mankind wanted it.'[47] But there is one fundamental obstacle: the utilitarian heresy. 'From the savage upwards,' Aitchison explains in 1886, until the middle of the eighteenth century, 'no one ever made anything without an attempt, however rude, to give it some beauty of form . . . [Alas] this desire ceased amongst civilised nations' with the advent of science, machinery and the market economy. 'From a toasting-fork to a steam-engine, things began to be made for . . . use, and use only.' As a result, 'we . . . have building, but not architecture'.[48]

Aitchison's conundrum – how to turn utility into beauty – went of course to the very root of the matter. Given the historicist mindset of his time, that meant how to make buildings 'beautiful without copying'. Aitchison's answer was hardly original: recapture not the style but the 'mental attitude' of the Middle Ages.[49]

But what did that mean? In Aitchison's eyes, architectural design should aim not at echoes of the tectonic product – as in the Renaissance – but at heightened expressions of the structural system, as in medieval times. According to this view Romanesque, Byzantine and, above all, Gothic represented authentic architecture; that is, evolving structural expression. By the same token, Classicism was not an image but a sham. His reasoning ran as follows. Architecture is above all a constructive art. Painting or sculpture imitate the appearance of nature, but architecture imitates its very process: 'it is an attempt to emulate the higher natural organisms, in the making of a shell for man's [own] use'.[50] In effect, forms evolve from function. But at this point in the argument alarm bells begin to sound: Aitchison seems about to enter a functional blind alley. Surely he was present, at the RIBA in 1863, when William Whewell of Cambridge explained that in fact 'the idea, not the reality, of constructive art governs the form of architecture'?[51] At the last minute, however, our critic regains his balance. He returns to the nub of the problem: 'the proper expression of a mere material need', he concedes, 'does not make architecture';[52] 'architecture appeals to emotions which no mechanical methods can produce'.[53] And it is the business of an architect to play upon those emotions as a musician plays upon an instrument. For architecture is to building as music is to sound; and its art is as 'inseparably bound up with' its science 'as the soul with the body'.[54] For effective imagery, for his means of communication, any architect has to draw upon the culture in which he lives. A Victorian architect, therefore, must express by his designs the mental 'turmoil' of his day.[55] Alas, Aitchison admits, 'we have abandoned the symbolic, the emblematic and the allegorical';[56] in fact, we live 'in an anti-symbolic age'.[57]

Thanks to the 'pernicious legacy'[58] of the 'abominable

Renaissance',[59] he believed, architects had been 'groping in the dark'[60] for half a millennium.[61] Somehow Victorian architects had to absorb the semiotic lessons of the Renaissance without copying its tectonic vices. 'If we use', he tells his students in 1894, 'as we eventually must use, iron and steel for those parts which are to bear great weights, great strains, or to bridge wide spans, and [if we] make the ironwork visible, we will not only find that those new materials will take new shapes . . . [they will] give rise to new advances.'[62] In other words, new needs, new materials, new forms, new aesthetic – in that order.

'No man', Aitchison told his students in 1883, 'can walk down the vast nave of the Crystal Palace and see its filmy construction and its flood of light without thankfulness and admiration.'[63] Here surely was a symbol worthy of 'the Second Iron Age'.[64] 'The difficulty in using iron aesthetically', however, 'is that from its very strength it tends to effacement, setting aside all the difficulties arising from its expansion and contraction, its condensation of damp vapour into water, its rusting, and the difficulty of making water-tight joints with . . . glass . . . [And of course] it involves four or five times as much time [in design] as similar work in the older materials.'[65] Not that the use of iron was in any way new: there had been wrought-iron girders in the Baths of Caracalla 1600 years before.[66] What was new was the attempt to give metallic forms appropriate aesthetic expression. Architects had traditionally 'joined the art of construction to the art of expression'. With the separation of the architectural and engineering professions, however, engineers 'simply solved the constructive problems, so that their structures bear the same resemblance to architecture that a woman's skeleton has to the Venus de Milo'.[67] For engineers appeal 'only to the intellectual and not the material side of man'.[68] Somehow the new technology had to be brought

5. Sir Joseph Paxton, Crystal Palace, London (1851–4):
'A single thought and some very ordinary algebra'

within the pale of aesthetics.[69] Conversely, architects must no longer be allowed to indulge in pictorial composition. All this involves risks: but 'eccentric ugliness is better than second-hand beauty, if it be the right step forward'.[70]

The most promising steps forward towards the end of the nineteenth century seemed to be visible not in London but in Paris. There Aitchison saw iron used for the first time convincingly, in architectural form, by Baltard, by Hittorf, by Labrouste, by Sédille.[71] Two passages from the writings of Émile Zola struck him as prophetic. First, the contrast between the sixteenth- to eighteenth-century church of St-Eustache and the nineteenth-century Central Market, Les Halles:

'This is a curious conjunction . . . this end of a chancel framed in an avenue of cast iron . . . One will kill the other; the iron will kill the stone; and the time is nigh . . . Don't you see, here is a whole manifesto; it is modern art, realism, naturalism, whatever you like to call it . . . grown big in the face of ancient art . . . In any case the church is of bastard architecture; the Middle Ages was dying there, and the Renaissance was only lisping . . . Have you noticed what churches they build for us now? They are like anything you please, like libraries, like observatories, like pigeon-houses, like barracks; but certainly no one believes the Almighty dwells therein. The masons of the Almighty are dead . . . Since the beginning of the century one single original monument has been built, a monument which has been copied from nothing, which has sprung up naturally from the soil of the epoch; and that is the Central Market . . . A swaggering work, and it is only a timid revelation of the twentieth century to come.'[72]

The second passage concerns the vision given by Zola to his hero Claude Lantier, of the birth of modern architecture:

'If ever there was a century in which architecture should have a style of its own, it is the century shortly to begin, the new century . . . the breeding ground of a new people. Down with the Greek temples; there is no use or place for them in modern society! Down with the Gothic cathedrals; belief in legends is dead! Down, too, with the delicate colonnades . . . of the Renaissance . . . [they can] never house modern democracy! What is wanted . . . [is] an architectural formula to fit that democracy . . . something big and strong and simple, the sort of thing that [is] already asserting itself in railway stations and market halls, the solid elegance of metal girders, developed and refined . . . raised to the status of . . . beauty.'[73]

But how? Where was this new vocabulary of form? There was no easy guide, even in the Paris of Émile Zola. For there could be no rule-of-thumb canons of architectural beauty. 'To some extent,' as Aitchison explained in 1897, 'our compasses must be in our eye.'[74] 'Aesthetic advance is possible, if we go the right way about it.' Following the American theorist Leopold Eidlitz, he suggests the following formula: first seek out statical solutions to constructional problems, then translate them into symbolic form.[75] 'That is easy to talk about,' he admits in 1891, 'but not easy to do; at present [it] . . . is mainly done by association.'[76] For a start, we lack some of the basic techniques: 'the art of moulding is as much neglected now as the science of statics.'[77] More important, society has become physically so materialistic, and intellectually so 'absorbed in physical science', that it no longer seeks to 'embody [its] aspirations in architecture.'[78] At present, 'our souls are full of deadness . . . to the highest forms of art'; and a rich man would prefer to give a banquet than build a house.[79]

★

This sense of gloom pervades Aitchison's lectures. 'It may be', he told the young men of the Architectural Association in 1884, 'that the grand gift of architectural invention is only to be found in what we call new races, barbarous races who . . . suddenly . . . find themselves conquerors . . . such races as the Arabs and the Normans. Amongst civilised nations, the Roman was the only one I know that slowly evolved a style . . . This style we now call Byzantine.' Today, he adds, our 'passion for change' has merely produced a 'Babel of architecture'.[80] And so, 'we have no national architecture', he notes glumly in 1886; 'whether anything . . . stable and progressive is to come out of the present chaos I cannot prophesy.' The relativistic approach of his contemporaries – a different style for each building type – he believed to be fundamentally wrong: 'an abominable heresy' produced by 'the present jumble of styles'.[81] And the 'mental fetters' which chained architects to the past seemed to be perpetually reinforced by the preferences of prevailing culture.[82] The Victorians, he believed, had got the architecture they deserved: new technology loaded with cultural luggage. 'We have no national architecture at present,' he repeats in 1887; 'many of us get our living by tinkering up old buildings . . . but it is archaeology not architecture.'[83] We have 'mastered . . . the bygone styles,' he notes again in 1891, and adapted them 'to the wants and uses of the present day . . . [But] we have [yet] to take [that key] step forward' – translating 'our sense of beauty and aesthetic fitness' into 'the foundation of a new style.' In particular, we have still to take our new materials, especially iron, and give them 'the vigorous stamp of architectural beauty'.[84]

'Must [then] we abandon ourselves to despair?' he wonders in 1892. Well, not quite: 'a new style is not to be enacted in a day nor in a lifetime.'[85] But by 1894 he is certainly getting restive:

'there is [still] no architecture in Christendom that . . . can be called good, true and distinctive of the present century.'[86] 'Surely we have something else to say in architecture than they had in the sixteenth century, not to speak of the thirteenth?'[87] By 1895 his patience is wearing very thin: 'there is not much time left' for the nineteenth century; let us pray that 'the twentieth century' at least will 'have an architecture of its own', not just 'a chaos of paraphrases'.[88] By 1897–8 he is 'almost in despair':[89] architecture is in a state of 'suspended animation';[90] still 'I am doing my best to dispel . . . dead styles . . . from . . . students' minds';[91] for 'if architecture cannot progress, it must be swept into the limbo where heraldry, necromancy, astrology and perpetual motion now moulder in peace.'[92]

By the turn of the new century Aitchison was becoming desperate. 'I feel ashamed,' he mourned in 1900; 'it is humiliating . . . It is too melancholy'; architects today are merely keepers of 'a fancy dress shop'.[93] Architects should be 'poets in structure';[94] and until architecture gets back to its structural roots, 'we are only groping around in the dark', stumbling among the debris of history.[95] 'I am not a prophet,' he admits in 1902, but as yet 'I see no signs' of 'something new.'[96]

By this time the editor of *The Builder*, which had patiently published hundreds of thousands of Aitchison's melancholy words, was also becoming restive. Repeated eulogies of the Crystal Palace, Statham complained, were really beside the point: after more than a hundred lectures, 'the problem' of iron, the mystery of its aesthetic properties, still remained 'to be solved'.[97] Professors of Architecture, he implied, are not much use if they merely teach us how to doubt.[98] Aitchison was unrepentant: 'when a man is lost in a wood', the best thing you can do is to 'direct him to the road out of it . . . Architecture has been [lost] in a wood since the fifteenth century.'[99] Even so, he was growing weary. The Jeremiah of the Royal Academy resigned his chair in 1905. He died in 1910.

For fifty years George Aitchison had wrestled with the burden of history. To what effect? His lectures cannot be dismissed as eccentric, irrelevant or peripheral. Generations of students listened; thousands of people read them at second hand. His anxieties represented the central concerns of the generality of thinking architects. There was immense confusion and deep concern. As Aitchison put it in 1885, 'the leaders of architectural criticism' are 'like the political leaders in [Ireland]; they do not know what they want, but they are determined to get it.'[100] Or as Viollet-le-Duc famously remarked, Victorian architects calling for a new style were like a chorus of opera singers all shouting 'Here we go' – and never moving an inch.[101] But in the end, after half a century of cogitation, Aitchison was no nearer an answer than he had been at the start.

And in a sense there could be no answer. All architects are born to search, and search in vain, for that magical, alchemical formula which turns 'the prose of building into the poetry of architecture'.[102] Aitchison's problem was the eternal architect's dilemma. 'Architecture', he explained in 1898, 'is above all things a constructive art; but . . . this construction must be clothed in the forms that will give the proper character to the building for the purpose it has to fulfil.'[103] Alas, here lay the great conundrum, first formulated by A.W. Pugin: propriety or truth? Aitchison never resolved that riddle. Nor did he supply an answer to T.L. Donaldson's challenge: 'Are we to have an architecture of our period, a distinct, individual, palpable style of the nineteenth century?'[104] He merely repeated the question, *ad nauseam*. As for social comment, Aitchison really adds nothing but repetition to Ruskin's diagnosis of the distintegrative aesthetic. In his favourite field, cast iron, he merely reiterates the dreams of Ambrose Poynter and William Vose Pickett which he absorbed in the 1840s.[105] In his own practice, he never approaches the prophetic achievements of his Parisian contemporaries. By the end of his life he had retreated to the less contentious field of interior decoration. As his interminable lecture series rolls on – through its half a million printed words – he finds little to add to Kerr's antitheses of archaeology and art, and even less to Fergusson's polarities of utility and beauty. Instead he falls back on Choisy's physiological analogy: architecture as organism, architecture as a microcosm of the evolutionary process. Armed with Choisy's conceptual microscope, he examined the architecture of his own day and found it methodologically defective. Then, re-armed with Eidlitz's teleological telescope, he conjured up an architecture of the future: statical equations couched in symbolic imagery; images of the structural process.[106] Nothing came of it, at least in his own lifetime. In that sense, Aitchison was a failure, and he shared that sense of failure with a whole generation of reluctant historicists.[107]

But the Victorians judged themselves too harshly. 'Failed', after all, as Ford Madox Ford pointed out long ago, is to artists but 'a small word'; for 'every artist when confronted by the immensities of [an] Art which is life [itself] must confess to failure.' Art in that respect – and architecture still more so – will always be 'a game that must be lost'.[108] Aitchison never found the architect's secret. But had he been able to look back at his own age from the vantage point of the twenty-first century, he would have discovered that his demand for a characteristically Victorian style had in fact been answered – though hardly in the way that he hoped.[109] For eclecticism was indeed the nineteenth-century style.[110] If there was a Victorian vernacular – and perhaps that is a contradiction in terms – it was an eclectic vernacular evolving in a complex, pluralistic culture. Gazing at the Victorian age through contemporary, Victorian eyes, Aitchison could see only architectural chaos. Looking at that chaos with modern – dare we say it, post-modern – eyes, he would still have seen chaos, but characteristic chaos: the rich, pluralistic chaos of an age of historicism.

2

The Reality of Brick:

William Butterfield and Benjamin Webb

'Glory be to God for dappled things.'

Gerard Manley Hopkins, 1877

THE LEGEND THAT Keble College, Oxford – in all its bricky glory – was somehow, aesthetically speaking, the responsibility of John Ruskin, is a legend that seems almost indestructible. The truth is that Ruskin had little to do with William Butterfield, and nothing at all to do with Keble. But both Ruskin and Butterfield had one thing in common. They belonged to the same generation, a generation looking for a style rooted in 'reality'; a mystical union of truth and beauty; an architectural Holy Grail. People called it modern Gothic. The difference between them was that Ruskin eventually gave up looking, whereas Butterfield never flinched. To the end of his life he remained a modern Goth. So the debate[1] as to whether Ruskin influenced Butterfield, or Butterfield influenced Ruskin, is really beside the point. If there was any influence, it was reciprocal and indirect. And they were not the only players involved. Both men were part of a larger eclecticism: the search for a new Victorian style, a fusion of past and present, medieval and modern; truthful in its use of materials, real in its relevance and utility. That meant, in the context of the Gothic Revival, a style which spoke

6. William Butterfield (1814–90):
'Thinking for myself'

the language of the new age, but which took its inspiration from the Gothic of both northern and southern Europe. At the end of *The Stones of Venice* in 1853, Ruskin had thrown out a hint as to what form this style might take: 'the pure and perfect forms of Northern [French and English] Gothic, [worked] out with . . . the refinement of Italian art in the details.'[2] It was a constructive proposal, but rather a gnomic utterance.

This movement towards 'reality', towards a modern form of Gothic, had already begun before Ruskin published his *Seven Lamps* in 1849 and his *Stones of Venice* in 1851–3. It was already gathering momentum before Butterfield conceived All Saints, Margaret Street, London (1849; 1850–9). Its origins are to be found in the mid 1840s, firstly in the writing of A.W. Pugin and secondly in the aspirations of the Cambridge Camden Society, better known as the Ecclesiological Society. Now, ecclesiology to early Victorian Anglicans meant the science of Christian worship; in particular, it meant medieval Catholic Christianity in three-dimensional form. And its implications went far beyond aesthetics. Pugin had set out, in words everybody could understand, the architectural theology of truth: form expressing material; layout expressing purpose; silhouette expressing plan; ornament expressing structure. In other words, the 'reality' of function. The ecclesiologists went one step further, turning architectural truths into theological symbols. What could be more 'real' than a pyramid, and what could be less Christian? Only Gothic, they claimed, could combine the symbolism of both architectural and religious truths. Henceforward, truth must have a moral as well as an aesthetic meaning. And sacramentality meant a combination of both: aesthetics and theology in one.[3]

The leaders of this Cambridge Movement – John Mason Neale, Benjamin Webb, Beresford Hope – were young, enthusiastic High Anglicans, aesthetic equivalents of their more theologically-minded Oxford Movement contemporaries. William Butterfield, by contrast, was not a university man: he was working in a builder's yard at the age of sixteen. Nor was he an Anglican by education: he came from a shopkeeping, Nonconformist background. He was not a gentleman. But by 1844 he was a member of the Ecclesiological Society. And soon afterwards he was invited to join an exclusive, secret group known as 'The Engagement' – Gladstone was its leading light – dedicated to Anglican observance and strict personal piety.[4] Thereafter he was always a high-churchman, though never a ritualist.[5] When he was elected to the Athenaeum in 1858, he was supported by the Archbishop of Canterbury and the Bishop of Oxford.[6] So Butterfield operated at the very heart of the Anglican Establishment. But unlike the Cambridge men, he was neither a theorist nor a publicist. He was a practising architect with a sense of mission; a practical idealist. He was 'that typically English combination', noted Goodhart-Rendel, a 'Puritan and Anglo-Catholic, suspicious of pleasure as presumably sinful, rigidly authoritarian, delighting in angular architectural modifications, and searing the eyeballs of his admirers with raw colours of raw materials, cunningly arranged to extricate truth from the enfeebling snares of beauty'. In Keble Chapel we see him 'at his bitterest and best'.[7] Well, maybe; but perhaps we should suspend judgement for a moment, while we examine the context in which Butterfield was operating.

At Balliol College, Oxford in the early 1860s, at least one undergraduate had the wit to see that Butterfield's chapel (1854–7) was actually not aggressive, but really rather 'graceful'.[8] In this he disagreed with the Master, Benjamin Jowett; still more with E.A. Freeman, who called it 'a personal injury' to all Trinity men, especially 'to me'.[9] The undergraduate in question was the 'star of Balliol', Gerard Manley Hopkins. At the time, he entered in his journal a prophetic comment:

'Note. There is now going on what has no parallel that I know of in [the] history of art. Byzantine and Romanesque Architecture started from [the] ruins of Roman [architecture], became itself [a] beautiful style, and died, as Ruskin says, only in giving birth to another [style] more beautiful than itself, Gothic. The Renaissance appears now to be in the process of being superseded by a spontaneous Byzantine style, [for example, Deane and Woodward's Trinity College, Dublin, 1853–7] retaining still some of [the] bad features (such as pilasters, rustic work, etc.) of the Renaissance. These it will throw aside. Its capitals are already as in Romanesque art, most beautiful. Whether the modern Gothic or this spontaneous style conquer does not so much matter, for it is only natural for . . . [this new Byzantine style] to lead to a modern spontaneous Gothic, as [ancient Byzantine once did] in [the] middle ages, only that the . . . [new Byzantine] is putting off what we might be or rather are doing now [i.e., developing modern Gothic. . . . Alternatively, Hopkins concludes,] the two [styles, Byzantine and Gothic,] may coalesce [in a new Victorian eclecticism].'[10]

Hopkins found a glimpse of this future in Butterfield's work. Remember his poem of 1877, 'Pied Beauty': 'all things counter, original, spare, strange'.[11] Visiting Butterfield's church at Babbacombe in Devon just after its completion in 1874, he began by thinking 'it is odd, and the oddness at first sight outweigh[s] the beauty'. But gradually he warmed to the details and the silhouette, and concluded: 'everything very solid and perfect'. Similarly, when Hopkins visited St Mary Magdalen, West

Lavington, Sussex (1850), he found it 'immature and strange'.[12] But – despite continuing unease at Butterfield's manner: the 'rather tiresome' wall mosaic, the overall 'want of rhetoric' – when he revisited All Saints, Margaret Street his original judgement in favour of the architect's 'genius' was confirmed.[13] What we see Hopkins beginning to untangle here is precisely that modern Gothic towards which Butterfield was working. Even so, the question still lingers: what, if anything, did Butterfield's modern Gothic – this new reality – owe to Ruskin?

Ruskin mentioned Butterfield only twice in print, and on neither occasion by name. In the *Seven Lamps* (1880 edition), he dismissed the cloisters of St Augustine's College, Canterbury as 'the stupidest traceries that can be cut cheapest'.[14] At the very end of *The Stones of Venice* in 1853, he had been a little more flattering. Referring to 'Mr Hope's church, in Margaret Street' in London – that is, Butterfield's All Saints – he remarks:

> 'I do not altogether like the arrangements of colour in the brickwork . . . much will depend . . . upon the colouring of [the frescoes; preferably they should be by] . . . either Holman Hunt or Millais . . . [Still,] this church assuredly decides one question conclusively, that of our present capability of Gothic design. It is the first piece of architecture I have seen, built in modern days, which is free from all signs of timidity or incapacity. In general proportion of parts, in refinement and piquancy of mouldings, above all in force, utility and grace of floral enrichment, worked in a broad and masculine manner, it challenges fearless comparison with the noblest work of any time. Having done this, we may do anything.'[15]

High praise, even if Ruskin's optimism turned out to be short-lived. But he was equally, perhaps more, generous about other architects, notably Benjamin Woodward, G.E. Street, S.S. Teulon and Alfred Waterhouse.[16] And on the rest of Butterfield's work – silence. On Keble – nothing at all. And yet, in 1939, a writer as perceptive as Christopher Hobhouse could still call Keble 'intensely Ruskinian'.[17]

By that phrase Hobhouse meant, presumably, 'Italian'; because Ruskin's name – although he did his best to deny it – is irrevocably connected with Italian Gothic.[18] Yet the more closely one examines Butterfield's style, the less specifically Italian it seems. The interior of All Saints has echoes of Italy – the upper chapel of Assisi was often mentioned at the time – but the scale and intensity of pattern is Butterfieldian rather than Italian or Ruskinian. And the details of sculptured or moulded work – the pier capitals modelled on Warmington church, Northamptonshire, for example – are still predominantly English. No doubt there are hints of Butterfield's technique in Ruskin. Under the Lamp of Sacrifice, for example, Ruskin recommended 'chequered patterns, and in general such ornaments as common workmen can execute [; these] may extend over the whole building'.[19] Under the Lamp of Beauty he famously decreed that colour – 'chequers and zig-zags', 'triangle . . . square or circle', 'zones as in the rainbow and the zebra' – should be independent of structural form, applied to plain, broad surfaces and not to points of studied significance.[20] In *Seven Lamps*, again, Ruskin insisted that colour was an attribute of architecture rather than of sculpture: 'sculpture is the representation of an idea, while architecture is itself a real thing. The idea . . . may be coloured by the beholder's mind; but a reality ought to have reality in all its attributes: its colour should be as fixed as its form . . . the colours of architecture should be those of natural stones . . . so put your variegation boldly on the flat wall . . . but be shy of it in capital and moulding.'[21] These instructions were reinforced in *The Stones of Venice* by a striking comparison between structural polychromy and geological formations. 'It is perfectly natural', Ruskin emphasised, 'that the different kinds of stone used in [a wall's] successive courses should be of different colours . . . [Indeed these] horizontal bands of colour . . . are valuable as an expression of horizontal space . . . and . . . in their suggestion of the natural courses of rocks, and beds of the earth itself.' Such analogies, he explained, 'metaphysically justify' the use of banded patterns of colour.[22] Finally, in *Seven Lamps*, under the Lamp of Life, Ruskin had also warned revivalists more generally against the use of *moulded* ornament: 'I believe the only manner of rich ornament that is open to us is the geometrical colour-mosaic . . . [and] much might result from our strenuously taking up this mode of design.'[23]

Well, perhaps: Butterfield's ornament is nothing if not strenuous. But is it Italian? Outside, the echoes at All Saints are rather of North German or Baltic origin: St Mary's at Lübeck, for example. And there are hints of Freiburg-im-Breisgau as well. These are medieval precedents. But comparisons with mid nineteenth-century north European work – that is, patterned polychromy of the early 1840s – could also be made, leading us to the Rhineland Palatinate and even to Copenhagen.[24] And, significantly, it was in February and June 1850 that Charles Fowler, Jnr presented the RIBA with two lectures on the medieval brick and terracotta buildings of north-east Germany and the Baltic coast.[25] The influence of Backstein or Baltic Gothic may be elusive, but it is clearly present. It was after visiting Lübeck that G.E. Street spoke most warmly of the sort of town church that might be a model for All Saints.[26] Nor need we be surprised at any of this. Pugin himself had conceived St Chad's, Birmingham (1839–56) in terms of German brick Gothic. But Pugin's Gothic remained English in spirit: his horizontal banding on the exterior of St Augustine's, Ramsgate (1845–50) echoes Kentish vernacular work in flint and stone. And it may be that to look for Butterfield in Lübeck – at St Katherine's or St Peter's – or at the Cistercian Church at Chorin, north-east of Berlin, without more specific evidence, is really rather speculative. Like Pugin, Butterfield actually preferred to think of his work as English. When *The Guardian* dismissed Keble College Chapel as 'fantastically picked out with zig-zag or chess-board ornamentation', Butterfield – as we shall see – rested his defence on East Anglian or Cotswold precedent: 'I know that I am in very good company.'[27] Aesthetically speaking, he was always a patriot. 'I have remained', he announced towards the end of his career, 'firmly English.'[28] Even his famous brickwork was usually laid in English bond.

Butterfield's tracery – Geometrical in spirit – does tend to be English in detail: first Decorated, then Perpendicular; and he clearly enjoyed working in the English Gothic tradition, as for example at Ottery St Mary in Devon, which he sensitively restored in 1849–50. When Hopkins visited Tintern Abbey he noted – correctly enough – that Butterfield had used its mouldings as a model for St Alban's, Holborn.[29] Similarly, echoes of Dorchester Abbey – notably its bulbous East window buttress – reappear at St Matthias, Stoke Newington (1849–53). And there are other sources too, English and secular: Tudor, diaper-patterned brickwork was clearly one of the prototype building styles upon which Butterfield could draw. Bricky diagonal patterns are famously found at Layer Marney Towers and at Leez Priory, both in Essex; and both were readily available to Butterfield. Similarly, if we look at the patterning of late medieval East Anglian buildings – at King's Lynn, at Barsham or at Walsham, for instance;[30] or if we examine an example of Midlands Gothic like Archbishop Chichele's Bede House at Higham Ferrers, Northamptonshire (1428) – we can mentally translate these vernacular patterns into the language of Butterfield's polychromy. But translations like that do have to be rather free. Butterfield's fondness for chevrons of white brick, for instance, has no medieval precedent. So we are thrown back in our search for prototypes to Italy, in particular to Verona (S. Fermo Maggiore), or Pavia (S. Francesco). And perhaps Butterfield did know them; though we in turn know very little of his travels. In 1854 he wrote to his friend John Duke Coleridge: 'You will think me odd of course but I am more than ever persuaded that an Architect gets but little by travel. I am only glad that I had made up my own mind about a hundred things in art before seeing Italy.' We do know that when Butterfield visited Sta Anastasia at Verona in 1854 – that is, *after* all Saints, Margaret Street had been built – he was delighted to find 'that what he did in simplicity as his own development of Gothic principles, had been done [there] before him'.[31] There is no reason to think that Butterfield was being entirely disingenuous. After all, as G.E. Street pointed out in 1855, All Saints, Margaret Street 'bears no great resemblance [to] ancient Italian work'.[32]

So our conclusion on this question is pretty clear: there is really little point in looking for exact precedents. Whatever the prototypes, Butterfield's synthesis is his own. That synthesis was in place by the early 1850s. His style was fully developed nearly twenty years before Keble College was built. If there is a link which binds that synthesis to Italy it is probably not Ruskin at all, but a writer now largely forgotten: the Reverend Benjamin Webb (1819–85), editor of *The Ecclesiologist*.

If he is remembered at all, Benjamin Webb is remembered today as a founder of the Cambridge Camden Society. But by the end of his life Webb's celebrity as a metropolitan liturgist – he became vicar of St Andrew, Wells Street in 1862 – had rather eclipsed his fame as a young Cantabrian ecclesiologist. Even so, it was the Ecclesiological Society which gave him his place in history. Of course he was not alone. From Cambridge – besides Neale and Hope – came Harvey Goodwin, later Bishop of Carlisle, Philip Freeman, F.A. Paley and Edmond Venables; from Oxford came William Scott and Sir Stephen Glynne, as well as the future Professor E.A. Freeman. Learned men, all of them; learned in ecclesiological lore. Still, it is Webb, Neale and Hope who will always be remembered. Of these three men – the founding fathers of ecclesiology – Webb is the one who tends to be overlooked. Neale was a romantic sacramentalist, first Tory, then Liberal. Hope was a romantic Tory. Webb was a Tory too, but above all he was a romantic ritualist. Like the others, his ideal was the beauty of holiness; but his temperament was less dogmatic than Neale's, less combative than Hope's. He could not afford to take up extreme positions: he was better-off than Neale, but worlds away from a plutocrat like Hope.[33] He needed a clerical income, and he reviewed regularly for money. In the end he left a goodly fortune: more than £20,000,[34] twice as much as Ruskin. But he never escaped from Hope's shadow. As a Cambridge undergraduate he seems to have been more than a little precious: 'his dress was very peculiar', wrote one contemporary, 'and intended to designate ultra-highchurchmanship' – so much so that he was known as the 'Blessed Benjamin'. As such, he might well have been forgotten: a fey young clergyman with rubrics on the brain. Hope took him up, and secured him employment; writing, for example, to Gladstone on his behalf in 1846:

'If he can get nothing he is thinking of the Colonies. [That] would be a very bad destination for him, as he is a learned clerk, and not capable of doing rough hedging and ditching, either morally or physically, as it must be done by a Colonial priest.'[35]

There was clearly more to 'the Blessed Benjamin' than book-learning, however. Throughout his career he regarded the growth of ecclesiology as part of 'a great moral movement'.[36] And he obviously had a very practical side: it takes a rather extraordinary freshman to set up an international society. First as secretary, then as editor, he handled the bulk of the Ecclesiological Society's day-to-day organisation, eventually operating from his own house in London, at 3 Chandos Street, Cavendish Square. He must have been supremely efficient. And thanks to his diary[37] – kept on a daily basis, sometimes in a form of dog-Latin code – it is possible to trace the progress of his thinking through hundreds of articles and reviews which would otherwise remain anonymous; articles in particular on the minutiae of ornament and liturgy, and more generally on the problem of style.

Through Webb's writings we can begin to grasp one key facet of the Victorian mind: its capacity to express its aesthetic sense, its spirituality – almost its very identity – through the art and architecture of the Middle Ages. It was by means of this process that the imagery of mid nineteenth-century Anglicanism became, increasingly, medieval. And Victorian church-building – or image-making – proceeded at an astonishing rate. In the twenty years ending in 1854, a quarter of the parish churches of England were restored.[38] Between 1840 and 1876, some 1,727 new churches were built in England and Wales; as many as 7,144 were rebuilt or restored; and the total cost ran to £25 million.[39] An astonishing programme, and it can be calculated more graphically still. Between 1800 and 1873, some 4,100 new churches were built; and between the 1850s and 1870s about £1,000 per day – say, £50,000 per day in modern money – was spent on church-building or rebuilding, at the rate of two consecrations per week.[40]

In its early years the Cambridge Camden Society followed

Pusey's theology and Pugin's aesthetic. The ecclesiologists were not the first to try to resuscitate the apostolic basis of Anglicanism. A pre-Tractarian High Churchman like Joshua Watson rightly complained of 'the impertinence of these Camdenians' in arrogating to themselves all the credit for this new conjunction of architecture and theology.[41] But on the architectural side they did speak loudest. Their favourite prototypes were fourteenth-century Decorated parish churches, preferably from East Anglia or the Midlands; their favourite architect was R.C. Carpenter, architect of St Mary Magdalen, Munster Square, London (1842–52). And in those days Butterfield followed suit, as at St Augustine's College, Canterbury (1844–8). Their favoured material was stone. Brick they abhorred 'most cordially . . . whether black, red or white'; and brick covered with stucco seemed infinitely worse: it was 'a kind of hypocrisy . . . because it professes to be what it is not'.[42] Such embargoes, however – at least as regards exposed brickwork – did not last long. Towards the end of the 1840s the ecclesiologists began to look elsewhere, to Europe, and in particular to Italy, for a new type of church: urban, liturgically planned and symbolically decorated, but using modern materials and techniques adapted to traditional liturgical and sacramental ends. Eventually even Albi cathedral came to be considered not quite beyond the pale: it might after all be suitable for the colonies.[43] This new aesthetic – Continental, polychromatic, experimental, utilitarian, progressive – had as its sponsor Beresford Hope; Ruskin became its prophet; but its immediate propagandist was Benjamin Webb, and his instrument of execution was William Butterfield.

Part of Webb's programme was the devising of an ecclesiological paradigm applicable to the worldwide Anglican community. The designs produced in 1843–44, for example, by J.M. Derick for the Afghan Memorial Church at Colabah, Bombay, and by

Anthony Salvin for the Anglican Church at Alexandria – both in English Gothic – were quickly seen to be quite unsuitable. Tropical churches demanded architecture appropriate to the tropics. So there had to be a new willingness to change. When church-building in Guiana came under discussion in 1848, Benjamin Webb – as editor of *The Ecclesiologist* – saw his chance:

'Brick is by no means a proscribed material for church-building . . . some of the most beautiful churches in Christendom are of brick alone . . . In Belgium, Bavaria and Italy, brick churches abound, and are always remarkable for the absence of stone dressings. Brick should be treated on a large scale: the architecture should be designed in bold and broad masses . . . [that is,] the brickwork must be thrown into masses on different planes . . . [as in] the brick church of St Cecilia, Albi . . .'[44]

Colonial projects in the Americas and in Australasia clearly offered interesting opportunities for this new, imperial ecclesiology. And Butterfield himself became part of the process, first with his plan for Adelaide Cathedral (1847), and then eventually with his scheme for St Paul's Cathedral, Melbourne (1877–91). New circumstances dictated new forms. But at the root of these novel attitudes lay a fundamental shift of perception, a change in the perceived potential of Gothic; and this in turn stemmed from a broadening aesthetic horizon, in particular a new appreciation of the Gothic architecture of southern Europe.

It was a Cambridge Professor of Natural Philosophy, Robert Willis – the man who first explained the Gothic vault – who in 1835 began the process of rescuing Italian Gothic from Neo-Classical 'contempt'.[45] But English Gothic Revivalists only began to show a serious interest from 1845 onwards. That was the year in which Benjamin Webb came back from Italy singing the praises of Italian Gothic: its colour, its massy forms, its simple detail, its brickwork and terracotta.[46] Webb's findings were definitively presented in *Sketches of Continental Ecclesiology* (1848), with plans and sections by William Butterfield.[47] In the previous year, 1847 – while working on Webb's book – Butterfield seems to have produced his first design in brick, a scheme for Adelaide Cathedral. Meanwhile there had been illustrated articles on Italian Gothic in *The Builder*,[48] and a pamphlet by the Reverend Thomas James *On the Use of Brick in Ecclesiastical Architecture* (1847), as well as a volume with shimmering colour plates, namely Matthew Digby Wyatt's study of Cosmati patterns – Roman, Venetian, Sicilian – entitled *Specimens of the Geometrical Mosaic of the Middle Ages* (1848).[49] All this was before the publication of Ruskin's *Seven Lamps*, before *The Stones of Venice*, and before the building of All Saints, Margaret Street.

Precise dates for this key episode in church building are important. Preliminary plans for All Saints were submitted to the Metropolitan Buildings Office in March 1850; the builder's contract was not signed until September. The cornerstone was laid on 9 November 1850; the church was in use from 1854 onwards; but consecration – originally planned for 1852 – was delayed until 28 May 1859.[50] There was plenty of time for second thoughts. The founding members of The Engagement – that secret clique of which Butterfield was a member – had been plotting the reconstruction of Margaret Street Chapel, 'in a more catholic style', since 1842.[51] First came a delay while negotiations proceeded for the freehold; then came a postponement on financial grounds, and a temporary refitting of the old chapel by Butterfield.[52] 'Margaret Chapel looks most wonderfully well,' Hope told Gladstone in November 1847; 'Butterfield has really

7. William Butterfield, All Saints, Margaret Street, London, pulpit (1856–8). The power of ornament: line *versus* volume; pattern *versus* mass

made a most religious place of it.'[53] In those days Hope was still thinking in terms of fourteenth-century Decorated; that is, 'Middle Pointed'. When All Saints was first envisaged as a practical project, in 1846, it was to have been 'constructed in the best English style of architecture'.[54] It was to have incorporated 'a college of priests'.[55] There was even to have been a competition, with Hope and Glynne as judges.[56] By 1850 that was no longer the case: the architect had been chosen, and the model church of the ecclesiologists was beginning to emerge as rather more exotic. In January 1850 Hope wrote in triumph to Freeman:

'The [parish] district is now formed, and the plans very forward. We are intending to make a great experiment of *constructional* polychrome in the shape of marbles, geometrical mosaic in tiles, and frescoes, and black and red brick on [the] exterior. Do you not approve?'[57]

By October 1852 Hope was urging Freeman to come to London and see what progress had been made:

'By the way, have you seen All Saints Margaret Street since the exterior has been completed and the spire up? It would I am sure modify your [hostile] judgement as to Butterfield. The exterior is completed, so is the *builder's* part of the interior nearly (saving the groining of the Chancel), and a great deal of the covering. But as it will not cost a little, and as subscriptions do not flow in much from general sources, we have no expectation of its being ready for consecration before 1854.'[58]

Even that suggestion proved optimistic. It turned out to be a very long campaign. Look again at those dates. First there had been Webb's *Continental Ecclesiology* (early 1848);[59] then Wyatt's

Geometrical Mosaic (late 1848); then Ruskin's *Stones of Venice* (May, 1849); and then the repeal of the brick tax (May, 1850). The exterior may well have been completed in mid 1851, but it was not until 1853 (nave arcades) and 1854–8 (pulpit) that the famous internal patterning was all in place.[60]

Clear enough; but such stylistic chronologies are seldom as simple as they seem. For example, Wyatt's *Geometrical Mosaic* was the product of lectures previously delivered to the Royal Institute of British Architects, the Royal Society of Arts and the Archaeological Institute. Its Introduction was dated August 1848; but its author had clearly been propagating the benefits of geometrical polychromy for some time.[61] We know there was actually a copy in Hope's library;[62] and Hope, in any case, had inherited an interest in the subject. As early as 1839 his father, Thomas Hope, had commissioned Blashfield to produce an elaborate mosaic floor for his own house, The Deepdene, near Dorking in Surrey. Again, 1839 was also the year when a friend of Whewell's, J.C. von Lassaulx of Coblenz, had published in German a *Description of a New Kind of Mosaic Composed of Brick*. The beauties of geometrical mosaic had thus been theoretically available in economical brickwork ten years before Butterfield's All Saints was planned. Could Hope and Ruskin have known of this? Could Webb and Wyatt? Possibly; very possibly. But there is no evidence. We are thrown back on what the ecclesiologists said, and wrote, and what they said they saw.

Thomas James, for example. He put the arguments in favour of brickwork with lucidity and force. Brick and terracotta were cheaper than stone, more durable than stucco, and capable of infinite variation in pattern and colour. This was something of a revolution in ecclesiological thinking. In 1839–40, *A Few Hints on the Practical Study of Eccclesiastical Antiquities* had ruled out the use of brick as inadmissable. In 1841 *A Few Words to Church*

Builders had dismissed the practice as corrupt: 'white is certainly worse than red, and red than black: but to settle the precedency in such miserable materials is worse than useless.'[63] In 1844 *The Ecclesiologist* had dismissed Edmund Sharpe's terracotta church of St Stephen, Lever Bridge, near Bolton (1842–5) as not 'a worthy offering to the glory of GOD'. Why? Because its material – 'fireclay, cut in moulds' – was deemed 'subversive of the variety and originality necessary for true art'. Better to settle for 'the honest ugliness of . . . red brick'.[64] But by 1847 James, a loyal ecclesiologist, could trumpet such cheap materials as the medium of the future. James Wild's Lombardic brick church on the borders of Brixton – better known today as Christ Church, Streatham (1840–2) – had at first aroused suspicion: its 'Moorish' forms – in fact as much Italian as Islamic – were felt to express 'only the spirit of a false religion'.[65] Now it came into its own. 'It is a most successful specimen,' James decided, 'and deserves more notice.' As for railway buildings, those on the Eastern Counties line – replete with red, yellow and black bricks – seemed exactly in tune with the modern age. And a new engine house at New Cross station on the Croydon–Brighton track moved him even to eloquence: 'in particular a tall round chimney, which would otherwise have been an eyesore, [had] gained great architectural beauty, by a bold coil of red and black bricks running spirally from the bottom to top of a round yellow shaft.'[66]

So, during the 1840s, English taste in Gothic was already changing, swinging away from fourteenth-century English Decorated towards more exotic prototypes. One sort of reality – Pugin's 'true thing' – was beginning to be replaced by another: ecclesiological eclecticism. In the previous decades English books on medieval Italian architecture – by Thomas Hope, Robert Willis or Gally Knight – had been concerned with history, typology and structure.[67] Now the accent was on materials, on decoration, on colour.

8. G.E. Street, St James-the-Less, Westminster, London, sedilia
(1860–1). The power of ornament: gravity diffused

1844; 'let deal be seen to be deal, not painted to resemble oak; let brick be known to be brick, not stuccoed to imitate stone.'[80] This obsession with honest building was a Puginian shibboleth propagated by *The Ecclesiologist* before it was romanticised by Ruskin. When Butterfield designed kneeling-hassocks for Christ Church, Hoxton in 1848 – 'low and long, and flat, and covered with leather' – the editor (Benjamin Webb) praised them for their 'reality', their 'working-day look'.[81] It must have been Webb, not Ruskin, who introduced Butterfield to Italy and first whetted his appetite for brick. Perhaps it was Webb who then interpreted Ruskin to Butterfield. The architect was certainly very close to the editor of *The Ecclesiologist*: apart from contributing plates to *Instrumenta Ecclesiastica* (1844–7) and *Sketches of Continental Ecclesiology* (1848), he also designed a muscular parsonage house for him at Sheen, Staffordshire in 1852. Unlike Gilbert Scott or even G.E. Street, Butterfield was never a publicist: he found his spokesman in Benjamin Webb. In return, Webb claimed Butterfield as his friend.[82] Thanks to Webb's diary, we know that it was in fact Webb who wrote the strikingly favourable review of *The Seven Lamps* in *The Ecclesiologist* for 1850; the more cautious survey of *The Stones of Venice* in 1851; and at least two of the abusive critiques of Ruskin's later social theories in the *Saturday Review* for 1858 and 1860.[83] Some elements in the Lamp of Truth, Webb noted approvingly – Ruskin's celebrated 'canons' of 'reality' – 'might almost have been taken from one of our own pages'.[84] Were it not for his '*monomania . . .* against Catholicity',[85] Ruskin might even have been welcomed as a contributor. But Webb never reneged on his early admiration for Pugin: 'a great artist', and 'a rigorous and independent thinker'.[86] He lived to doubt whether even Pugin could have 'kept pace' with the generation of Goths who came after him; but in the end, it is Webb who turns out to be the link between

Puginian truth and Ruskinian reality. And finally, thanks again to his diary, we know that it was Webb who wrote one of the most famous pieces in the whole of nineteenth-century architectural criticism, *The Ecclesiologist*'s commentary of 1859 on All Saints, Margaret Street.[87]

In that much-quoted essay, it was Webb who made the famous comparison between Butterfield and Millais.[88] It was Webb who referred to Butterfield's 'deliberate ugliness'. Webb's was the notion – borrowed from Coventry Patmore – of 'Pre-Raphaelitism' in architecture: 'its coarse but honest originality', its 'dread of beauty'. Outside, the red and black bricks offset by Whitby stone; inside, the alabaster, the serpentine marble, the Peterhead granite – all this seemed to Webb both sumptuous and challenging. At All Saints, above all, he spotted from the start the relevance – the 'reality' – of brickwork in an urban context; the infinite potential of brick, and tile, and marble, for polychrome pattern; the 'sublime' abstraction of reductive geometry.

> '[Butterfield] was the first to show us that red brick is the best building material for London, and to prove to us that its use was compatible with the highest flights of architecture. In the matter of banding his red brick with black and other colours, we chiefly admire his moderation. His numerous imitators in this popular style of constructional polychrome have often overlooked his example of discretion.'[89]

Webb did not approve of everything. Some of the colouring – the green voussoirs, for instance – seemed to him over-strident; the patterning over the chancel arch appeared 'fragmentary and crude', the clerestory glass mere 'gaudy bits of colour'.[90] In fact he agreed with Beresford Hope that in some ways Butterfield had 'parricidally spoilt his own creation with . . . fanatical . . .

colour doctrines'.[91] And yet, for Webb, this was indeed a memorable church: '*the* original work of modern English art . . . a tentative solution of the problem [of] what the architecture of the future [is] to be'.[92]

At much the same time, Beresford Hope was sponsoring a critique of All Saints for his own journal, the *Saturday Review*. We shall hear more from him in due course. At this point we must limit our reference to this one review. Again, the hand is Webb's, though this time with more than a touch of the journal's proprietor. In the first place – and this is worth remembering, in view of Hope's quarrelsome record – the *Saturday Review* acknowledges 'Mr Butterfield's genius'. But the line of argument is much the same as *The Ecclesiologist*'s: the church's pioneering 'reality' had been spoilt by too many of Butterfield's 'crotchets'. But because Hope, as patron and 'co-originator', had seen his own scheme 'parricidally spoilt', the criticisms this time are predictably bitter. Here was 'the most ornate and sumptuous [parish church built] since the Reformation'; 'the first attempt . . . [at] a true and genuine style of brick construction' worthy of Flanders or Lombardy; a harbinger indeed of 'that bolder style of design which has opened up so hopeful a future for English architecture' – all undermined, apparently, by 'crudeness' of colour and 'grotesqueness' of form. Outside, the adjacent clergy house was 'gloomier than a dungeon', with 'iron girders of incredible coarseness'. Inside, the pulpit and chancel screen were 'a perversely ingenious confusion of coarse contrasts'; the patterns of spandrels and chancel arch 'a fortuitous jumble of colour patches'; and the clerestory windows – 'spotted with blotches of staring colours' – quite 'simply barbaric'. And yet something of the 'model church' programme had survived. The materials, in texture and colour, were 'naturally' employed, in line with Ruskinian theory. 'Nearly all the polychrome', the *Saturday Review* explained, 'is constructional . . . most of the colour is indestructible. Fresco and mastic, polished marbles and alabaster, and the glazed tesserae of Staffordshire may be almost said to defy time.' *The Ecclesiologist*'s programme of reality – 'in God's house everything should be real' – had survived even Butterfield's mannered 'principle of coloration'.[93] Webb's manifesto was still intact. And flat-pattern ornament even defied accusations of popery: there were no three-dimensional images.

So, for a hundred and fifty years, through his reviews in *The Ecclesiologist* and *Saturday Review* – written, incidentally, on successive days – we have been seeing Butterfield, without realising it, through the eyes not of John Ruskin but of Benjamin Webb. It was Webb, through his publications on Italian Gothic, and through his influence with Beresford Hope, who first led Butterfield in the direction of Continental Gothic, probably even before the architect himself had set foot on the Continent. It was Webb who then – again with Beresford Hope – turned against Butterfield's idiosyncracy, coining the critical language of 'ugliness' which has persisted ever since. Webb never rejected the spirit of Butterfield's work: as late as 1880 he still thought the church at West Lavington 'beautiful'.[94] They remained on good terms, dining regularly at Nobody's Friends and the Athenaeum. And – like Beresford Hope – the editor of *The Ecclesiologist* continued to defend Butterfield against the criticisms of E.A. Freeman.[95] But the legend of Butterfield as a kind of aesthetic sadist – a legend immortalised by Summerson in his lecture of 1945[96] – turns out to be a legend largely created by the Reverend Benjamin Webb.

In any case, the very notion of ugliness is hopelessly compromised by subjectivity. If by ugliness we understand a willingness to shock rather than a desire to please; an anti-classical instinct for discontinuous forms and contrasting colours; a taste for 'volumetric violence',[97] for planar conflict, broken lines, exaggerations and juxtapositions of texture; an obsession with honesty, primitivism and vigour – the very stigmata of 'reality' – then we are fully in agreement with Butterfield's contemporaries. They saw elements of ugliness – the studied angularity of Pre-Raphaelite art, for example – in much of Butterfield's best work. Ugliness in that sense does not represent a deficiency of genius, still less a barrier to appreciation. In grappling with Butterfield's ugliness, we are merely encountering the visual vocabulary of High Victorian aesthetics.

But there is yet another set of factors to add to the equation. Architecture is a matter of technology and economics as well as a matter of taste. High Victorian Gothic – and Butterfield's Gothic in particular – could never have happened at the moment it did, and in the way that it did, without a combination of fiscal and technological change. In the first place, the increasing use of cast and wrought iron – and the development of plate glass – threatened to overturn the whole basis of traditional aesthetics. The time was ripe for a new approach to style. The end of the 1840s was just the moment for a new wave of architectural theory, and a new wave there certainly was; one purpose of these lectures is to untangle at least a little of its complexity. And then there was climate: we have records of a documented sequence of very bad weather in the 1840s and 1850s. Ruskinian polychromy was as much an answer to Dickensian smog as a reaction against Neo-Classical purity.[98] Butterfield's church of St Augustine, Queen's Gate, London (1865–71), for example – blue bricks from Staffordshire, red bricks from Suffolk – sets at defiance any hint of gloom; it seems almost to cry out, Why should the Devil have all the best colours? In the third place, as if to demonstrate to every art historian the interaction of aesthetics and socio-economic trends, the duties on glass were repealed in 1845;[99] the tax on bricks went in 1850;[100] and the window tax in 1851.[101] Finally, in 1858 came the invention of the Hoffman coal-fired kiln.[102] The scene was set for a High Victorian breakthrough into plate glass and polychromy.

Unlike Ruskin, Butterfield always preferred sash windows to casements; again unlike Ruskin, he preferred machine-shaped brick and engine-polished marble to any amount of hand-crafted material. He was neither a dogmatic medievalist nor a prototype of the Arts and Crafts movement. He was simply a mid Victorian realist. But his brickwork was never cheap. It was chosen wherever possible from the relevant locality – Rugby bricks at Rugby, for example – though not solely on grounds of economy. G.E. Street thought that the brickwork at All Saints, Margaret Street – hand-moulded, originally pink rather than red, and very precisely laid – was unnecessarily expensive.[103] Even so, Butterfield clearly saw the potential of industrialised polychromy. And 'Mr Hope's church' was rather a special case. Elsewhere, he was at one with the preferences of the wider building profession. In December 1849, with technical and fiscal changes succeeding one another fast, the *Civil Engineer and Architect's Journal* sensed the dawn of a new age: 'Polychromy will be a feature of the Victorian era, as stucco was of the Georgian.'[104]

In the mid nineteenth-century cult of brickwork, aesthetics and economics went hand in hand.[105] The age of stucco – which of course disguised cheaper bricks – coincided almost exactly with the existence of the brick tax between 1784 and 1850: a fact curiously ignored by architectural historians. The ending of stucco owed as much to fiscal policy as it did to Puginian invective. And as regards Butterfield, the timing is uncanny. When was the tax on bricks repealed? – May, 1850. When was the decision taken to make All Saints, and its clergy house, not of stock brick but of a hitherto more expensive patterned brick? – late 1849, or very early 1850. Beresford Hope, MP, might talk about the aesthetic potential of different materials; about the choice between tiling and fresco; about colour deriving from '*construction* and not from *superaddition*'.[106] But he also knew about fiscal trends. By 1848, repeal of the brick tax was widely regarded as inevitable. Perhaps the patron saint of modern Gothic was neither Ruskin nor Butterfield, but the Whig Chancellor of the Exchequer, Sir Charles Wood, later Viscount Halifax.

During the later 1840s the campaign for the repeal of the tax on brick had quickly gathered momentum. George Godwin spoke for *The Builder*:

> 'The duty was but 5s. 10d. per thousand, but [it] . . . had the effect of nearly doubling the price of bricks to the public . . . Since the reign of George III the price of brickwork had risen from £7 15s. per rod to (say) £12 . . . The duty was levied [on green, or unbaked, bricks: that is,] as soon as the bricks were stacked, and before they were burnt. The manufacturer, therefore, had to pay upon all that were spoiled in the burning, and this led to the use of bricks of the most infamous quality . . . [bricks in fact which were] abominable rubbish.'[107]

Apart from questions of health and security, the decorative possibilities of moulded and vitrified brickwork were limitless. Repeal[108] opened up immense opportunities for 'artistic treatment'. And the use of brickwork fulfilled to the letter the Puginian concept of truth. That was why Butterfield preferred bricks which were coloured throughout – salt-glazed, coal-fired Staffordshire 'blues', for example – to any amount of surface-coloured, wood-fired brickwork. Unlike Street's polychromy at All Saints, Boyne Hill, Berkshire (1854–7), for example, Butterfield's brickwork never faded. 'Don't', he once remarked, 'give me a brick with a smear on the surface.' It was its permanence of colour which guaranteed the truthfulness – the reality – of polychromy. 'There is nothing', noted H.B. Garling, 'so likely to produce a meretricious style in art as the use of an *artificial* and *inconstructive* material for decorative purposes'; whereas 'architectural decoration in constructive material . . . suggests . . . the union of decorative features with constructive requirements . . . a sort of homage . . . to the truths and reality of this last great principle of propriety in architecture [, namely,] . . . that art be the handmaiden of necessity.'[109] In other words, it was – as it always has to be – the architect's duty to turn utility into beauty. And that aesthetic message could be made to carry spiritual force. 'Let us use [brickwork] plainly and boldly,' James concludes; 'not covering it with whitewash or stucco, but in the sincerity and reality that becomes the house of the God of Truth . . . In variety of colour it may be made to exceed marble . . . It is economical; it is easy of carriage; . . . above all, [its material] is almost universally, under our feet. Hitherto the restrictions of the excise have debased [brickwork] to its rudest and most forbidding form, and having been used only in our commonest buildings, we have associated with it ideas of poverty and coarseness. Let us once make it by beauty of form, and colour, and expression, worthy of the highest works of man in the service of his Maker, and nothing which has been thus sanctified to the House of God, shall any henceforth call common.'[110]

This cult of reality in ecclesiastical design clearly appealed to Butterfield. His first ecclesiastical design in brick – for an Australian cathedral, remember – had been made in 1847, the very year of James's manifesto. And as larger commissions came his way, he was able to develop reality of composition with full

Puginian rigour. When the first Warden of Keble suggested in 1872 that chimney stacks might be out of place in a college chapel, the architect's reply was uncompromising:

'As regards these chimneys, I must say most distinctly that I not only don't think them undesirable, I positively like them . . . One . . . is [actually] a flue . . . to the furnace room . . . and if it's not wrong to warm the chapel, this flue ought to be honestly avowed, and not wasted. It will not draw well if there is any attempt to hide it. [Anyway,] five flues make a better object than one flue which would be stalky.

There are bodies as well as souls in the Chapel.'[111]

Pugin himself could not have put it better. Appropriately, when Butterfield began work at Rugby in 1859, he found polychrome brickwork already there: blue bricks in a nearby railway viaduct; yellow bricks and blue tiles in a water tower on Barby Road.[112]

So much for the ecclesiastical context. For the secular context we have only to look to the *Civil Engineer and Architect's Journal*. This publication had no time for ecclesiology. It called the Cambridge men 'a clique of overgrown school-boys'.[113] Its focus was on utility, not symbolism. As the new railway system developed, so the traffic in bricks and tiles increased: there was obviously scope here for fast-expanding production.[114] In 1851 the same journal celebrated the abolition of brick tax on purely practical grounds:

'The removal of the *brick duties*, the *glass duties* and the *window duties* [will transform] the architect's powers of action. The old brick duties limited him to bricks of a certain size, and virtually deprived him of sculptured, coloured or hollow bricks; the glass duties deprived him of plate-glass for external purposes, and of coloured glass for internal effects; and the window duties restricted him in the number, position, dimensions and superficies of his openings. Thus, whatever might be the ideas or wishes of the architect, he was at every point bound down by a code, dependent on no artistic considerations but on the dictates and convenience of the excise. This is a system of monstrous absurdity, which has confined our architects to a kind of Chinese conventionalism, and very much injured the practice of architecture. [All this must now change] . . . In fact, the whole model of architectural practice must be re-modelled. [And in this respect] the French, Flemish and High Dutch examples . . . [developed] free from the restrictions of [brick tax and] window tax [may well have something to teach us].'[115]

Within a year, James Wild had built the ultimate monument to brick-tax repeal: the new Dock Tower at Grimsby, three hundred feet of red brick, hugely outscaling its venerable prototype at Siena. Its structure contained no fewer than one million bricks.[116]

By the mid 1850s the prospects for brick seemed limitless. Young George Aitchison – still years away from his later phase of disillusion – saw no end to its possibilities:

'We have at hand an inexhaustible supply of plastic material that merely asks us to mould it in any form of beauty that we love: it asks us to indulge in that [key] instinct of our nature, [namely,] never to repeat [ourselves] . . . [For] in every foliated moulding, slab, panel, or spandrel . . . [we have in vitrified clay a substance with] the facility of plaster [and] the durability of granite . . . We may point and gild in imperishable colours the fronts of our houses; we may fill them with the finest fretwork, purer than alabaster, and as enduring as adamant; we may set them over with jewels that shall glow like the liquid fire in the setting sun . . .'[117]

Whatever the context, secular or ecclesiastical, the compass of progress seemed set fair for brick.

In Butterfield's work we see both these contexts in combination, ecclesiastical and secular. Milton Ernest Hall, Bedfordshire (1854–8),[118] Keble College, Oxford (1868–83) and Rugby School, Warwickshire (1859; 1867–85),[119] all embody the same revolutionary potential. The conventions of design in all three works are closely related. And in two of these commissions – Rugby and Keble – Butterfield even employed the same contracting builder: Parnell of Rugby. It is time to look a little more closely at these designs, especially the design for Keble.

Milton Ernest is a fairly early work, built for Butterfield's brother-in-law. The occasional trefoiled arch, the occasional shouldered lancet, still hint at domestic ecclesiology. But the ruthless asymmetry of its plan, those uncompromising sash windows, the insistent polychromy, all point to a precocious maturity in Butterfield's own style. Outside, the coloured brick-work – pinkish rather than red – operates in counterpoint to the buff and brown of stone and tile; inside, geometric marbles, pale and underplayed, dapple each chimney-piece with purple, green and grey. And the scale is domestic. At Rugby there was no need for such restraint. There the silhouette is made up of blocky, reductive shapes, shaken together in glorious asymmetry; and the bricky patterns of the walls – red and yellow, blue and black; increasingly complex as they rise – act out their role as linear abstracts, solvents of weight amid so much compositional mass. As at Keble, these abstract elements of design – the endless counterpoint of horizontal and vertical – can best be understood

9. William Butterfield, Milton Ernest Hall, Bedfordshire
(1854–8). The power of ornament: gravity domesticated

by a spectator who is not only perceptive but mobile. Pattern succeeds pattern; silhouettes compose and re-compose parallactically, in shifting sequences of lines and shapes. There is revolution embodied in these forms, and its language is the myriad potential of brick.

Triggered by fiscal changes, the 'brick revival' of the early 1850s gathered momentum quickly, thanks to changing technology. Between 1830 and 1854, annual brick production more than doubled; and the figure for invested capital rose to £2 million. By 1856, the total number of bricks produced each year in the United Kingdom topped 1,800,000,000.[120] At Thomas Cubitt's brickyard at Burham on the Medway, Ainslie's mechanised process was soon spewing out 1,000 bricks per hour.[121] At Oldbury, Birmingham, Oates's brick-making machines not only doubled the crushing strength of brick; they could actually produce some twenty bricks per minute.[122] A decade later, deep in darkest Coalville, Leicestershire children were already baking the bricks which would one day build St Pancras:

'Troops of children . . . ragged, thin, shoeless for the most part, hungry eyed and in colour like the clay they work in . . . These are the brickworkers . . . [for] St Pancras [Station].'[123]

There was indeed a darker side to all this polychromy. The cost of Gripper's patent bricks could be measured in other ways than by the registers of conventional accounting. Meanwhile, the chemistry of brickwork seemed inexhaustible. Salt-glazed 'blues' from Birmingham and Shropshire; glaring 'French-whites' from the Architectural Pottery Co. at Poole in Dorset; bricks of green and maroon, yellow and black, from Leicester and Stafford, from Manchester and Dudley: English brick-production expanded mightily in those frenetic years after repeal. By 1868, forty-seven

English and Italian sources.[126] This synthesis was the result neither of ignorance nor of malice; still less was it the product of Procrustean archaeology. He was simply playing the eclectic game, and playing it by a set of rules known only to himself. In Coventry Patmore's words – thinking of All Saints, Margaret Street – it is all most 'peculiar'; but it is fundamentally 'Gothic in spirit', and a product of 'real genius'.[127] Just how delicate was the touch required – the balance between success and failure – can be shown by a comparison between the genuine article – a late design like the Chanter's House at Ottery St Mary, Devon (1884–3) – and a stylistic derivative which collapses into parody: two houses in Banbury, Oxfordshire (1866) by William Wilkinson of Oxford. At Chanter's House, Butterfield combines archaeology and invention with extraordinary subtlety and skill. By comparison, the houses at Banbury are crude and gauche. To adapt Gilbert Scott's epigram, Wilkinson's work may well be 'Butterfieldism', but this is surely 'Butterfieldism gone mad'.[128]

Part of Butterfield's skill lay in holding English and Continental forms in some sort of equilibrium. By 1861, when his style had settled into an identifiable routine, Benjamin Webb felt sure that although Butterfield was a 'distinguished leader in the polychromatic party', his works revealed 'by their architectural detail, that in the mass they are decidedly northern and specially English'. In this respect Butterfield's stylistic emphases were different from those of George Edmund Street. 'Mr Butterfield,' Webb explained, 'throughout all his experiments with Italian systems of decoration, has remained staunch to English architecture, while . . . Mr Street has drunk deep of the Italian and Early French springs.' And yet, Butterfield's polychrome was beginning to appear curiously obtrusive: 'Mr Butterfield, in wielding constructive colouration, acts as one who spoils the Egyptians, and makes foreign architecture surrender its one superiority to the otherwise more excellent English.'[129] The dangers of excessively polychrome brickwork were becoming increasingly obvious. In 1856–7 *The Builder* was openly campaigning for colour; but by 1868 there were widespread calls for caution.[130] In the mid 1850s, G.E. Street went through an acute phase of enthusiasm for the 'truthfulness' and 'reality' of brickwork; that is, brickwork used 'fearlessly' in the north Italian manner. Not until 1861 did he decide 'this hot taste is dangerous'.[131]

Any type of brickwork operates – in visual terms – on at least two levels: pattern versus volume; two dimensions versus three. Throughout Butterfield's career we can trace this ambivalence at work: linear pattern versus volumetric mass. That explosive pulpit at All Saints – conjuring mazy patterns out of recalcitrant marble – illustrates the process in almost caricatural form. And Butterfield never quite forgot that skill. His later designs for fonts – at Braunstone and Hagnaby, for instance – retain a startling geometrical clarity. But there is a gradual change of effect. During the 1850s Butterfield's composition begins to shift in emphasis, from mass to linearity; from primal geometry – Ruskin's Lamp of Power – to colour, light and flickering shade. The weight and force of three-dimensional shapes dissolves by the end of his career into patterns of two-dimensional form. In all his buildings, however, brick and marble, stone and glass dance an endlessly-intricate measure. String-course and dripmould, dentil and chamfer – to say nothing of those artful, unnecessary buttresses – act and react in pursuit of tectonic imagery. By manipulating the Victorian language of reality – always an aesthetic rather than a strictly functional concept – Butterfield turns structure into an image of structure, in this case an image of volume delineated, of gravity defied.

★

10. William Butterfield, Keble College, Oxford (1868–83). The power of ornament: gravity dissolved

What then of Keble? The college had an austere beginning. It set out, in 1868, to offer first-rate academic teaching to High Anglicans with low incomes. In the language of its charter, its aim was 'sober living and high culture of the mind'. Yet, as Pusey put it, 'not poverty, but simplicity of life, Christian simplicity, was to be its chief characteristic'.[132] Austerity and High Churchmanship, ritual with a touch of muscularity: no architect was better fitted for such a commission than this austere Anglican bachelor, this staunch defender of the Athanasian creed. Butterfield was the ideal choice. Thirty years before – under the spiritual direction of Keble himself – Butterfield had relished the secret pieties of The Engagement. Religious conviction went to the core of his being. He came from an ecclesiological generation, remember, that saw in architectural reality at least a hint of eternal truth. Not for nothing was he christened 'the Fra Angelico of nineteenth-century architecture'.[133] For reality was a matter of morals, as well as a mere exercise in technology and aesthetics. In one remarkable lecture, R.W. Church, Dean of St Paul's, set out the qualities of national character – the distinctive characteristics of the Teutonic race – which responded to the ethos of Christianity; in particular, the virtues connected with truth and the virtues connected with manliness:

'I mean by the virtues connected with *Truth*, not only the search after what is true . . . but the regard generally for what is real, substantial, genuine, solid . . . the taste for plainness and simplicity . . . the deep moral indignation at shams and imposture . . . the dislike of overstatement and exaggeration . . . Under the virtues of Manliness I mean . . . the duty of hard work; the value and jealousy for true liberty; independence of soul . . . the temper not to make much of trifles . . . [and above all] moral courage . . .'[134]

There is something of Butterfield in each of these observations; something which lies at the root of what it meant to be Victorian; something which goes to the heart of Keble. As Pusey explained at the dedication of the chapel in 1876, 'this school of faith . . . this school of simplicity' was conceived as a visible rebuke to the self-indulgence of richer colleges.[135] In 1894 Murray's *Handbook* noted: 'it is not to be in any invidious sense a poor man's college, though it will be possible to live there on a smaller income than elsewhere.'[136] Or, rather, to live *and pray* there: in Paul Thompson's words, 'Keble College Chapel was conceived as a statement of faith; as a Te Deum, strictly ordered but manifestly triumphant.'[137]

There was a tone of austerity and rectitude in the air almost from the start. Butterfield's respect for the credal authority of the church – 'backbone' in a 'subjective' age – was reflected in his didactic schemes for the chapel's mosaics.[138] He opposed the installation of Holman Hunt's *Light of the World* on the grounds that the chapel was a place of prayer, not a public picture gallery.[139] Even the chapel benches were specifically designed *not* to be too comfortable. Butterfield disliked traditional English hassocks; he preferred benches, as in Italy or Germany, equipped with a fixed kneeling board and a low back, which made it impossible to slouch.

'The hassock and carpet are the rich man's tradition, and they usually mean [rented pews]. A hassock is a stumbling block . . . It is always in different stages of decay, raggedness, and nastiness, and in town churches at least it harbours vermin. It can never be cleaned. [And in any case, hassocks are never provided for] the poor . . . Overmuch effort has often been made [in the past] to produce a too easy and lounging seat . . .'[140]

Clergymen of Butterfield's persuasion endorsed this view. One incumbent assured him '*you* have made my people kneel'. But at least one rival architect, H. Roumieu Gough, described such benches as 'instruments of torture'.[141] Generations of Keble sportsmen must have suffered penitential torment at the hands of Butterfield Procrustes.

So Keble's characteristics – cheap and churchy, and perhaps a little muscular – were set firm from the very start. And as if to make its novelty manifest, the college was built upon a plan which broke decisively with Oxford tradition. For centuries collegiate planning – apart from Wilkins's campus paradigm at Downing College, Cambridge – had been based on the conjunction of two medieval traditions: the lateral grid of the manorial courtyard, and the vertical stacking of the lodgings staircase. Hence the collegiate Picturesque – a random grouping of staircases and quadrangles, punctuated by hall and chapel – all the way from William of Wykeham to A.W.N. Pugin. In 1858 Butterfield chose a radically different alternative: the corridor plan. Hawksmoor had toyed with this in his early schemes for All Souls; Wren had supplied a primitive prototype – private cubicles opening off a continuous corridor – at Chelsea Hospital in 1682–92. But what Butterfield probably had in mind were the corridor plans of religious seminaries: Pugin's buildings at Handsworth (1840–1) and Maynooth (1845), for example, or his own St Augustine's College, Canterbury (1844–8). Keble, after all, was conceived as an Anglican training-ground. Ironically, it turned out to be the new women's colleges – in Oxford, Cambridge and London – which, from the 1880s onwards, adopted Butterfield's system, on grounds of order, security and economy. Keble had little influence on the planning of colleges for men, at least until the emergence of the modern university hall of residence.[142]

In Oxford itself Keble's 'impudent' brickwork quickly became the butt of dons and undergraduates alike. In 1875 Butterfield was stung into thinking of a reply. In a draft letter to *The Guardian* he pointed out that he had used almost as much stone as brick. The chapel, he claimed, 'might nearly as well be called a stone building as a brick one. It is, in fact, neither one nor the other, but a mixture of both, to the great advantage of each material.' In any case, he explains, on this occasion he had a particular eye to economy; making use of 'materials such as the nineteenth century and modern Oxford provides'. And then comes the caveat. These modern materials, he asserts, were employed in accordance with English precedent: the diapers were 'a common decoration upon old red brick walls'; the chequer patterns could be seen throughout East Anglia, as near to Oxford as Burnham or Reading, indeed in 'hundreds of churches in the flint and stone districts of England . . . Taking my place in a long line of worthy predecessors,' he therefore concludes, 'I am content.' But in making this defence – his bricks, in fact, came from Wheatley, Oxfordshire – Butterfield refused to place himself in any form of archaeological strait-jacket. 'As long as I continue to work,' he announced, '[I shall] take the responsibility of thinking for myself.'[143] Now there's an epitaph for an architect: '*thinking for myself*'. Keble's 'gay walls' – Butterfield actually used that phrase in a letter to Philip Webb[144] – could hardly be further from copyism; they come down to us as a peculiarly Victorian legacy, a triumph of free-range historicism.

Anyway, who paid? It was the Gibbs family of Tyntesfield, Somerset who made Butterfield's building possible. To William Gibbs (£30,000 donation), Keble owes its chapel; to his sons Anthony and Martin Gibbs, Keble owes its hall and library. The chapel alone cost about £50,000 (say, £2.5 million today).

Others gave generously, notably Frederick Lygon, sixth Earl Beauchamp.[145] But it was the Gibbs family who shouldered the bulk of the cost. By the 1870s Anthony Gibbs and Sons Ltd was an established merchant bank, run by a family of Tory landowners. But the origins of the firm were rather more murky. It is one of the ironies of Keble's foundation that it was funded by a firm whose initial wealth came from their monopoly of Peruvian guano; and guano dug out by what can only be described as native slave labour. William's nephew, Henry Hucks Gibbs, first Baron Aldenham, was a learned bimetallist and philologist whose great-uncle, Vicary Gibbs, is remembered for the *Complete Peerage*. And all the family, in different degrees, were patrons of Anglican church building. But that didn't stop the messenger boys at the Stock Exchange singing rude rhymes about

'The House of Gibbs that made their dibs,
By selling the turds of foreign birds.'

By the mid 1850s, profits from the guano monopoly were about £100,000 a year,[146] the equivalent of perhaps £5 million today; and that was profit, not turnover. These huge proceeds found their way, from the 1860s onwards, first into merchant banking and then eventually into the building of Keble College.

Keble has always been a test of taste. When the chapel was finished in 1876, reactions were very mixed. *The Guardian* was sympathetic,[147] *The Spectator* enthusiastic; even Gladstone called it 'noble'.[148] But *The World* despaired at its 'unspeakable ugliness': 'an anomaly in idea', it complained, the college had now emerged as 'a monstrosity in appearance'.[149] *The Hour* dismissed it as 'hideous . . . vividly suggestive of a workhouse or county lunatic asylum'. No wonder Liddon warned Warden Talbot in

1872 that Butterfield's design was 'throwing down the gauntlet to Oxford opinion'.[150] *The Times* hedged its bets by praising the interior and excoriating the exterior:

> 'The style . . . appears to be 13th c. Gothic . . . [But] the materials . . . red and grey bricks, pointed by Bath stone . . . are quite out of harmony with all the architectural glories of Oxford . . . [Unfortunately] ivy and other creepers [do] not seem to be liberally encouraged . . . [However, as to the inside,] there is no ecclesiastical interior in England, of proportionate size, so richly decorated and so glowing in colour . . . The roof is of a noble height; the proportions recall those of the *Sainte Chapelle*.[151]

The *Illustrated London News* merely noted that 'ivy and other creepers . . . should be liberally encouraged'.[152] By 1894, Murray's *Handbook* was telling visitors to beware: 'the buildings are bizarre in appearance and quite alien to the spirit of Oxford architecture . . . [though perhaps the chapel's] proportions are fine . . . [while] the decoration throughout is elaborate, and by many admired.'[153] Curiously, none of these comments focuses on the prime factor in Keble's Oxford setting: the contrast between blushing pink brickwork and cool evergreen foliage. Viewed from across the University Parks, the chapel rises – brick on brick, stone on stone – to explode in an efflorescence of pattern high up above a sea of fir and cypress. No ivy there; just trees – and very good they look, too.

Of course, like all major buildings constructed over a long period of time, Keble ran into criticism because it was old-fashioned before it was complete. Conceived in the 1860s as a High Anglican statement in High Victorian Gothic, it was born into a very different world, the world of the Aesthetes in the 1870s and 1880s. Butterfield was an easy target in the Oxford of

Walter Pater and Oscar Wilde.[154] By the time of the First World War, modern Gothic – as the mid Victorians conceived it – had become rather a stale joke.

The year 1927 – just before the publication of Kenneth Clark's *Gothic Revival* – was perhaps the low point in Keble's architectural reputation. 'Block after block', noted the *History of the University of Oxford* in that year – 'block after block has been gradually added . . . all unhappily in the same vivid and unsatisfying style . . . A great opportunity of building a beautiful College [has been] thrown away. The Chapel . . . [may be] costly in its marble [and] conspicuous in size but [it is] strangely wanting in judgement, dignity and repose. Its crude colouring [makes for] distressed spectators. Its [stained glass] windows [are] deplorable in execution and in tone. But time has mellowed the worst of its misfortunes.'[155]

By 1939 the pendulum was beginning to swing. In that year Christopher Hobhouse decided that though it was composed of 'unspeakable materials', it was at least built in 'heroic proportions . . . [Butterfield's] scale is superb, and his proportions are manly . . . there is nothing timid or mean about Keble . . . Only a crank could like his work, but it is a mistake not to admire it.'[156] That judgement stood at least until my own time as an undergraduate in the later 1950s, when the first stirrings of Brutalism – and thus of a revived interest in Butterfield – began to be felt.[157]

Perhaps it is more helpful to look at Keble through Butterfield's own eyes; and at Butterfield through the eyes of his contemporaries. When Butterfield described the chapel's virtues, in a letter to the Warden of Keble in 1873, he emphasised 'the restfulness and strength, and sense of communion that come of quiet order, completeness and proportion'.[158] In addition he made it clear that abstract patterning also had for him a distinctly religious resonance: naturalistic figures would appeal to the senses rather than the intellect; 'we must stamp upon [the chapel's decoration] what is divine rather than what is human'. God as divine geometer can never have been far from Butterfield's conception of form.

As for Butterfield's contemporaries, four comments are worth repeating. The first has to be from Ruskin, whose thinking overshadows the whole debate. In November 1873 he delivered his sixth Slade Lecture of that year, only yards away from Keble. He made no mention of the new college, still less of Butterfield. But there are clues in his text with which we can begin to unlock the architect's secret.

> 'Architecture consists distinctively in the adaptation of form to resist force . . . by the ingenious adjustment of various pieces of solid material; . . . the perception of this ingenious adjustment, or structure, [must] be always joined with our admiration of the superadded ornament . . .; but . . . the beauty of the ornament itself is independent of the structure, and arrived at by powers of mind of a very different class from those which are necessary to give skill in architecture proper . . . [And so] the noblest conditions of building in the world are nothing more than the gradual adornment, by play of the imagination, of materials first arranged by this natural instinct of adjustment.'[159]

The subtlety of this revision of Puginian simplicities was clearly too much for Oxford undergraduates. 'Bad day altogether,' Ruskin noted in his diary; 'thinnest audience I ever had.'[160] But here, in this explanation of the semiotic principle – the imaging of tectonic force – lay just that heuristic mechanism by which Oxford critics might well have decoded Keble's mysteries. Ruskin himself never developed these hints into a systematic explanation of architectural form. For that we must turn – as we will in chapter four – to Coventry Patmore.

Meanwhile, the second comment – this time directly about Keble – is a simple expression of admiration. It was written by F.T. Palgrave, one fine summer evening in 1875. Palgrave was Professor of Poetry at Oxford, editor of the *Golden Treasury*, and an art critic of considerable range and formidable power of expression. He had travelled widely in France, in Italy, in Switzerland, Germany and Holland. His judgement is not to be sniffed at. On 5 June 1875 he took his family to see Keble, newly built and freshly pink. 'We sat long in the quad of Keble,' he wrote, 'where Butterfield's new chapel seems to me decisively the most beautiful church built within my knowledge – proportions, details equally lovely and original; the whole with a shrine-like air, yet also with a look of size and power most rarely united.'[161]

The third comment – a year or so later – comes from Butterfield's first critical patron, Benjamin Webb. By the 1870s, Webb seems to have sensed that Butterfield's promise had been not entirely fulfilled.[162] Even so – thirty years after the inception of All Saints, Margaret Street – he willingly acknowledged quite a few of Butterfield's idiosyncrasies as the acceptable insignia of genius.

'In the Chapel of Keble College, a single learned and inventive mind has had its full play, and the result is a work of great beauty and lofty instruction, not without its imperfections, but successful enough to form an aera in English church-decoration . . . Mr Butterfield has made his own style, and done it gallantly, and with beautiful result.'

In daylight the mosaics might seem too weakly tinted for the windows, the windows themselves too glaring for the walls. But by the light of flickering tapers 'the mosaics have their way and show their power . . . [For] in their severity and splendour they make one understand what real and good Christian art is . . .

rich, genuine, imposing, and historic, intelligible to learned and unlearned; weighted with meaning and devotion; full of the grandeur of sacrifice . . .' Outside, in arch and wall and chimney-stack, Butterfield's stippled patterns had managed somehow to signal – first one way, then another – architecture's universal counterpoise of vertical and horizontal force. Perhaps those patterns had indeed become too dominant, turning an accessory detail into a leading characteristic. But the totality of Butterfield's conception evinced persuasive power. 'Within the walls he has his high-pointed stonework upwards, and his altogether lovely flower-cornice in white alabaster all round. Without, he has his lofty buttresses, high niches and pinnacles, and his horizontal bands along the building: the principal one a zigzag, which combines pointedness and horizontality.' In this way, by combining the principles of northern and southern Gothic, Butterfield had set out to reconcile – through the charge and counter-charge of ornament – architecture's two eternal opposites: vertical thrust and horizontal mass. 'The results', Webb concluded cautiously, 'are, or will be, beautiful.'[163]

The fourth comment, from a decade later – 1885 – is rather more sharp, and gets a little closer to the bone. It was written by J.D. Sedding, a Goth, but a Goth of a softer, Arts and Crafts kind. He recognised that Butterfield was – to use a modern cliché – an original: an artist without provenance or posterity. 'Keble College', writes Sedding, 'can never look mellow. No one supposes that it ever will look less startling and raw than its talented author took pains to make it. Mellowness is a quality it ever must lack. Nature – who is a soft-hearted creature – will try her best to throw her charitable cloak over its crude walls; but Keble will be a nature-puzzling, time-defying object till the crack of doom, and will stare with its peculiar nineteenth-century stare straight into the eyes of eternity.'[164] That peculiar nineteenth-century stare – the enigma of the Victorian mind – remains for twenty-first-century historians a challenge and a delight.

In the end, Butterfield went his own way. He was never the leader of a school.[165] His dogmatic muscularity, his syncopated polychromy, his capacity for endless geometrical invention – all this is entirely his own. He worked intuitively, and in his own way he found an answer to the architect's secret: gravity distilled in line and pattern, pattern dissolving weight and mass. Pugin had first set out the doctrine of reality, based on the gospel of truth. Ruskin may have supplied the explanatory aesthetic; Webb the archaeological framework; Hope the moment of opportunity. But Butterfield was always his own man. His buildings prove that, without question. He found his style in 1850, and it never changed. We know the context – the cult of 'reality' – from which it sprang, and in that context Pugin, Ruskin, Webb and Hope (to say nothing of the Gibbs family) all had a part to play. But without Butterfield's quirky talent those particular buildings would not exist. That is why, in 1948, Goodhart-Rendel made him his principal Rogue: his chief rogue-elephant architect, foraging alone, away from the herd.[166] Goodhart-Rendel even managed, in his own designs, to echo something of his hero's bricky genius.[167] But it was a genius uniquely individual; and this individuality – this streak of sacred cussedness – shines steadily, throughout Butterfield's work, particularly at Keble. So too that element of 'Pied Beauty': 'all things counter, original, spare, strange'. We began with Gerard Manley Hopkins; so let Hopkins have the last word:

'Glory be to God for dappled things.'[168]

RT. HON. ALEXANDER J. B. BERESFORD HOPE, M.P., 1874.

11. A.J.B. Beresford Hope (1820–87):
'Progress through eclectism'

Progressive Eclecticism:

the Case of Beresford Hope

'Englishmen are the most eclectic of the human race.'

Building News, 1858

ALEXANDER JAMES BERESFORD Beresford Hope (1820–87) –
he doubled his surname in 1854 but preferred not to use a
hyphen – was almost predestined to be an architectural pundit:
he was the youngest son of Thomas Hope, Neo-Classical Hope
of Deepdene. He inherited a fortune in 1841, a great London
house in 1843, and sizeable estates in Kent and Staffordshire in
1854. All his life he remained an independent, High Tory MP,
an articulate high-churchman, and a key patron of the Gothic
Revival. And he loved a good argument. There is 'nothing I
desire more', he told E.A. Freeman, 'than fair controversy'.[1]
Committees and public meetings were his bread and butter. He
was President of the RIBA in 1865–7, proprietor first of the
Morning Chronicle and then of the *Saturday Review*, and for many
years Chairman (1846 onwards) and President (1859 onwards) of
the Ecclesiological Society. He was rich, he was learned, he was
religious, he was solemn, and he was more than a little absurd.
Disraeli's description of Hope's maiden speech in the House of
Commons is damning:

'I had the pleasure last night of seeing the great Mr Alexander Beresford Hope make a great fool of himself. I never knew such an imbecile – no voice, and the manner and appearance of a cretin. But when he quoted a line of Greek, the universal chatter ceased, and there was a general laugh.'[2]

No doubt there was a touch of envy there; and in any case, as an ally of Henry Thomas Hope ('our Hope'), Disraeli automatically placed himself in opposition to his hated brother, Alexander. Later, much later, antipathy turned to respect. Even Gladstone learned to treat him with wary regard.[3] But there is no getting away from it: Beresford Hope struck many people as pomposity personified.[4] The story goes that one day his wife, Lady Mildred – daughter of Lord Salisbury and sister of the future Prime Minister – tumbled into a fountain on the terrace of his house at Bedgebury in Kent. Beresford Hope re-fixed his monocle, strolled back into the house, and rang the bell for the footman: 'Go and pick her ladyship out of the fountain.'[5]

Absurd or not – G.J. Shaw-Lefèvre described him more favourably as 'romantic, humorous, generous, unconventional'[6] – Hope's status in architectural history is secure. In the first place, he was a churchman. He supported the Established Church 'both as a divine institution, and as an estate of the realm'.[7] That institution, he believed, should bear an appropriate architectural image. In the second place, he was committed to architecture in its political aspect; in particular, he looked for an evolving architectural expression of England's burgeoning imperial identity. And what he had to say struck a chord with many mid Victorian audiences. Academic audiences, too: not for nothing was he MP for Cambridge University. In some ways, of course, Hope embodied the prejudices of the Establishment. The editor of *The Builder* dismissed him in 1876 as 'an educated

Philistine'.[8] Goldwin Smith – never a friend – was equally dismissive of his ownership of the *Saturday Review*, which he likened to 'a sort of literary yacht'.[9] But in architectural circles Hope did have a loyal following. Robert Kerr ranked him with Fergusson, Ruskin and Pugin.[10] Even so, as a politician, as a writer, as a churchman, as a leader of taste, he ended his life in the wilderness. For fifteen years after its consecration, he could hardly bear to go inside his own church – as he thought of it – All Saints, Margaret Street. Its services were far too High. The Tory party turned to Disraeli. High Anglicans turned to Ritualism.[11] The Gothic Revival turned to Queen Anne. The RIBA never elected another layman as President. 'I could have imagined myself', he lamented late in life, 'measuring swords with Gladstone, or Disraeli, or Carlyle, or Tennyson, or Montalbert. Now I shall die a second rate notoriety, "the rich Mr Beresford Hope".'[12] Towards the end of his career, saddened by the deaths of Burges, Street and Benjamin Webb, he was even unable to see that his own pet theory – Progressive Eclecticism – had in fact been vindicated by time: it emerged, full-blown, as the architecture of Free Classicism.

In several ways – socially, intellectually, financially, politically – Beresford Hope was the leader of the Gothic party. He supported it for half a century, 'by voice, pen and purse'.[13] In the heyday of ecclesiology he was a 'potentate' of taste, whose disapproval could break an architect. In 1840, at the age of twenty, he installed a stone altar – revolutionary in its ecclesiological implications – in his own family church, at Kilndown, Kent.[14] From 1840 onwards in Cambridge, and from 1845 onwards in London, he was the mainstay of the Ecclesiological Society, putting his wealth and influence – and his London mansion, Arklow House in Connaught Place – at the committee's disposal. For years he was a compulsive reviewer, and now at last his anonymous reviews are gradually being unmasked.[15] It was Hope, for example, in *The Ecclesiologist*, who hailed Butterfield's Balliol College chapel as a triumph, and damned Skidmore and Woodward's Oxford Museum as a failure.[16] It was Hope who first warned the Ecclesiological Society away from Pugin, and then – in effect – after his death apologised for having done so.[17] It was Hope, through the *Saturday Review*, who fired a frantic broadside against Ruskin's theories of political economy: 'empty sophisms', 'windy hysterics', 'repulsive', 'revolting'.[18] All these are instances of his determination to manipulate taste. Most famously, he was Butterfield's patron at St Augustine's, Canterbury and again at All Saints, Margaret Street. He was Scott's advocate in the battle for the Foreign Office. He was Burges's champion in the Law Courts competition. And in matters of restoration he had plenty to say as well.

As in politics, Beresford Hope favoured conservative principles in church repair. But he was by no means a blanket conservationist. His voice was invariably on the side of creativity. 'The *primum mobile* of ecclesiology', he wrote in 1861, 'is practical progressive conservatism . . . our policy must be eclectic, and every case [must] be dealt with on its own individual merits.' That meant occasional prohibitions. When Butterfield proposed to tamper with the sacred stones of Merton College, Oxford, for example, he received a magisterial reprimand: why interfere with antiquity when an alternative site was available? After all, the nineteenth century – unlike the fourteenth – was uniquely blessed with 'feelings of historical association'. By that he meant a 'new sense . . . created [by] Providence . . . as a compensation for what our generation [has] lost in other ways'. Hence the 'good conservative element in the *ethos* of this nineteenth century of ours [, namely a] feeling of historical association'.[19] Conversely, when arguments for change were strong, Hope was prepared to accept them. Even when the Gothic Revival began to wane, he remained in church-building matters an adherent of 'creative restoration'. He denounced the SPAB's 'anti-scrape' doctrine as 'a gospel of despair and death'.[20] Such views led him into many a battle. His support for Butterfield's abstracted polychromy was rather too 'progressive' for many Goths; and his support for Burges's plan to complete St Paul's Cathedral with a full-blown scheme of early Renaissance decoration was rather too creative for most Classicists.[21]

But although Hope was 'a Gothicist to his heart's core', he was a Goth with more than a sneaking respect for Classicism. 'I am a Goth,' he admitted; 'more than that, a Northern Goth, but I am anxious to beautify the Northern Gothic with the best points of other styles, namely Italian Gothic and Italian Italian.' That is, he was willing to fuse Italian Gothic with Italian Renaissance. 'I am a Northern Goth', he explained, 'in conviction, not prejudice.' And so he managed to discover Gothic in the most unlikely places. He found Gothic principles – in skyline, composition and planning – in Venice and Amsterdam; in Greenwich and Brussels; in seventeenth-century Paris and in fifteenth-century Bruges. Almost everywhere, in fact, except in Palladianism and Neo-Classicism. When he came to re-model his own house at Bedgebury, Kent, in 1854–9, he told Carpenter and Slater to make it – even the private chapel – Louis Quatorze.[22]

Finally, as a collector, Hope's tastes were omnivorous. In 1857 G.F. Waagen visited Arklow House and commented: 'Mr Beresford Hope belongs to that yet limited number of collectors in England whose taste for art embraces a very universal standard.'[23] After his death, the sale of his library alone lasted six full days.[24]

★

As chief political pundit of the Camdenians, Hope's principal role in the later 1840s was to mark out clear water between ecclesiology and popery. This he did by criticising Pugin's work in architectural terms, leaving Neale and Webb to distinguish between Puginian reality and Camdenian sacramentality. Then, when Pugin fell foul of the Oratorian ambonoclasts, he felt able to suggest that the distance between Puginism and Anglicanism was not, in fact, so very great.[25] All this he managed to do, at the same time neutralising the Ecclesiological Society's Evangelical critics by changing the society's name and transferring its headquarters from Cambridge to London, in effect to his own palazzo overlooking Hyde Park. It was a very calculated performance, culminating in his favourite project − developed, of course in tandem with Benjamin Webb − for a Camdenian model church.

It was this latter scheme, the building of All Saints, Margaret Street, which − as we saw in chapter two − enabled Hope to formulate a programme of structural polychromy, a programme which brought him intermittently into conflict with his chosen instrument, William Butterfield.[26] At this point it has to be said − and said again − that Hope's attitude to Butterfield remained supportive. In 1858 he could still describe Balliol College Chapel as 'an excellent example of [the architect's] best style, grave, somewhat startling, but dignified and religious.'[27] The tensions at All Saints must have been as much personal as stylistic. With Ruskin, however, Beresford Hope never enjoyed easy relations. Here the trouble seems to have been not only personal but aesthetic, and political as well. He resented Ruskin's appropriation of Italian Gothic. 'I beg to repudiate [the adjective] "Ruskinian",,' he wrote to E.A. Freeman in 1858; 'my father [Hope of Deepdene] had written . . . [on] Italian Gothic while Ruskin was still in the nursery.' In fact Ruskin's appropriation − in the public mind, at

least – of the very notion of Gothic was to Hope a constant vex-
ation. 'The only misgiving I can have about Gothic', he assured
Freeman, 'is the fact that Ruskin patronises it.'[28] As Ruskin's
interests moved further and further towards radical social change,
Beresford Hope took up a position of total hostility. Through the
Saturday Review he mounted a campaign of ferocious criticism,
culminating in denunciation of *Unto This Last* as a recipe for total-
itarian socialism.[29]

Now, the growing cult of polychromy had received enormous
impetus from the writings and designs of A.W. Pugin. But Pugin's
interiors – notably at St Giles, Cheadle (1841–7) – depended for
their effect primarily on painted decoration. When Hope visited
Cheadle in April 1850, he saw a chance – using Ruskinian ammu-
nition – to mount an aesthetic counter-attack:

> '[Amidst] this sea of glowing diaper . . . We asked ourselves,
> Why all this paint? Why not higher art and costlier materials?
> . . . We very much wish that [Mr Pugin] had . . . entered into
> the question, which has not yet received the consideration
> which it deserves – of *constructional polychrome*. We are every
> day more and more convinced that this is one of the problems,
> which the revived Pointed architecture of the nineteenth
> century, enterprising and scientific as it is, will have chiefly to
> work out, if it means to vindicate its position of being a living
> and growing style.'[30]

The problem was, how to move beyond Pugin – and beyond
Ruskin, too – towards this new, evolving style: a style which we
now can recognise as Victorian eclecticism.

Eclectic was not a word which mid Victorians used lightly.
Beresford Hope himself began as hostile to the very idea. In the

early 1840s, he regarded eclecticism of taste – that is, plurality of styles – as aesthetically corrupt. In January 1845, for example, he dismissed 'the *revival* of Romanesque in these days' as merely 'an eclectic notion'.[31] But a year later he had begun to move towards acceptance of a different sort of eclecticism, an evolving synthesis of historic forms. We can watch him struggling to achieve this intellectual somersault in an anonymous review of September 1846:

'Christian architecture attained the highest degree of perfection . . . in the early days of Late Middle Pointed [i.e., the fourteenth century] . . . [And] the wonderful comprehensiveness of the Middle Pointed . . . renders it our fitting starting-point. Even "Perpendicular" will probably . . . have to do it visible homage by contributing something . . . to future Christian architecture. Such absorption is wholly different from eclecticism; [for absorption] incorporates [whereas] eclecticism [only] borrows . . . [In fact, absorption] appropriates all it touches . . . Eclecticism raised the Pavilion at Brighton, and the Egyptian Hall in Piccadilly. Absorption helped to develop the Basilic[a] of Trèves into the [Cathedral] of Cologne.'[32]

Once Hope had made that leap – from authenticity to development – there was no turning back. Henceforward, any objection to the principle of change – the notion of 'boundless improvement' – became almost heretical: 'like attempting to limit the power of Omnipotence'.[33] But what to call it, this new momentum for architectural reform? A word like 'absorption' could never be a battle cry; 'development' was accurate enough, but suspiciously anodyne. 'Eclecticism' was different: somehow it had the ring of credibility. So eclecticism it had to be, and preferably conjoined to the very watchword of enlightened nineteenth-century thinking: Progress.

It was through the construction of All Saints, Margaret Street – as we have already seen – that Beresford Hope aimed to realise these theories in tangible form. In particular, he saw the use of eclectic polychromy – English and Continental, first by Butterfield, then by Street – as 'a contribution to the solution of that great problem – an architecture of the future, worthy, in its aesthetic development, of the intellectual and material resources of the age we live in'.

> 'England is a brick-making country – London, *ante omnia*, a brick-built city. But our island also produces marbles – the rich-coloured and enduring Serpentine in Cornwall – and the dark, shelly, but very crumbling "Purbeck", "Petworth", and "Bethersden", in Dorsetshire, Sussex, and Kent – while the varieties which Devonshire produces need hardly be alluded to. Again, in Derbyshire we find alabaster . . . and a shelly species of marble more durable than Purbeck, beside a store of fluoric spars available in delicate inlaying – not to mention a red marble closely rivalling the Rosso Antico . . . Anglesey also yields specimens of a dark-green colour – so does Connemara – and Aberdeen and Peterhead respectively abound in grey and rose granite . . .'

It was through the use of these native materials – compounded with foreign forms – all marshalled in eclectic splendour, that Beresford Hope dreamed of creating 'the future . . . architecture of England'.[34]

The consecration of All Saints in 1859 coincided with Beresford Hope's most famous battle: the duel with Lord Palmerston over the Foreign Office in Whitehall. The Gothic principles he relied upon on this occasion turned out to be – despite all his earlier reservations – the *True Principles* of A.W. Pugin. In the early days of the Cambridge Camden Society, Hope had taken the lead in damning Pugin's achievements with faint praise. But when he attacked Palmerston in 1859 for displaying architectural ignorance, his invective had the true Puginian stamp:

> '[Lord Palmerston] thinks that art is like his own political performances . . . he thinks all art and architecture proceed on the same principle . . . [with] the trickery, and finesse, and sham of his own political morals. True art makes the apparent and the real coincide – makes the external elevation display honestly its construction and purpose. Ground plan and elevation, outside and inside, construction and ornament, must match and express each other. Art must say what it means, and mean what it says. Art does not Machiavelise, or deal in constructional ambiguities, or diplomatic evasions . . . And until Lord Palmerston has grasped this fundamental fact, that an elevation is not a thing to be nailed on to any interior, like a scene in a play, but must be the real expression of the inner intention and object, he has not mastered the very first principles of taste.'[35]

Two styles, and two alone, he contended, attained the highest status: 'pure Greek art, that is, honest, earnest, severe, horizontal art; and pure Pointed, that is honest, earnest, truthful, vertical art . . . [For] Roman is a mere debasement [of Greek. And] Italian is only a debasement [of Gothic] . . . Whatever there is good and true in Italian [for instance, its occasional felicities of composition and planning] is only Pointed in masquerade.'[36] But of these two models, Greek architecture was totally unsuited to the varied demands of the nineteenth century. That left only Gothic. And at this point Hope reveals his true colours: no other style was permissible.

'In this single word "style" lies the root of the evil. It cannot be that Greek art is altogether right for certain things, and right in its way, and that Pointed art is suited for certain purposes, and right in its way. This, which affects to be Liberalism, is, to use the nomenclature of another subject, Indifferentism. It is the resource of intellectual idleness and critical incapacity – there must be an exclusive and prohibitory art in the architecture of every period of society and civilisation.'[37]

Such an art would transcend ephemeral style; for here was a vision of tectonic truth.

In the propaganda of ecclesiology, Beresford Hope was certainly persuasive. The movement, he admitted in old age, might not have had 'the *chic* to gain general popularity'; but it did represent a vital step forward in pursuit of 'architectural truth'.[38] And for this propaganda coup he should certainly take some credit. As for forms of worship, he had no doubt that the Cambridge Camden Society had indeed triumphed: '[we] affected a revolution in the idea of worship throughout the Church of England. We . . . turned minds upside down.'[39] Throughout the world, Anglican churches had come to embody the full range of Camdenian principles. In effect, the ideal of a Christian church had been re-established, incorporating 'the great truths of reality, symbolism and perpetual prayer'.[40] An Anglican church was no longer to be 'a sermon-house', but 'a temple of the MOST HIGH'; no longer a 'Protestant Auditorium' but a 'Catholic House of Prayer'.[41] In all this, Hope was at one with his Oxford and Cambridge allies. 'We are all fellow workers,' he wrote to E.A. Freeman in 1845; fellow workers 'in a common and holy cause'.[42]

Well, maybe so; but in the politics of ecclesiology, Beresford Hope played out a somewhat ambivalent role. Although he will be for ever linked with Benjamin Webb and J.M. Neale – the trinity of Trinity College, Cambridge – his churchmanship was rather different from theirs. He was less of a sacramentalist than Neale, less of a ritualist than Webb. What he longed for was a restoration of Archbishop Laud's 'beauty of holiness', 'the palmy Caroline days of the English church'.[43] What he hated was the imagery of Counter-Reformation Baroque: sacramental theatre, without even the decency of a rood-screen. This he christened Oratorianism, and its revival in Roman Catholic circles seemed – paradoxically – to point a way towards *rapprochement* with A.W. Pugin. Both men, Hope and Pugin, could unite in selective medievalism; in hostility, above all, to Dr Newman and the ambonoclasts. 'Mr Hope's anti-Catholicism', concluded the Reverend J.M. Capes, 'is of the *aesthetic* species. He is a Protestant on ritualistic and architectural grounds.'[44] Hope was prepared to endow the modest services conducted by Webb at Sheen in Staffordshire, but not the more elaborate rituals of St Andrew, Wells Street. And for years he absented himself from services in Margaret Street, because of their Romanising tendency: his connection with that famous church, he insisted, was 'purely architectural'.[45] In the end, Hope's relations with its incumbent, W. Upton Richards, became positively painful. 'Richards', he assured Gladstone in 1853, was not only a ritualist: he actually had 'a crooked turn of mind'.[46]

One obituarist neatly remarked that Hope was 'a High Churchman of the Hook and Hooker type, which is a very different thing from [being] . . . a ritualist'. Perhaps; but not surprisingly so. He was, after all, a layman. Hope's Anglicanism was establishmentarian, moderate, paternal and Tory. Neale thoroughly disapproved of his 'inveterate . . . spirit of compromise'. Hope, in return, regarded Neale as unwisely dogmatic. 'Neale,' he once remarked, 'with all his genius, was not judicious.'[47] For Neale, Gothic was a spiritual symbol; for Webb it was a sacred text; for Hope it was more an evolving language of form, hungrily assimilative and endlessly adaptable to circumstance. All three agreed that the architecture of the mid nineteenth century had achieved a new 'spirit of reality'; but for Hope that spirit represented just another phase in 'the onward march of improvement'.[48] By 1859, he had learnt his lesson as a patron: having burnt his fingers in Margaret Street, he settled for influence rather than control. And, in stylistic terms, his outlook came to assume an increasingly evolutionary stance. Ever since 1846 he had been an adherent of 'development'.[49] He had been forced to admit that 'Late Middle Pointed was only an approximation to perfection'.[50] By the 1850s, he had clearly moved on from the early antiquarianism of his Cambridge days towards a viable eclecticism of form. In this he took Benjamin Webb with him; but he failed to shift the Gothic fundamentalism of John Mason Neale.

'We are a medieval party,' Hope reminded the ecclesiologists in 1862. 'Why? Because we find that there are many things which make medieval art the most serviceable in the present nineteenth century. We greatly respect archaeology and we gladly study antiquities; but we study medieval art with a view to the benefit of the present age, and the edification of succeeding generations.'[51] 'We took up the Gothic movement', he repeated a year later, 'because we believed that that was the movement most practicable for the material, and the social, and the political, and the religious needs of this progressive and agitated century.'[52]

Unlike James Fergusson, who believed that a new style would one day replace all its predecessors, Beresford Hope realised that such a cultural cataclysm was unlikely to happen again. Total styles were the product of primitive civilisations. And even in these, style is a slow, accretive growth: we do not look for the phenomenon of spontaneous generation in the anthropology of built form. But by the nineteenth century there had been a change of gear; a 'counteracting influence' had emerged, 'the creation, thanks to a modern civilisation, [thanks] to printing, engraving, increased locomotion, and so on, of the feeling of *association*, that is, of archaeology made popular.'[53] Or, as Gilbert Scott once put it, 'the peculiar characteristic of the present day, as compared with all former periods, is this – that we are acquainted with the history of art.'[54] Hence 'the Babel of schools'. Hence the search for 'a real style embodying the wants of the living and not of any dead age'; 'the aim [in fact] of all philosophic writers on architecture in modern days.'[55]

For Beresford Hope, there was in the end only one way out of this conundrum: 'Liberal' or 'Progressive Eclecticism'. This, he explained, is 'the very key-stone of our system . . . it . . . makes the [Ecclesiological] Society a living power'. What they hoped to develop was a 'type of art . . . which, though called medieval, [was] still modern and progressive'.[56] He had long realised, for example, that when it came to architectural sculpture, 'so-called classical and so-called medieval figure-drawing slide into each other'.[57] The next step was to unify both traditions in compositional terms. That involved an endless commitment to eclecticism, but eclecticism in a European context. 'The style for Europe as it is', he contended in 1863, 'must have some principle to start with, and . . . this principle can only be found in the successive teachings of collective Europe since the day that Christianity set its seal on the civilisation of the West.'[58] Gothic was, after all, in Gilbert Scott's unguarded phrase, 'the Christian architecture of the Teutonic race'.[59] But how could it be both Gothic and modern at the same time? Somehow the Victorians had to steer their way 'between the rocks of unreal antiquarianism and an unfettered originality which unkind critics might even call eccentricity'.[60] In its origins, Hope saw the new style as necessarily international; but in its formulation it would be English: 'this style, while boldly eclectic in its details, must, in its main principles, vividly embody the historical characteristics of England, for whose material uses it will come into being.'[61] Nationalist feelings, evolutionist thinking, cultural imperialism: all these would have their part to play. 'In the style of the future,' he explained in 1856, 'very much will be borrowed from Gothic . . . [But] it will incorporate the beauties and conveniences of all other styles . . . it will be as massive as Egyptian . . . or light as Saracenic . . . and . . . proportioned like a Grecian temple. But that Gothic *must* be the main ingredient appears to us demonstrable from the fact that Gothic was the universal emanation of the mind of Christian Europe, or at least of its active portion, in the days when that polity which is now overspreading the world was cradled. It was European – it was Christian – it was conclimatic with the chief regions of organised civil polity. With such an origin, we believe that it must prove itself a germinating power in the germination of Europe, in both hemispheres, just as the [Saxon] Wittenagemot has been the seed from which have sprung the Parliaments of Belgium, Holland, and Sardinia, Legislatures (such as they are) in Spain and Greece, the Congress of the United States, and the Colonial Assemblies of the Cape, Australia, and Jamaica.'[62] 'The only style of common sense architecture for the future of England', Hope concludes, 'must [therefore] be Gothic architecture, cultivated in the spirit of progression founded upon eclecticism. But here', he admits – and he is speaking at this point in 1858 – 'our difficulties only begin . . . [for] what are we to eclect?'[63]

At this stage of the argument, Beresford Hope has to admit that – like most of his generation – he developed his architectural sensibilities pragmatically. The founders of the Cambridge Camden Society had fought the good fight for Middle Pointed, and they had won. In those days they were Catholic rather than eclectic. In the 1830s and early 1840s, he explains, we chose our native Gothic as 'our point of departure', 'the starting point for that which was then our only dream, the development and perfecting of our English Gothic'. In the battle between first, second and third Pointed, victory went to second – Decorated – 'the golden mean of English Gothic'. And that was a good thing. Why? Because in Decorated Gothic 'the principle of verticality was . . . triumphant, but not despotic'. In other words, the balancing of gravitational images was well understood. The revival of such a style, Hope concluded, 'certainly flattered our insular pride. We were the best men in the world – nobody was like us – nothing [was] like our style.'[64] In the writings of A.W. Pugin – whom Hope eventually came to see as 'an honest, a true, a loving and a loveable man' – English Gothic thus found its prophet.[65] The model for ecclesiologists in those days was 'the typal rural parish church'. And this stylistic ideal was difficult to shake off. 'We planted [those churches]', Hope later admitted, 'most impartially in town or country.' That was because 'we had got hold of certain theories, very true in themselves, but like all theories, somewhat misleading when pushed to abstract *doctrinaire* principles.'[66] Gradually the need for a different sort of town church emerged: taller and wider – with triforium galleries or an apse, if necessary – as in 'Old Rhenish churches', or in 'the large churches of Belgian cities'. By 1864 – twenty-five years after its foundation – the Ecclesiological Society was beginning to be more interested in Cuypers' new church in Amsterdam than in the rustic monuments of Heckington or Snettisham. No wonder old Archdeacon Thorp was starting to feel confused: 'I begin to ask myself where I am – in what age do I live?' His old pupil Beresford Hope seemed to be 'saying exactly contrary to what he used to say. It is all new, all heretical.'[67]

It was during the later 1840s that this new generation – Thorp's cleverest Cambridge pupils – moved into full control of the ecclesiological movement. Soon English Gothic alone was no longer enough. They began to look abroad. In 1847 George Truefitt published *Architectural Sketches on the Continent*: dedicated, significantly, to Beresford Hope. And early that very year Hope himself had already been heard calling for an expansion of Gothic sources. At this point, however, he had yet to adopt the banner of eclecticism.[68] But in the 1850s the basis of revival widened inexorably: Italian, French and even German Gothic were all absorbed. Speaking at Oxford as early as 1846, Hope had demanded the broadest of all possible bases: 'We must be as familiar with San Clemente, Santa Sophia, and the church of the Holy Sepulchre, as with Heslington and York Minster . . . We should remember that Great Britain reigns over the torrid and the hyperborean zone, that she will soon have to rear temples of the True Faith in Benares and Labrador, Newfoundland and Cathay.'[69] At that stage he was still looking for a way out of the strait-jacket of Middle Pointed. He found it in a semantic conjuring trick: 'Eschewing . . . eclecticism, our aim is to be Catholic.' That last capital letter was a piece of typographical ambivalence which lured his Tractarian readers on to the next phase in the dialogue. Grecian architecture might have been perfect, he contended, but it represented 'pure intellect, unsanctified by higher grace'. Romanesque architecture, by contrast, did embody Christian values; but reviving its details could never be more than an 'arrant piece of impractical antiquarianism'. Only as a mine of visual principles – 'a storehouse of models' – could it play a part in the revival of Gothic practice. 'We do not anticipate', Hope concludes – this is 1846, remember – 'any development which shall not be Pointed'; because 'Pointed Architecture is [the] true correlative to Christian doctrine'. Even so, the nineteenth century could still look forward to a limitless development of the Gothic system: to shrines, indeed, which would outdazzle Cologne, even as Cologne outshone Torcello. 'Do not the achievements of modern science, do not our increased acquaintance with the products of all lands, their marbles, their woods, their ornamental work; do not our increased means of commerce all point to fresh stores of artistical wealth, which may hereafter be devoted to the service of the sanctuary? Christian Architecture has not yet incorporated them, but is Christian Architecture to be tied by a statute of mortmain?'[70]

One year after that, still seeking a foundation 'more broad and comprehensive', Beresford Hope definitively crossed the Rubicon of eclecticism. On 18 May 1847, in a debate on church restoration prompted by a pamphlet by E.A. Freeman, both Hope and Webb 'avowed [themselves] Eclectic'.[71] From that point onwards a tempting path stretched irresistibly upwards, from Conservative (that is, restorative) Eclecticism to the higher polemics of Eclectic Progression. Over the next ten years Beresford Hope built up a theoretical position which could encompass all possible forms of change. 'To be truly eclectic,' he announced in 1858, 'we must be universally eclectic – we must eclect from everything that has been collected; and we must assimilate and fuse everything that we eclect, for without such fusion the process remains after all only one of distributive collection . . . And even then we may only be storing up material for our successors. Ours is only an eclecticism of the past . . . I imagine there will be an eclecticism of the future.'[72] The new style, he explained, would draw upon 'resources unknown to the fourteenth century. There will be the knowledge of all the architecture of all the ages and countries, out of which to absorb a variety of materials, every day augmented to an extent almost bewildering; and there will be processes, gigantic as steam power, or minute as photography, to abridge labour, or to facilitate invention.'[73] New materials, both decorative and structural, 'must in time revolutionise all architecture; but I believe it will be a peaceful . . . revolution [supplementing] . . . the good tradition of the old time.'[74] And where will all this collecting stop? 'I will stop', Hope sagely concludes, 'where common sense tells me to stop. When I can no longer assimilate I will cease to absorb.'[75] Meanwhile, 'absorption is the thing to be aimed at'; for absorption is 'conducive to invention'. And the criteria for absorption were, of course, the ones he had learned from A.W. Pugin: 'those realities of construction and those realities of decoration which derive their life and vigour from Gothic'.[76] For Beresford Hope, therefore, the lesson for the Victorian age was by 1858 quite clear: 'truth . . . progress, and common sense'. Let the message go forth: 'progress through eclecticism'.[77]

Now, eclecticism was a risky business. There would be the occasional blind alley. Hope's own involvement in the development of a prefabricated iron church – first for Ireland, then for more remote colonies – came in the end to nothing.[78] And eclecticism, even within the territory of traditional materials, was inevitably fraught with error. The men Goodhart-Rendel eventually labelled Rogues clearly managed to overstep the mark. The turning of engineers – and even gardeners – into architects additionally compounded the problem. When in 1856 Sir Joseph Paxton produced his designs for Ferrières, the Rothschild palace near Paris, Hope's rebuke was magisterial: 'He once made a hit in the Crystal Palace – let him rest content with this, and not damage a life of prosperous horticulture with an old age of reprehensible architecture.'[79] That was more than a little unkind. But there was something in it. Victorians like Paxton were cultural autodidacts. And they taught themselves too much. Their architecture came close to dying from a surfeit of prototypes. 'Eclecticism, Eclecticism,' muttered J.P. Seddon, 'what horrors have been perpetrated in thy euphonious name.'[80]

Still, Beresford Hope remained optimistic, at least into the 1860s. At the very least, he announced, 'our architects have begun to think', and to think 'in an empiric spirit'. At present there might be confusion. The state of English architecture might even be 'chaotic'. But remember: '*Splendide errare*'.[81] Creative eclecticism necessarily involves creative error. 'There may be here and there exuberance, if not extravagance; but this is only the natural recoil from the *malebolge* of stock-brick and cement in which we have so long been wandering.'[82] Polychromy, for instance: 'if you go into this style at all, you should do so boldly'. The aim must be an evolving synthesis – mere multiplicity is not enough: 'the choice of styles is Babel'.[83] 'A real style' will only emerge if its base becomes 'conservative . . . not destructive, retrospective no less than prospective, national rather than cosmopolitan, and yet encircling its native tradition by the imported and assimilated contributions of other lands.'[84]

In his belief in Progressive Eclecticism Beresford Hope could at least claim to speak for the majority of his architectural generation in England. John Sulman defined it as 'not . . . the haphazard jumbling of incongruous fragments but a judicious combination or modification of forms'.[85] 'This judicious, and indeed inevitable eclecticism', claimed Benjamin Webb, 'is the distinguishing glory of our English architects. Nothing of the sort has yet been seen in France or Germany.'[86] In France voices could still be heard demanding absolute fidelity to a single style. In his *Entrétiens* of 1863, Viollet-le-Duc warned that a new style could only be based on a new constructive system: without that, eclecticism – on the nosegay principle – would merely produce 'a macaronic style'.[87] In 1856 Lassus denounced eclecticism as 'the Plague of Art . . . the common enemy . . . the scourge of our epoch'.[88] In England such views found little support. Was not eclecticism in architecture the natural product of a liberal society and a *laissez-faire* economy?[89] 'Englishmen', announced the *Building News* in 1858, 'are the most eclectic of the human race.'[90] Over the years any number of critics toyed with eclecticism as an answer to the problems posed by evolutionary thinking and technological change: Goths like Gilbert Scott;[91] rationalists like James Fergusson;[92] syncretists like H.N. Humphreys,[93] Samuel Huggins,[94] James Boult[95] and James Knowles;[96] pessimist classicists like T.L. Donaldson;[97] pessimist Goths like J.T. Emmett;[98] eternal optimists like Robert Kerr.[99] And their ultimate, collective aesthetic goal was still that same eclectic goal set out by Beresford Hope's father – Thomas Hope of Deepdene – in 1835: 'An architecture . . . at once elegant, appropriate, and original . . . "Our Own".'[100]

Beresford Hope's trumpet-call to eclecticism, 'The Common Sense of Art', was delivered in 1858. The lecture theatre at South Kensington was 'crowded in every part'; the lecturer himself was 'warmly applauded'.[101] But how exactly would this persuasive principle operate? In that year, two experimentally eclectic combinations of new materials and historic forms could be directly compared: Benjamin Woodward's University Museum at Oxford and Sydney Smirke's Round Reading Room at the British Museum. The first was Gothic, the second Classic. Hope

began by being predisposed to Woodward; but he ended by pre-
ferring Sydney Smirke.[102] Four years later current design was put
under a microscope at that 'saturnalia of art', the International
Exhibition of 1862.[103] The exhibition building itself had been
designed by Captain Francis Fowke, an engineer not an architect, and a rather different sort of eclectic. Fergusson welcomed
Fowke's characteristic *mélange*: 'neither Grecian nor Gothic, but
thoroughly nineteenth-century'.[104] But for Beresford Hope the
building was an 'architectural fiasco': its walls displayed 'that particular combination of Venetian and emasculated Byzantine
which might be termed the Cosmopolitan-Governmental architecture of this century';[105] its brick-based glass domes – 'dish-
covers . . . cucumber-frames' – were 'the basest and most
purposeless crystallo–chalybeate bubbles which earth has yet
regurgitated';[106] its construction might indeed be 'a triumph of
engineering', but its triumph was merely the triumph of a 'fifth-
rate railway station'.[107] Unlike Paxton's Crystal Palace, Fowke's
composition appeared to embody no single ruling idea, no
intrinsic sense of scale. It seemed to Hope to be merely an illustration of the eternal functional fallacy: the equation of utility
with beauty. In this 'monstrous bazaar', he concluded, England
had created 'a thing of ugliness which is . . . a grief for ever'. Oh
for 'the euthanasia of Captain Fowke'![108]

Clearly Beresford Hope found engineers' eclecticism a little
difficult to swallow. Still, he believed that in 1862, from many
different routes, 'a new style' was actually germinating, 'derived
from, but not servilely following, existing systems'. At the
International Exhibition many styles were certainly on display;
enough to undermine the resolution of any medievalist. But did
that mean that the Goths were in confusion, all at 'sea, without
. . . a haven . . .? By no means so! The moral is that . . . art is
one . . . New ideas can be gathered from every school . . . but

. . . ours [is] the most liberal . . . the best suited to the requirements of the age . . . the . . . most patient of help from every
quarter.' Gothic principles, he still believed – 'progressive architecture . . . architecture illimitable'[109] – could absorb almost anything. Lined up, facing each other 'like rival armies', the British
exhibition of architectural drawings emphasised that the mid
Victorian age was at the very least 'an epoch of vast material and
intellectual activity in the pursuit of architecture.' There they
were, 'the Gothic on one side, the classical and the renaissance
on the other, but peacefully commingled in the . . . galleries . . .
devoted to the Scotchmen.' Scots Baronial: here indeed was
eclecticism with a vengeance. But here too was historicism in
labour: 'the eager, sometimes exuberant, oftener healthy, search
after originality'; the battle of ideas from which, one day, One
Style would come. But whatever form it took, Beresford Hope
believed, architecture one hundred years later would eventually
owe more to Gothic principles than it did to Classic.[110]

Meanwhile, there was an increasing range of new materials
available, in particular durable finishes in ceramic ware. At
Burslem in Staffordshire, at the centre of the Potteries, Hope
called in 1863 for ceramics more valuable in the long run than
vases and statuettes. 'There was another, more solid and more
eternal sort of pottery,' he reminded his audience, namely 'architectural pottery'. Its ceramic finish might take the form of
'mouldings in terracotta'; or 'Della Robbia panels'; or even
'mosaics in tesserae'. There were various possibilities; but this
was no 'vague dream'. The manufacturers of Staffordshire had it
in their power to outshine the potters of medieval Milan.[111]
Hence Burslem's Wedgwood Memorial Institute (1863–9). This
experimental building – resplendent in polychrome brick and
terracotta, pullulating with sculpture by Rudyard Kipling's
father – seemed to Hope to embody Progressive Eclecticism at

12. G.B. Nichols, R. Edgar and J. Lockwood Kipling,
Wedgwood Memorial Institute, Burslem, Staffordshire
(1863–9). Progressive eclecticism: the arts applied

the heart of industrial England.[112] And it was not the only example. Down south in London, at the Langham Hotel in Portland Place – designed by Giles and Murray in 1863 – a very different sort of building was exploring progressive principles in a very different sort of way.[113] There was less polychrome at the Langham; but its silhouette embodied just that 'pyramidising of the skyline' which filled eclectic pundits with glee.[114] And its style was indeed eclectic: Trecento in its fenestration, mixed Renaissance in its cornice, French Pavilion in its silhouette.

So was this the hope of English architecture? 'We have everything the thirteenth and fourteenth centuries could give us,' Hope explains in 1863, 'together with all that is our own, and all that the invention of printing and the spread of literature have opened up. Art is in a transitional state; the minds of men are in a transitional state; politics are in a transitional state. We live in a century . . . of revolutions . . . Empires are crashing, new worlds are forming . . . And in the midst of all this zeal and turmoil, there is the grand figure of Christian . . . Art, progressive, . . . European, . . . English, rising higher and higher from the dark and surging waves of the ocean.'[115] It was the destiny of Gothic, therefore, to become one day the unifying focus for all other styles. 'Whatever beauty any other style possesses, that beauty we embrace; and we hope, or dream . . . that in some later day the hidden link that joins it to the seemingly rival developments may be discovered. Art we believe is one, only man has not yet mastered the secret of its unity.' Meanwhile, 'first-rate imitation [is] better than second-rate originality'.[116]

In the brickwork of Butterfield and Street, in the sculptural genius of William Burges, in the versatility of Gilbert Scott, Hope sensed something of the endless possibilities of this new visual language. And in all this he was at one with Benjamin

13. Thomas Cundy Jnr, Grosvenor Mansions, Grosvenor Place, London (1864). Progressive eclectism: 'pyramidising the skyline'

Webb. In particular, both men looked to Butterfield – at least until the later 1850s – as the rising star of English Gothic. At the Exhibition Building of 1862, Captain Fowke's design seemed to have been strangled by its engineering aesthetic: 'the blank, vast, solid, helpless inanity of the endless, featureless block of piled-up bricks'.[117] Butterfield, by contrast, had seized upon the true magic of brick: its capacity to atomise mere weight and mass into endless patterns of line and colour. Butterfield at the very least had shown the way, by 'inventing an eclectic style [somewhere] between Southern Byzantine and Northern Gothic': a magic synthesis of brickwork, tile and mosaic.[118] But how many could follow that particular lead?

By the end of the 1860s the dream of a new Victorian Style – the Holy Grail of nineteenth-century architecture – had begun to look a little thin. Benjamin Webb still clung to Hope's progressive vision; it was 'the salt', he believed, 'which . . . preserved the . . . Ecclesiological school from the moral stagnation of an effete dilettantism'.[119] But could they carry the architectural profession with them? In 1865 Hope at last became President of the RIBA. He had been defeated by the Classicists in 1861;[120] they defeated him again in 1863.[121] Now he had a major platform to propagate his views. In his inaugural address he proposed that one solution to the conundrum of style might be the professional integration of architecture and engineering. 'The Institute', he explained, 'ought to be the central regulating Areopagus of Architecture – of architecture as a science, and architecture as an art';[122] Paddington Station, after all, had been the triple achievement of Matthew Digby Wyatt, Owen Jones and Isambard Kingdom Brunel. That argument postulated an institutional approach, and a dramatic one at that. Had it succeeded, the history of western architecture would no doubt have been rather different. But it was far too big a step, and nothing came of it. A year later, in his second presidential address, Hope scaled down his ambition, calling merely – 'in the name of progress and eclecticism' – for the application of modern techniques and materials to Gothic Revival design.[123] That was a more modest proposal, but it proved equally unproductive. So, the year after that, in a farewell speech, he was reduced to speculating again on the progress of architecture, looking back to his father's time, and forward – presumably – to an endlessly eclectic future.[124] But time was running out for the Gothic Revival – the New Law Courts Competition of 1867 marked its climax – and Beresford Hope refused to concede to Queen Anne the freedom he so willingly granted to Gothic.

What Hope objected to in the Queen Anne revival was not its eclecticism – Dutch, French, Flemish, German, English, Japanese – but the fact that its decorative matrix was Classical, not Gothic. The best elements in what he regarded as this heretical synthesis – 'the honest use of red brick, the frequent resort to something like window tracery, the indulgence in constructional decoration . . . the conspicuous and pyramidising . . . skyline' – all these might certainly be traced back to medieval roots. But to take 'the prosaic comeliness of a Queen Anne house in some dull suburb, and then to trick it out with gables from Amsterdam, tile-facings from Kent, chimneys from Essex, and sgraffito from Italy' – to do all this, and then hail it as a new style – seemed to him the ultimate absurdity.[125]

Ironically, the propaganda of the pundits over so many years – and Hope was the doyen of architectural pundits – had merely succeeded in replacing the monotony of developer's Georgian with the mendacity of developer's Queen Anne.

'Take a row of houses [Hope had suggested in 1863] in Hanley, Birmingham, Manchester, or Bradford, . . . no outline, no

skyline . . . the same dread, dreary, uniform, colourless square
block, the same square doors, brass knockers and door-plates,
the same sash windows, the same stone slabs under the
windows, the same chimneys – and . . . inside, the same
rhubarb-coloured oil-cloth in the passage, the same rooms with
the same paper on the walls, the same Brussels carpets, with the
same flowers [on them] . . . the same mixture of oil-cloth and
carpet on the stairs, the same chimney-piece . . . [and, sitting
there, the owner, wearing] that most extraordinary and
uncouth dress, which . . . no . . . Feejee Islander or any savage
in the world . . . ever invented the like of – the swallow-tail coat
. . . [and] chimney-pot hat. By his side . . . the partner of his joys
and sorrows, in a shawl, . . . crinoline and . . . coal-scoop bonnet
. . . [What a] dreadful Sahara [of taste].'[126]

So much for spec. builder's Georgian. That was what the Gothic
Revival – in its secular manifestation – set out to abolish. And its
influence – in colour, in materials, in carving, in silhouette – was
by the 1860s omnipresent. Even in London's most mixed
Renaissance monuments – Cundy's Grosvenor Mansions in
Grosvenor Place (1864); the Grosvenor Hotel designed by J.T.
Knowles in 1860–1; or the London Bridge Hotel, of 1861–3 – in
all these buildings some glimmerings of Gothic virtue were dis-
cernable.[127] At Longman's great warehouse in Paternoster Row,
even in Upper Brook Street, in the house of Harry Emanuel the
jeweller – Italian detail; Gallic roofline – Hope sensed some vestiges of Gothic spirit. Each of these buildings, he believed,
showed some understanding of 'that prime essential of all
effective civil architecture – skyline'. Even the Charing Cross
Hotel – designed by E.M. Barry in 1863–4 – could boast at least
a 'semi-Gothic outline'.[128] After all, 'Gothic principles' could in
practice be reduced to a bare handful of essentials: 'the reality of

material . . . free, aspiring skyline . . . [composition] symmetrical or broken; . . . staircases [freely planned, with] . . . varieties of window and . . . door . . . [plus a willingness, of course, to use] every kind of wood and stone . . . pottery and iron'.[129] It was a pretty comprehensive list: what, at the end of it all, was thereby excluded from the Gothic canon? Scarcely anything, it seemed.

In practice, all this talk of assimilation was stretching Gothic principles to the limit. And Hope had no time for the style which eventually emerged from so much dilution: Queen Anne. Besides, even if a viable style were indeed to emerge, where were its masters to come from? The problem, as Hope saw it, was that the Gothic Revival had multiplied the demand for artists and craftsmen; but no adequate system of training had been developed to meet that demand.[130] The result was multiplied vulgarity. If only the art-workman could be replaced by the working artist. That was why he endeavoured to draw the Royal Academy into the training of craftsmen; and why he consistently championed the training programmes of the Architectural Museum. 'Though it has no obligatory credo,' he concluded, the museum 'is mainly Gothic. It does not exclude other styles, but it has a strong Gothic bias . . . [whereas] the Institute of Architects has no credo at all.'[131]

Beresford Hope's ambitions in respect of architectural training were never to be fulfilled. In 'the Queen Anne Craze', as he saw it, a few misguided 'schismatics from the Gothic church' had led English architecture astray. They had produced, or so he thought, not style but negation of style. Its enthusiasts might call it 'free classical'; but its history, he predicted in 1875, would surely be 'written on water.'[132] Because its characteristics were essentially 'factitious': it denied the truths of vernacular building.[133] It was not 'real'.[134] The result, therefore, was 'unbridled eclecticism'.[135] 'Something', he concluded sadly in 1884, 'may come of all this hurly-burly at some time or other; but at present the results are merely negative.'[136]

In effect, by the end of his life Beresford Hope had only one set of architectural rules to hold on to: the *True Principles* of A.W. Pugin. 'Why', he asked in 1880, 'are [the] younger generation so forgetful, or . . . so ignorant of . . . [– or even] so ungrateful to – Pugin's great services to architectural truth?'[137] As a young man, Hope had built up ecclesiology by playing down Pugin's influence; in middle age, he had back-tracked in Pugin's direction, while calling for Progressive Eclecticism as an escape from a surfeit of Ruskin; and now, in old age – after half a century of debate – we find him summoning up the armoury of *True Principles* once more to do battle with the 'unbridled eclecticism' of Queen Anne. It was a curious irony.

At his death in 1887, the editor of *The Builder*, H. Heathcote Statham, commented on the fact that Beresford Hope's plea for Progressive Eclecticism, delivered so optimistically in 1858, had borne some very curious fruit: 'eclecticism has run wild since then'.[138] Wild or not, had it produced a Victorian Style? More to the point, had Victorian critics moved any closer to understanding its secrets? When Hope's RIBA obituary came to be delivered, his obituarist simply set out the question – 'whether we have really evolved a Victorian style' – and urged the audience to look about them.[139] The audience, apparently, was not disposed to look: the speeches were heard with 'manifest impatience'.[140] Hope, after all, had been known as a hard-line Goth; his name had little resonance for the Arts and Crafts generation, still less for the founding fathers of Edwardian Baroque. But in that very year, 1887, Basil Champneys produced a Jubilee assessment of 'The Architecture of Queen Victoria's Reign', and he came to the conclusion that eclecticism had indeed triumphed,

14. R. Norman Shaw, Alliance Assurance Office, St James's Street, London (1881–3). Victorian Free Classicism: 'a Teutonic counterpart of Jacobean'

but in a novel, 'free classic' form.[141] He chose three recent buildings: Norman Shaw's Alliance Assurance Office (1881–3) on the corner of Pall Mall and St James's Street; Bodley and Garner's School Board Offices (1872–9) on the Embankment;[142] and T.G. Jackson's Examination Schools at Oxford (1876–82; 1887).[143]

Now, Hope himself had little good to say about any of these. Shaw's office building, he admitted, was Picturesque. But it would have been even more so in seventeenth-century Gothic. Instead it embodied 'that Teutonic counterpart of Jacobean' occasionally found 'in the Low Countries and in Heidelberg'.[144] As for Jackson's Schools quadrangle, that seemed a prime example of eclecticism without assimilation, justified only on the grounds of local loyalty.[145] But Champneys – a master of what Hope preferred to think of as 'post-Gothic' design – could in fact see further than his mentor. In all three buildings Champneys identified a union of Gothic and Classic – Classic forms and Gothic principles – 'the germ of an original and harmonious style in the future'.[146] And in a way this had been the essence of Queen Anne: by reviving hybrid formulae – François Premier, Flemish or Jacobean – it suggested an escape from the stylistic deadlock, a truce in the Battle of the Styles.[147] That was certainly a theme taken up about the same time by other critics. For here – in the work of Norman Shaw and Ernest George, T.G. Jackson, Aston Webb and T.E. Collcutt – was a 'transitional style', a style both 'Victorian' and 'Modern'.[148] The nomenclature of the new approach might be confused: 'Queen Anne', 'Old English', 'Dutch William', 'Free Classic', 'Mystic', 'Neo-Classic', 'Re-Classic', 'Stuart', 'Re-Renaissance'. Some of the detail – even in a civic triumph like Collcutt's Imperial Institute at South Kensington – seemed to qualify only too well as 'Bric-à-Brac'. But here, in an eclectic fusion of both major western traditions, seemed to lie a way out of the dilemma of style. Right at the end of Victoria's reign, the Imperial Institute (1887–93) seemed to sum up all the optimism – and all the uncertainty – of so much Victorian thinking. 'The style', wrote one critic in 1893–4 – without a trace of sarcasm – 'is indescribable . . . [This] is a building which is essentially Victorian . . . and . . . truly modern.'[149]

Beresford Hope never found quite what he was looking for. In fact, he regarded Aestheticism and the Queen Anne Revival as a reversal of all his aims: an eclecticism which was not progressive but chaotically atavistic. Nevertheless, he was nearer to the Holy Grail than he realised. And two years before his death, he publicly admitted that the stylistic phenomena foolishly known as Queen Anne added up – at least in the hands of 'men of progress' – to 'free manifestations of the European architecture of Christian civilisation'. In other words, Progressive Eclecticism. At the very least, this tendency seemed to Hope in his declining years to embody a little more promise than the 'sterility' – the decomposing Classicism – of Leeming and Leeming's Admiralty building of 1894–5 on Horse Guards Parade.[150] That lame performance – 'woefully disappointing . . . vulgar [and] commonplace'[151] – seemed to many critics the end of the line for unitary composition. Eclecticism – crossing and re-crossing the boundaries between alternative stylistic traditions – seemed to be a much better bet. And so it proved. For eclecticism was indeed the Victorian Style, Robert Kerr's '*omnium gatherum Victorianum*'.[152] And Beresford Hope had actually identified its secret. He had sensed in all architecture that ambivalence – that multivalence – which is inseparable from sophisticated design. Alone among the fine arts, architecture combined elements of objective and subjective form – utility and beauty – within a single eclectic union. For architecture should be the poetry of building, and eclecticism is best understood as the vernacular language of sophisticates. 'Architecture', Hope told the RIBA in 1865, 'is the calling

15. T.E. Collcutt, Imperial Institute, South Kensington, London (1887–93; largely demolished). Eclectic progression: 'essentially Victorian and truly modern'

which, next to that of poet, dives deepest back into the young world's gulf of ages. As it moves on it spins out as part of itself that golden chain of association which ties together the ancient and the new, the foreign and the home-born, the beautiful and the useful.'[153] In a nutshell, eclecticism in an age of progress – a philosophy which first re-created the Gothic Revival and then destroyed it.

With Beresford Hope we have moved a little closer to the architect's secret. Through all his contradictory writings – and no doubt he wrote too much – he sensed the power of the semiotic principle. But he failed to conceptualise its structural basis. That was reserved for the fourth member of our critical quartet: Coventry Patmore. Without a notional link between decoration and structure, without some understanding of the indicative function of ornamental form – the power of ornament as metaphor – architecture will flounder in what Goodhart-Rendel christened 'the empiric hedonism of picturesque indiscipline'.[154] Victorian critics were clearly in need of a rather more rigorous aesthetic. As it happened, there was just such a theory available – a comprehensive way of seeing – and Patmore was its unsung hero. It is time to turn from the vocabulary of eclecticism to the metaphysics of beauty.

4

The Architect's Secret:

Coventry Patmore and the Image of Gravity

'Art is the mediatrix between time and eternity.'

August von Reichensperger, 1861

HOW SHOULD WE judge a building? As scenery, as structure, as ornament, or simply as the enclosure of space? Should we think of architecture as a form of social manipulation? As basically an art? Or simply as machinery? No doubt a building is all of these things. Architectural criticism is scarcely an exact science, and the nature of architectural judgement is notoriously elusive. Somebody once asked Lutyens, 'What is the secret of good architecture?' 'Just remember', he replied, 'that water runs down hill.' What he meant – apart from the advisability of damp-proofing – was that all building necessarily obeys the law of gravity; all good building turns gravitational thrust to aesthetic advantage; and all great building converts the imperatives of gravity into soaring expressions of the human mind. In this, architecture is unique among the arts.

One man, alone among English critics, saw this truth, and explained it clearly. His name was Coventry Patmore.

In 1848 the Pre-Raphaelite Brotherhood decided to draw up a 'list of immortals', each with an appropriate number of stars. Jesus Christ received four stars and Shakespeare three; two each

16. Coventry Patmore (1823–96):
'The great natural law of gravitation'

went to Browning, Keats and Shelley; and one apiece to Raphael, Tennyson and Coventry Patmore.[1] Since then, Patmore's reputation has been rather less buoyant. Sometimes he is remembered as a precocious Pre-Raphaelite poet, as in John Brett's romantic portrait of 1855:[2] a friend of Rossetti, Ruskin, Browning and Tennyson; the author of one domestic masterpiece – *The Angel in the House* – plus a handful of obscure odes.[3] Sometimes he is remembered in 'apocalyptic old age': an arrogant, thrice-married Catholic visionary, the metaphysician of wedlock, glaring out of Sargent's portrait of 1895 'like a wild crane in the wilderness'[4] – an image, incidentally, re-used by Sargent for the Prophet Ezekiel in Boston Public Library.[5] Rarely does the name Coventry Patmore ring bells in architectural circles today.

Patmore was an architectural critic of extraordinary power. He had learning, fluency and perception, the mind of a mystic and the eye of a poet. He was perhaps our most eloquent expositor of architectural style. And it was he who first set out for English readers the secret of all great architecture, in all places, and at all times. That secret was not ornament but symbol, not structure but an image of structure: the expression of gravitational thrust.

Patmore's architectural criticism was never presented in a single, definitive publication. Over the years he tried several times to compress his thinking into book form. In 1847 he was reported to be doing so.[6] In 1850 he was beginning to fear that he might be 'forestalled' by 'others' who were already thinking along similar lines.[7] In 1852 he actually offered 'a small volume' to the publishers of his poems.[8] Nothing came of it. Instead, between 1846 and 1858, he developed his ideas spasmodically, in fragments, in a dozen separate essays in eight different journals. All these were anonymous, as were further articles rehearsing similar themes in 1872 and between 1886 and 1888. Not until he collected a few of these later, and slighter, reviews in a slim volume entitled *Principle in Art* (1889) did the public discover – what the *cognoscenti* had known all along – that they had been written by the author of *The Angel in the House*.[9]

Forty years of procrastination: due partly to a perfectionist temperament, partly to a radical change of circumstance. Patmore's father, P.G. Patmore, was a Grub Street *littérateur* with talent, good connections and the instincts of a gambler. Before fleeing to France to escape bankruptcy, he introduced his son to the world of journalism, then left him without a penny. Between 1846 and 1866, Coventry Patmore worked in the Department of Printed Books at the British Museum.[10] During those years he married the original angel in the house – the daughter of Ruskin's tutor – fathered six children, and supplemented his salary by acting as a reviewer and translator.[11] His wife's death in 1862 lead to a drastic change of direction. In 1864 he became a Roman Catholic, married for the second time in 1865, retired and became a country gentleman, exchanging a world of north London lodgings[12] for Heron's Ghyll at Buxted, near Uckfield in Sussex, designed for him by J.F. Bentley in 1866–8.[13] Thence he transferred in 1880 to the Manor House, Hastings, opposite which he commissioned from his future biographer, Basil Champneys, a major church, Our Lady Star of the Sea (1882–3).[14] His final home – with his third wife, whom he married in 1881 and by whom he had a seventh child – was The Lodge at Walhampton, near Lymington in Hampshire.[15]

These biographical details are important. Patmore's second marriage made him, for the first time, financially secure, and confirmed his allegiance to Catholicism.[16] Before 1864 he had no time to finish his book; after 1865 he had no need to. Building activity at Heron's Ghyll and Hastings served perhaps as sublimation for that unwritten masterpiece of architectural criticism. We are left with *obiter scripta* from which to piece together his thinking.

When Patmore began to wrestle with architectural theory in the 1840s, he was faced with a choice between two perennial aesthetics: decoration as autonomous form, and decoration as structural expression. The first of these, basically the Renaissance tradition, made – to a rationalist – the mistake of regarding ornament as independent of construction. It was a tradition translated into very different Gothic terms by Ruskin. The second viewpoint – broadly speaking, the Neo-Classical tradition, translated into Gothic by Pugin – made the equally fatal mistake of restricting ornamental validity to forms which were tectonically determined. Hence – to an anti-rationalist – the great error which has bedevilled modern criticism: 'the notion . . . that, if the architect takes good care of the useful, the beautiful will take care of itself'.[17]

Both these views Patmore rejected. Neither was entirely wrong; but neither could be more than a partial truth. Was the glory of antique building explicable only in terms of arbitrary mathematical proportion? Was the relationship of that harmony to human or natural form anything more than allegorical? Was our understanding of the Orders increased in any way by the application of subjective terms like 'simplicity', 'purity', or 'classicality'?[18] Was a Gothic spire – to use Pugin's notation – decorated construction or constructed decoration? Or was it something else? Clearly, the conceptual vocabulary available to architectural critics was insufficient.

Steering his way between both fallacies – the arbitrary and the determinist – Patmore set out to demonstrate his own criterion of excellence: the quality of 'architectural expression';[19] that is,

17. Sir Robert Smirke, Council House, Bristol (1822–7): style as an image of structure

the expression of gravitational control. 'Without forcible expression of security and permanence . . . in appearance as well as in reality,' he announced, 'no building can rightly be called architectural.' And the 'constant condition of good architectural expression' is 'that it should have some allusion to the law of gravitation'.[20] His sequence of priority in building was therefore as follows: first, 'constructive obligation'; second, 'appropriate expression'; third, 'symbolical value'.[21]

To Patmore there were only three architectural styles which embodied this 'criterion of a true style',[22] this single controlling idea or 'unifying principle':[23] the Egyptian, the Greek and the Gothic. In each of these he identified the operation of the idea within material boundaries dictated by the laws of physics. The resulting ethos he categorised in turn as Material, Rational and Spiritual. Thus – and this is a preliminary summary – the Egyptian style turned deadweight into a totem of material power; the Greek made equipoise a symbol of rational harmony; and in Gothic a system of vaulting became etherealised in pursuit of spiritual aspiration.

Patmore restricted serious consideration of architecture to those three styles. His reasoning ran along the following lines. Any good architect has his own manner, but style is integral not just to one building but to a whole culture: it is both an outward sign of inward strength, and a symbol of collective ideals. Each of the great stylistic triad – Egyptian, Greek and Gothic – was both expressively and symbolically related to 'the great law of gravitation'.[24] Most of the so-called styles – notably the whole Renaissance tradition – failed, in his eyes, the test of expressional character and/or the test of ideological symbolism.

Roman architecture, he believed, failed on both accounts. The Romans had abandoned Greek construction but retained its ornamental expression: hence that 'revolting sense of anomaly

18. Sir Frank Wills, City Art Gallery, Bristol (1899–1904);
Sir George Oatley, University of Bristol, tower (1925):
alternative images of gravity

19. William Burges, Castell Coch, Glamorgan (1872–91).
Gravity triumphant: the imagery of power

and falsehood' which – for Patmore, at least – deprived Roman architecture of all aesthetic merit.[25] Engineering and art had moved in fatally different directions. 'Vague and arbitrary notions of symmetry, simplicity, variety etc., took the place of a steady and intelligent reference to the powers of gravitation and support.'[26] Those much-vaunted systems of proportional harmony were based merely on codified preference and not on 'the only right basis, namely the expression of the due proportion of power of support to power of gravitation'.[27] The result was a 'hellish architecture' worthy of Dante's Inferno,[28] in which three great principles of construction were confused: the wall, the arch, and the beam.

Renaissance architecture, Patmore admitted, though 'full of error and barbarism' inherited from the Romans, 'really was an art, having certain comprehensible and consistent artistic principles'.[29] Its details were often crude: he especially disliked Vignola's Tuscan,[30] to say nothing of Giulio Romano's eccentricities. The 'itching' of Renaissance architects for 'inexpressive variety' produced rustication which was 'gross and tautological',[31] and alarming confusions of voussoir, lintel and arch.[32] London, he remarked, had miles of such 'unmitigated architectural nonsense':[33] Burlington House, Piccadilly, for instance, where the entrance columns seemed to be festooned with rusticated sheepskins.[34] But at least in Palladio, Patmore noted, 'there is not much utter nonsense'; his detail even had 'a faint reminiscence of constructive meaning'.[35] Indeed – looking at Barry's scholarly Reform Club – Patmore had to confess that 'the faults of [the Renaissance] style may almost be said to constitute its principles'.[36]

There were two other styles, however, that merited serious consideration: the Romanesque and the Islamic.

In the first of these – 'the Romano-Byzantine or Lombard', as

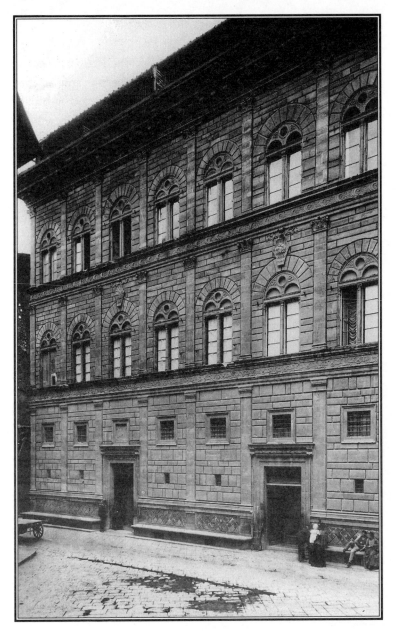

20. L.B. Alberti, The Palazzo Rucellai, Florence (1446–51).
Gravity abstracted: falsity codified as principle

21. T.E. Knightley, Queen's Hall, Langham Place, London (1891–3; bombed 1941). Gravity perplexed: 'unmitigated architectural nonsense'

Patmore called it – the semicircular arch (which is not, of course, self-supporting) achieved at last its true expression by being wholly subordinate to the encompassing wall.[37] It was 'this power of the wall' which Patmore saw as 'the theme of the Lombard system of expression'[38] – a power emphasised by panelling, plating and arcading; a power epitomised by the Lombardic circular window, its 'radiating . . . spokes' and 'deep . . . decorated chamfer' emphasising the 'vast power' of the wall 'to which by its form, it expresses its infinite power of resistance'.[39] But, at least until it became Norman, this was all too much of 'a mongrel mode', 'an incongruous hybrid', stemming ultimately from the Roman mixed-marriage of arch and beam.[40] Such 'organised chaos' might be paralleled in the 'pseudo-architectures of India, Mexico, China etc.', but it could never rank as tectonic excellence.[41] Indeed, it was closer to sculpture.[42] Its basis was less an expression of superincumbent weight, more a reference to the mass and modulation of masonry walling: 'thickness within thickness, arcade within arcade', exploiting 'artistically' its thickness and might.[43] Its columnar formation – 'twisted . . . contorted . . . knotted together' – seldom bore any valid proportional relationship to structural necessity.[44] The subordinate arcades were just 'Lilliputian mockeries of the Attic shaft'.[45] And minor ornaments – chamfer and panel, billet and chevron – were all designed to reveal the texture of the masonry rather than the dynamics of its construction. Romanesque, Patmore concludes, 'well conveys the solemn expression of a calm eternity . . .'; but for religious purposes 'it will not bear the least comparison with the flamelike Gothic'.[46] In other words, whatever its plastic quality, it lacked the dynamic element – structurally and spiritually dynamic – of Gothic. The Norman arch, a 'cavernous gap in masses of . . . all-sufficient masonry',[47] awaited the arrival of its pointed successor.[48]

Meanwhile, the Byzantines had tried 'to create a style . . . in which the semicircular arch should afford, not only the main principle of construction, but also the theme of expression'. However, 'the object of the circular arch is the distributed weight of the wall; just as the object of the column is the entablature, or the wall concentrated upon its capital by means of the arch. The Byzantines . . . made the arch the chief object to the eye, setting little importance upon the chief object of the arch; and the consequence is . . . an unpleasant sense of imperfect purpose . . . A great resisting power [the arch] . . . is . . . ostentatiously displayed . . . and . . . given . . . little . . . to do.' Its surplus energy is vented in 'fantastical tricks' like the dome of Sta Sophia. That dome's 'chief boast' – its apparently miraculous means of support – is in fact its chief artistic defect: 'the wonder is but a lying wonder; for that which the uninitiated spectator gapes at, as a vast mass of legitimate masonry, unaccountably suspended in air, is a structure of Rhodian bricks and pumice-stone, possessing only a small proportion of the supposed force of gravitation, and exerting a lateral thrust which is met by a vast and hidden buttress-system. This species of falsehood attained its climax in the dome of St Vitale, Ravenna, which, while it claims credit for being constructed of stones, put together on the principle of the all-prevalent arch, is, in reality, a kind of grotto, formed by a coil of empty earthen jars.'[49] Patmore eventually admitted that Sta Sophia was 'perhaps the greatest triumph of architectural skill ever attained'.[50] But he continued to believe that falsified construction – as, later on, in Renaissance domes – could never rank highly as symbolic form: it was merely illegitimate expression.[51]

The 'aimlessness' of the Byzantine arch, Patmore thought, appealed powerfully to 'the vivid and excitable Arabian temperament'. In the resulting Islamic style – he called it Moresque

or Saracenic – the mechanical properties of the arch are translated into a system of expression which surpassed even Gothic in
transcending tectonic reality.[52] The honeysuckle domes of the
Alhambra seem to hang in the air as pendentives – almost with
the ease of clouds. At Cordova the arcades are superfluously
multiplied in a way which confuses tectonic and atectonic in a
veritable trellis of masonry. 'Gravitation,' Patmore explains, 'con-
solidated by the Egyptian, adequately opposed by the Greek, and
turned into aspiration by the Gothic architect, was by the Arabian
boldly and simply negatived. The form of the arch is repeated in
his buildings without end; but it seldom . . . appears to have any
work to do. And this ostentatious idleness in a powerful means of
support, together with a most curious and elaborate system of
real or apparent lateral thrusts, by which the idea of gravitation
in all the masses is hidden or confused to the eye, is the grand
source of the marvellous effects of the Alhambra and the Mosque
of Cordova.'[53] An image of tectonic truth had been counterbal-
anced into nothingness; turned, indeed, into a 'fairytale'[54] from
the *Arabian Nights*. For Patmore this conquest of gravity by
sleight-of-hand posed an interpretive puzzle. He recognised its
virtuosity, but he doubted its symbolic meaning. Here he saw no
ultimate significance 'for the human race and its religions'.[55]

Perhaps he preferred not to look too hard. His aesthetic per-
ceptions were conditioned by his Christian perspective. But,
given that conditioning, he found neither Romanesque nor
Islamic could match the big three styles – Egyptian, Greek and
Gothic – in terms of conceptual significance. Each of these three
great styles achieved heights of structural and moral symbolism
by exploiting in three dimensions 'the great natural law of gravitation'.[56] And once those three great ideals – the Material, the
Rational, the Spiritual – had found utterance in stone, what
fourth abstraction remained to inspire a new art?[57] Gothic – 'the

purest expression of sacramentalism' – would last as long as Christianity.[58]

In other words, Patmore made no provision in his aesthetic for the emergence of a new style. New materials, new techniques – be they cantilevers of steel or vaults of glass – might well manifest new mannerism. They did not guarantee that elusive new style. Anyway, he believed, when 'the Gothic style . . . was invented' – maximum strength, minimum material: a pointed arch never rests – 'all others became forever obsolete'.[59] No doubt, Patmore concluded, iron and glass would continue to be useful – each in its proper place – in suspension bridges and railway stations.[60] But if employed in the higher levels of building they would surely result in 'the abolition of architecture as a fine art[61] . . . [Indeed,] iron architecture is like the unmanageable mechanical man of Frankenstein . . . now that our architects have "developed" him, they are at a loss to know what to do with him, or rather how to prevent his destroying them!'[62]

Such a gloomy prophecy was neither more nor less perceptive than that of many contemporary Victorians. Ruskin felt much the same.[63] So did William Morris.[64] But Patmore did foresee a little of the future, and in a more positive light. He realised that 'the artistic law of architecture' was not limited to style: it simply 'adapts, perfects and displays with the utmost degree of ostentation the essential, but nothing else'.[65] 'Iron and glass', he suggested in 1857, 'are the only materials in which [Gothic] can ever attain to the full development of the effects aimed at by the architects of Strasbourg and Cologne. The upward cataract of the Gothic spire, which in Strasbourg cathedral probably attains its utmost practicable limit in . . . stone, could easily be continued 500 feet higher in iron . . . although the impressive element of hand-carving would have to be sacrificed in the details.' Such a 'final adoption' of Gothic, 'with certain modifications', he

22. Alfred Waterhouse, National Liberal Club, London, staircase (1885–7; bombed 1941, rebuilt in altered form 1952). Gravity denied: conjuring in steel and marble

added, 'we regard as inevitable'.[66] Metallic construction might well turn out to be the logical conclusion of the Gothic system. In that respect, Patmore's thinking proved to be prophetic. But prophecy was not his business. Not for him the glories of transcendent technology. He glimpsed, far off, the skyline of Manhattan; then preferred to look the other way – back to Egyptian, Greek and Gothic. It is time therefore to piece together his analysis of those three styles.

Firstly, Egyptian.[67] Architecture on a large scale is one of the prerogatives of power. It assumes control of an economy, control of a political culture. The architecture of the Pharaohs – that is, 'the ruling idea'[68] of the rulers of ancient Egypt – came to exhibit not only power but the permanence of power, a power exercised from beyond the grave. A pyramid – an 'organised cone'[69] – is secure against the injuries of time. The pyramidal form – the shape of a mountain: 'nature's own architecture'[70] – suggests a heap of masonry thrown down by the Almighty. Its shape, a passive symbol of gravity, indicates weight unrelieved by construction: 'the simplest architectural expression of mere ponderosity'.[71] The obelisk is 'a sort of shorthand expression of the same idea';[72] that is, the idea of 'weight in the abstract'.[73] Similarly, concave cornices; twin towers tapering like decapitated pyramids; walls scored with hieroglyphs, and sliced into converging planes; a superabundance of columns, massed together like troops of masonic infantry; columns and capitals which themselves seem to bulge under an intolerable burden – all these subtleties of 'constructive expression'[74] act as indicative images of unrelieved weight. There is no balance of support and superincumbent mass: somehow these buildings are all base. But their concatenation of planes – upright, angled, canted, battered; their volume multiplied by pattern, groove and moulding – seemed to Patmore one of mankind's 'most remarkable efforts of architecture'.[75]

No doubt such forms derived in practice from the imperatives of primitive technology: burrowing temples out of solid rock, or compensating for tectonic naivety with a superfluity of stone. That, however, is only one level of explanation. All architecture makes virtue out of necessity; but it also transmits the instincts and values of its creators. What began as defective science was surely retained as emotive symbol.[76] In an age of ephemeral existence and crushing material might, these buildings defy eternity.

In Greek architecture Patmore also discerned an idea of permanence and a perpetual allusion to gravitational thrust. But this time the symbolism goes beyond mere ponderosity. Away with the burdens of material power; these temples breathe a new-found tranquillity, and their medium of expression is an overt equilibrium of force.

Doric columns, through multiple flutings, assume a form which – both mechanically and aesthetically – achieves a level of optimum function.[77] They impress Patmore's eye as though by 'a torrent of power rushing up to meet the [downwards] gravitating mass of the entablature. [That] mass, and its supporting power, [are] each expressed with elaborate artistic science, and [historically] the different ways in which this was done gave rise to the different "orders".'[78] In the Doric order the deadweight of the entablature is triply expressed: *simple weight* in the architrave; *weight depending* in triglyph and hanging guttae; and *weight impending* in a cornice projecting and undercut. Again, the 'vast active power which the eye at once recognises . . . in . . . the Doric shaft is shown to be fully competent for its task by being proved to be rather more than competent':[79] at the weakest point of the column, just below the capital, there are three horizontal channels; the column thus throws away a token of its strength, while boasting of superincumbent power – performing its supporting role as nonchalantly as the caryatids of the Erechtheion. Similarly, the 'quirked ovolo' of the Doric capital, by flattening itself into parabolic curves, seems almost to invite the entablature's superincumbent weight. Such parabolas, or conic sections, multiply through entasis the tensile effect of the entire fabric.[80] And at a key point of balance in the whole structured image, the abacus acts as a visual fulcrum: a neutral 'point of rest and indifference between the opposing powers of [upward] support and [downward] gravitation'.[81]

Such details create not structure but an image of the structural process – what Patmore vividly calls the 'ostentation of active energy'.[82] Thus the purpose of antifixae along the cornice is not stability (they bear no precise relation to the lines of the roof tiles), but simply an impression of stability.[83] Again, 'the business of the shaft is to support weight; the aim of the Greek architect was to make it express, as well as perform, that business.' In the Doric order this expressional power breathes 'from every curve and cut of shaft and capital'. In the Ionic order it is there too 'in all the features of the entablature, in the dead unbroken mass of the architrave, in the frieze, with its hanging row of triglyphs and guttae, in the impending corona of the cornice, and, finally, in the low pyramidal pediment'.[84] As for the Ionic column itself, 'instead of channels diminishing its power [at the neck], it was ornamented where it was weakest; and its power, on meeting the weight of the entablature, distributed itself into two streams, which rolled over in elastic curves'.[85] Throughout both orders codified patterns – egg and dart, fret, et cetera – play minor, but significant, roles in defining members or intensifying outlines, and in capturing through the eye that all-important sense of gravitational tension.[86] Finally, the semiotic import of all these forms is heightened by indicative polychromy.[87]

Thus the Doric order, in Patmore's eyes, had – strictly speaking – no decoration at all, only expressive form.[88] In the Ionic order decoration does occasionally appear. But it is ornament in harmony with 'the leading sentiment': in particular, in capital and base, it adds a key element of elasticity; in fasciaed architrave, it adds 'impension and recession'. This makes 'almost every member . . . at once agent and re-agent', so maximising that sense of harmonic energy in which Patmore divined the Attic balance between material and intellectual force.[89] These orders are thus allegories of mind: brute mass controlled by reason. The medium of the allegory is equipoise, not just of structure but of structural expression. 'There is not a moulding in base, capital, or cornice, not an ornament of any sort whatever, but has for its chief object the intensification of this beautiful expression of weight competently supported.'[90] 'It was not', Patmore concludes, 'until the Attic spirit was wholly quenched, that "decoration" proper made its appearance . . . This was the case with Roman architecture.'[91]

Of course, all these optical devices embody echoes of half-forgotten functions. In primitive timber structures, the shaft of a proto-Doric column was no doubt hung round with bark or spears and strengthened by a triple banding near the top. But in terms of aesthetic validity such hypotheses are irrelevant. The significance of these mouldings is not their origin but their meaning,[92] not how they were invented, but why they were retained. Whatever the style, Patmore points out, 'all the most remarkable architectural effects can be traced to the *suggestion* of some accident or necessity'.[93] The key point is that they survived, in terms of stylistic evolution – utility evolving into art – because of their contribution to some preponderant *idea*. In Greek architecture that idea – that instinct for form – was harmony through gravitational expression.[94] Omit any of the subsidiary details – a triglyph here, a set of guttae there – emasculate its ornament, as in Roman Doric – and the order loses much of its expressional power, and much more of its aesthetic impact.

And therein lay the rub. After two thousand years, perfection made a poor model. Smirke's British Museum (1823–58) Patmore knew well. He admitted its grandeur, but pointed out that the omission of one or two crucial refinements – entasis in stylobate and terminal columns, for instance – meant 'the omission of half the glory that ought to have sent its subtle beams from [that] still noble façade'.[95] In practice, all those subtleties of entasis – by which the apparent concavity and convexity of straight lines is optically adjusted[96] – made impossible any apt translation from the antique. And literal replication was an aesthetic cul-de-sac. It is perhaps significant that the only Greek Revival monument in Britain which made full use of entasis – Cockerell and Playfair's National Monument in Edinburgh (1824–9) – remained unfinished. The very self-sufficiency of Greek architecture – perfection within strict limits – unfitted it for modern use. Like the perfect monotony of Greek music, its forms were not designed for export. More important, its central 'idea' – the balance of matter and mind – consorted ill with a Christian culture based on notions of an infinite deity and unfathomable mystery.[97] Coventry Patmore had to look elsewhere.

Greek architecture had been an expression of weight in equipoise: a statical adjustment of burden and support. Gothic architecture was based on the principle of resisted thrust: a system not static but dynamic. The Lombardic column had been 'constructively superfluous'. The Gothic pier was both functionally and symbolically valid, a symbol first ascendant then transcendent. It had 'to bear burdens', Patmore explains, 'and yet appear to be doing nothing of the sort, the burden and bearing members being alike transformed into portions of the great vertical stream

23. Sir Robert Smirke, British Museum, London, colonnade (1823; 1842–7). Gravity controlled: the discipline of archaeology

of piers, pointed arches, groined vaults and vaulting shafts'.[98] Unlike the round arch, the pointed arch is self-supporting: it does not have to be 'embedded in heavy masses of wall in order to make it constructively good and artistically beautiful'.[99] It was, therefore, adopted for constructive reasons. But it was retained, developed, cherished for reasons of symbolism: it embodied the principle of aspiration.

This central theme of aspiration – spirit triumphing over material weight – is expressed alike in pointed arches, clustered columns, groined ribs, pinnacles, crockets, pitched roofs and spires. The Egyptian column was expressively crushed, the Greek visually balanced; but the Gothic pier 'flies up like a shaft of arrows',[100] 'without the least diminution of its substance, and without swelling either under sufferance or gathering of strength by entasis . . . to the commencement of the arch; where [with no more than a token hesitation in the capital] it divides itself, sending up the streams of its clustered shafts, some into the lines of the arch and others to the top of the clerestory wall; then dividing again to follow the lines of the vaulting, there to meet like fingers in prayer, but still having no thought of the weight of the roof they really help to carry'.[101] Gothic forms, in short, resulted from their builders' desire to intensify 'the simple result of a peculiar constructive system'.[102] Hence the transparency of Gothic, especially in Germany – to Patmore 'the country in which Gothic architecture attained its most ideal perfection'.[103] Cologne, for example: all glass, no wall; almost a cat's-cradle of piers, mullions, tracery and light. 'The whole mass soars, the material itself becoming the simplest and most forcible expression of the spiritual by the entire reversal of the primary characteristic of matter.'[104] In other words, that primary characteristic – weight – is dissolved in 'a semblance of ascendant energy'.[105]

But there is more to Gothic than simple perpendicularity.

24. William Burges, St Mary, Studley Royal, Yorkshire
(1870–2). Gravity transcended: the imagery of prayer

Horizontal forms have a part to play as well. String course, base or capital do not mark (as they might in the Greek system) a notional counter to overall verticality. They are moments of hesitation, brief gatherings of strength in a continuous and co-ordinated upward thrust. Hence the interrupted verticals in the towers of York or Canterbury. Compare those towers with the spires of Freiburg or Salisbury. A spire may be 'the finest spire in the world', but it 'evaporates as it soars'; in a tower the motion, 'the sense of ascension', does not diminish: 'the great steady, heavenward current' is strengthened rather than tempered by intermittent checks, to culminate, via arch and battlement, in a 'solemn . . . heart-expanding sense of infinite aspiration'.[106] Spires, however prominent – as at Lichfield or Cologne – are but partial escape valves for that 'vast current of vertical force' bottled up in the mass of a great cathedral, then gloriously released in a veritable 'geyser of ascending life'.[107] Like 'jets of . . . flame' flickering above a furnace, spire, cresting and crocket act as points of release for the pressure accumulated below in 'thousands upon thousands of soaring lines'.[108] All that pent-up verticality is bounded, shaped, moulded to form one vast spiritual metaphor: 'the infinite bounded . . . by the finite [and thus] . . . the true character of the life and worship symbolised'.[109]

To Patmore this theme of aspiration in Gothic is twice modified: by 'foliation' and by 'contented truncation'.[110] These neologisms he explains in terms of symbolic tension. Contented trucation meant interrupted ascension: vertical thrust, or perpendicularity,[111] not impeded but controlled. Foliation – as in cusped and floral patterns – meant naturalistic detail shaped, not stifled, by geometrical form. The key factor – as in the Decorated Gothic of Lincoln – was the counterpoint of foliation and aspiration.[112] At last 'the enigma' of Gothic was becoming clear: its secret lay in *'the graceful union of a spontaneous energy and a restraining law'.*[113]

Without it, '*it is not Gothic*'.[114] The mystery is laid bare in the major metaphor of Gothic structure, in the minor metaphor of Gothic ornament. For example, 'the special aim of fourteenth-century ornamentation', Patmore explains, 'is to show vigorous life playing with perfect freedom in severely geometrical forms'.[115] Hence the splendour of Decorated tracery – before it loosens into French Flamboyant or hardens into English Perpendicular: the sinewy patterns swirl outwards and upwards like bubbles of liquified light or tongues of petrified flame. This reconciliation of life and law – mortal will and immortal destiny – is to Patmore 'the consummation of Christianity'.[116] And its symbols – in structure, terrestial limits bounding the 'potentiality of infinite ascension'; in ornament, nature perfected by constraint – these symbols are to him the essentials of Gothic.[117]

In short, Patmore here combines two traditions: Classical notions of order and law, plus Romantic ideas of expression and aspiration. The result is a vision of Gothic conceptually antiphonal: an endless dialogue of freedom and law, spirit and matter, energy and form, male and female, human and divine. In terms of Patmore's Catholicism this is not just symbolic, it is 'highly symbolic'.[118] The Gothic system – gravity defied – becomes for him 'a symbol of the world overcome':[119] a symbol first of Incarnation, then of Resurrection.[120]

Of course there will be those who doubt. Patmore refutes them thus: if a Gothic spire did not symbolise a sentiment, then what on earth was it for?[121] 'For us,' he announces, 'seeing is believing'; all doubts dissolve before that 'upward cataract of shafts, and mouldings, and canopied figures which left us breathless when we first found ourselves before the piers of Cologne Cathedral'.[122] Patmore had little time for 'the whole medieval system of *arbitrary* symbolisation' – the system of Durandus so beloved by 'Puseyite clergymen'; but he remained convinced

25. William Burges, All Saints, Fleet, Hampshire, Lefroy monument (1861): Gravity compressed

that Gothic forms involved not only 'artistical effect' but 'an *artistic and essential symbolism*, which must retain its efficiency as long as the human mind retains its present constitution'.[123]

To recapitulate. Weight of material is 'the great fact of building', and 'the primary source of architectural symbolism'.[124] The Egyptian style was an expression of unrelieved weight; the Greek of weight in equipoise. It was left to Gothic to complete the syllogism, to demonstrate in three dimensions the conquest of spirit over matter; that is, '*weight annihilated*; spire and tower, buttress, clerestory and pinnacle, [rising] to heaven, and [indicating] the spirituality of worship to which they are applied'.[125] 'Weight, support and ascension', Patmore concludes, 'are ideas which, in all times and languages, have been accepted as the most direct and forcible material images of the three great phases of sensuality, intellectuality and spirituality; and those three phases are precisely those which it was desirable to express as adjuncts of the Egyptian, Greek and Christian worship.'[126]

Well, how much of this is original, and how much derivative? Clearly the German Idealist tradition of aesthetics played a part. During the 1840s, English interest in the German school increased significantly.[127] G.H. Lewes noted in 1842: '*The Times* has quoted Hegel. The *Spectator* has had articles on *Aesthetical Economy* – and in the *Atlas* for 20th March, the question is asked: "Why is there no Professor of Aesthetics at Oxford?"'[128]

For someone of Patmore's generation there would be two obvious routes for the transmission of German philosophy: Coleridge and Carlyle. Coleridge ranked high in his calendar of saints, Carlyle not quite so high.[129] But Patmore was unusual in also being equipped to go back to the original sources. We know he was a competent linguist, as well as an amateur scientist.[130] His father trained him in English literature; he trained himself in

French theology and German philosophy. He read Lessing,[131] Goethe[132] and Fichte[133] in the original, as well as Schiller[134] and Schelling.[135] He even tackled Hegel. 'The acquisition of great stores of the purest gold' in the works of that 'metaphysician', he noted, was well 'worth the trouble of [a little] quartz-crushing'.[136] Indeed, he placed Hegel with Aristotle as 'the two great expositors of the relation of the emotions to art'.[137] Sitting at his desk in the British Museum, Patmore was indeed ideally placed. 'During my twenty years' service', he recalled, 'I read tens of thousands of books.'[138]

From Coleridge he learned the aphoristic method, the holistic vision;[139] from Lindsay the progressive, dialectical triad of sense, intellect and spirit;[140] from Freeman the statical trinity of immobility, horizontality and verticality;[141] from Reichensperger the eternal relevance of Gothic;[142] from Pennethorne and Penrose he derived his knowledge of entasis;[143] from Aristotle and Aquinas came the ideal of encompassing law;[144] from Goethe, Gothic's Teutonic soul;[145] from Hegel the dialectic of master and spirit, as well as the trinity of true styles;[146] from Kant he learned the dialogue of freedom and constraint;[147] from Schlegel the idea of organic form;[148] from Hegel again – this time via Whewell and Pugin – the key notion of aspiration;[149] from Schopenhauer came a crucial insight, first suggested by Hegel: the aesthetic imperative of gravity;[150] in Kugler he found that all-purpose explanatory device, expression;[151] in Brandon, innumerable examples of foliation;[152] in Willis the idea of Gothic as a structural image;[153] in Pugin the law of constructive decoration – ornament's own verification principle.[154] It is a formidable list – enough to make an empiricist cry out for Occam's Razor.

Patmore never suffered from false modesty. He aimed to show the world 'the spirit . . . of architecture'; to supply 'the as yet unanswered demand for a system of architectural aesthetics'.[155]

In other words, to explain the significance of tectonic form, to decode Hegel's tower of Babel.[156] In this enterprise he found his predecessors of little help. Vitruvius was a primer of prototypes, not a handbook of aesthetics. Renaissance theorists – Palladio, Scammozzi, Vignola – had merely codified falsity, turning tectonic truth into the mumbo-jumbo of proportion, symmetry, variety and harmony.[157] French critics, notably Quatremère de Quincey, had skirmished with the subject; but most of them – Batissier, for example – were working from 'insufficient or inaccurate data'.[158] English scholars, chiefly those sponsored by the Dilettanti Society, had greatly increased our knowledge of antique detail; but that was 'all they seem to have attempted'.[159] Writers as diverse as Chambers,[160] Gwilt,[161] and Alison[162] had all swallowed – in different degrees – Renaissance notions of proportional harmony. 'This view', Patmore noted curtly, 'is now exploded.'[163]

If there had been an explosion, it was due to the Germans. Patmore had no time for insular 'English critics . . . impregnated with John Bullism' who regard everything beyond 'the finite-logical school of Locke' as 'a cloudy dream-land – a foggy region fit only for crazed idiots or frenzied madmen'. We are held back, he explained in 1845, 'not by the ignorant vulgar, but by the ignorant learned' who dismiss German philosophy as 'rubbish' merely because it is 'abstruse'.[164] Even so, he was suspicious of too much Teutonic 'science and system'.[165] He preferred to make use of Germanic insights – especially those of Hegel, Kugler and Schopenhauer – without pursuing too far the metaphysics of aesthetic psychology. 'Truths which are *combinations* of instinctive convictions', he concluded in 1852, are ultimately inexplicable. 'These convictions are the postulates of life, and the data of action and art. The grand error of . . . Germanising critics, has been that of demanding data for the data.'[166]

It was Kugler[167] – Burckhardt's teacher and Semper's mortal enemy[168] – who, in Patmore's eyes, 'first glimpsed the secret' of Greek building: 'the aesthetical development' of the principle of trabeation.[169] His *Handbuch der Kunstgeschichte* (Stuttgart, 1842; 1848; 1856)[170] owed much to Hegel, and was in any case too wide-ranging to deal with architectural theory in any detail; but at least it gave 'a vivid glimpse or two' of 'the elements of architectural character'. These glimpses had been shaded into 'a dim glimmering' by E.A. Freeman,[171] but otherwise ignored in England. Meanwhile Patmore had sailed beyond Kugler, beyond Mueller,[172] beyond Hubsch,[173] beyond 'the high-watermark of German architectural aesthetics'.[174] Studying Hegel – the root of all these thinkers – he had located the secret for himself: Greek ornamental forms were neither an allegory of nature nor a proportional code (as Renaissance theorists presumed); still less were they dependent for their aesthetic value on some antecedent constructive validity (as maintained by the Neo-Classicists).[175] The architectural mouldings of the ancients were sign-manuals of gravitational force; each element played its part in expressing the statical harmony of dependent pressure and ascendant thrust. Here – not in the formulae of associational aesthetics[176] – lay the key to the beauties of Greek architecture. And not just Greek: all the buildings of the world could now be judged by the same yardstick – their aesthetic relation to Newton's 'paramount and universal . . . law'.[177] The riddle had been unravelled. From Hegel's hint, from Kugler's glimpse, from Schopenhauer's gloss, came Patmore's general theory of tectonics. 'They are the first discoverers of truths', he announced triumphantly, 'who first understand their general extent and importance.'[178]

Much of this thinking was developed in a series of reviews, purportedly of Ruskin's *Seven Lamps* and *Stones of Venice*. Patmore's relationship with Ruskin was never easy. They agreed in their contempt for the Renaissance, though for rather different reasons. They respected each other's genius, they admired each other's style;[179] but they disagreed fundamentally in matters of aesthetics[180] and theology.[181] When Ruskin told an Edinburgh audience that cast iron in building should be outlawed on biblical grounds, Patmore thought it 'the most imbecile kind of argument that ever came out of a sane man's mouth'.[182] And there were other disagreements more crucial still. Ruskin was cut off, by language and by temperament, from the whole school of German aesthetics. His forte was description, Patmore's was analysis.

When in the late 1840s Patmore began to review Ruskin he had, first of all, to explain the 'enigma' of Gothic. He found the way to the secret lay not in archaeology (despite Grose,[183] Milner[184] and Carter),[185] nor in engineering (despite Willis), nor in expressional truth (despite Pugin).[186] Still less did it lie in classification (despite Rickman);[187] and certainly not in profile and section (despite Brandon,[188] Bloxham[189] and Paley).[190] The answer to the enigma did not lie in perspectival harmony (despite Schnaase),[191] nor yet in optical device (despite Semper);[192] it did not even reside in symbolism (despite Boisserée,[193] Michelet[194] and Neale).[195] All these routes to understanding were plausible enough, but none of them explained the essence of Gothic. Each was applicable to any style, as indeed were all seven of Ruskin's *Lamps*. 'There are other lamps,' noted Patmore, 'and of these Mr Ruskin tells us nothing.'[196]

It was William Whewell of Cambridge, the first man to call himself a scientist,[197] who – thinking along Hegelian lines[198] – gave Patmore the clue: 'the whole secret of the expression of Gothic architecture is to be found in its aspiration'.[199] But how? Whewell stopped short of an answer, so did Freeman. Patmore went back to Kugler. There – as in Kugler's analysis of Greek architecture – he discovered the germ of an explanation: *empor-streben* (the expression of vertical effect). So Ruskin, Patmore concluded – unblessed by the Hegelian tradition[200] – had missed the essence of 'the Gothic idea':[201] the transcendent symbolic potential of the pointed arch. And that omission made Ruskin's notion of Gothic rather like *Hamlet* without the Prince.[202] Hence Ruskin's enthusiasm for north Italian Gothic, a useful urban synthesis but a synthesis which turned the sublime principle of pointed vaulting into just another system of secular decoration.[203] As for Patmore's theory of foliation, here he did succeed in converting Ruskin.[204] But at bottom Patmore's whole approach to ornament was quite different: its significance in his view was not decorative at all, but operatively expressive.[205] In Patmore's opinion, ornament in building – that is, 'artistical expression', vernacular or polite – was only a means in the creative process, not an end.[206] Ruskin's writing provided the occasion for Patmore's pyrotechnics, but Hegel supplied the combustible materials; from Kugler sprang the necessary spark, and from Schopenhauer came much of the cosmic conspectus.

How then can we sum up his achievement? Patmore's position among the immortals is likely to rest on the metaphysical poetry of his later years – those mystical works which led Gerard Manley Hopkins to remark: 'for insight he beats all our living poets'.[207] This chapter reclaims only one portion of his life-work, but one that has been very largely ignored – his architectural criticism. Patmore's achievement here was to seize upon the imagery of strength as an explanation of architectural form. In 1844 a hugely influential but now forgotten book had postulated a single, fundamental division of the natural world. The book was Robert Chambers's *Vestiges of the Natural History of Creation*. In it he declared that the inorganic world 'has one final, comprehensive

26. Sir Edwin Lutyens, Marsh Court, Hampshire, entrance
porch (1901–4). Gravity subverted: allusion and illusion

law, GRAVITATION . . . the organic [world] . . . rests in a like manner on one law, and that is – DEVELOPMENT.'[208] Gravitation and development: in effect, by transposing the language of natural science into the language of architectural principle, both Hope and Patmore had opened up new territory in the field of architectural aesthetics. Hope chose development, Patmore chose gravitation, as the key to the architect's secret. And Patmore won the argument hands down. Henceforward, architectural theory would translate physics into aesthetics. Patmore had produced a simple answer to an impossibly difficult question. And in composing it – form as a metaphor of force – he forged a conceptual key of formidable explanatory power. In the whole of English architectural writing, there is no more eloquent exposition of architectural style.

But where are Patmore's disciples today? In a waspish article in the *Dictionary of National Biography*, Richard Garnett claimed that Patmore's 'attitude to other men's ideas was that of Omar towards the Alexandrian library'.[209] In fact, his intellectual methods were closer to the Jackdaw of Rheims than to Attila the Hun. 'Genius', he decided, lies in 'the synthetic eye', 'the unitive vision', which draws together all the strands of knowledge in pursuit of a deeper understanding.[210] Undeterred by accusations of amateurism – after all, you scarcely need to be a cobbler to know when the shoe pinches – Patmore set out to establish principles of architectural criticism. That meant tackling the hardest questions of all: the nature of aesthetic judgement; the origins of style; the secret of beauty in architecture. He did not expect an easy ride. 'English readers', he noted, tend to react to such 'transcendental' notions with 'repugnance and suspicion'.[211] 'Let no one', he added ruefully, 'who is afraid to be laughed at by fools and knaves undertake to define the relationships of art and religion.'[212]

As regards the architectural world, Patmore was never an

influential critic: epigrams seldom persuade, repeated platitudes often do. But he must be the only poet whose obituary was written by the President of the RIBA. He left behind no volumes of aesthetic theory, just a random scatter of notices. 'But those pages', noted Paul Waterhouse, 'are so replete with . . . thought . . . that one is forced to realise in him one of the very few minds who, without any professional connection with [architecture], yet see and can express something more than the surface of its mysteries' – in particular, the mystery of 'that eternal theme of all legitimate structural design – gravitation and its counteraction'.[213] In other words, the imagery of perceptible strength: the secret of beauty in architecture.

Postscript

EVERY ARCHITECTURAL GENERATION lives, of necessity, in hope: in hope of finding the architect's secret. The mid Victorians searched harder than most. George Aitchison looked longest, and found least. His reward lay in the future, in the folk-memory of early modernism. Benjamin Webb at least had the satisfaction of seeing his critical ideas reflected in the work of one contemporary, William Butterfield. Not so Beresford Hope. He perhaps looked furthest. He saw the whole of architectural history as an engine of eclectic progression. But his intellect over-reached itself; and when he failed, his disappointment was appropriately great. In the end it fell to Coventry Patmore – a critic with a poet's eye – to unravel the secret of beauty in architecture: in all architecture, at all times. That secret was neither space nor volume; neither line nor mass; neither proportion nor purpose; neither utility nor plan. It was simply the image of gravity.

Notes and Bibliographical References

(Place of publication: London, unless otherwise stated)

Introduction

1. See *Dictionary of National Biography* (J. Summerson), and A. Powers, ed., *H.S. Goodhart-Rendel* (Architectural Association, *c.* 1987).
2. For obituaries, see *The Times* 12 Nov. 1992; *Daily Telegraph* 13 Nov. 1992; *Architectural Review* Jan. 1993, 9–10 (J. Mordaunt Crook); *Proceedings of the British Academy* xc (1995), 467–95 (Sir Howard Colvin). Summerson lectured regularly on the History of Architecture at the Architectural Association from 1949 to 1962, and at Birkbeck College from 1950 to 1967. He was Slade Professor of Fine Art at both Oxford (1958–9) and Cambridge (1966–7), and Ferens Professor of Fine Art at Hull (1960–1). He delivered the Page-Barbour Lecture for 1972 at the University of Virginia; the Walter Neurath Memorial lecture for 1973 at Birkbeck College, London; and the Russell Van Nost Black Memorial Lecture for 1974 at Cornell University.
3. J. Summerson, *Victorian Architecture. Four Studies in Evaluation* (1970), 6.
4. *Ibid.*, 10.
5. J. Summerson, 'Vitruvius Ludens', *Architectural Review* March 1983, 19–21; 'Vitruvius Ridens', *ibid.* June 1987, 45–6. For differing interpretations of Summerson's attitude to the changing face of modernism, see P. Mandler, 'John Summerson: the architectural critic and the quest for the Modern', in S. Pedersen and P. Mandler, eds, *After the Victorians: private conscience and public duty in modern Britain* (1994), 229–45; and A. Powers, 'John Summerson and modernism', in *Twentieth Century Architecture and its Histories*, ed. L. Campbell (SAHGB, 2000), 153–75.
6. J. Betjeman, *Letters*, ed. C. Lycett-Green, i (1994), 386: 15 March 1946.
7. J. Grant, *The Saturday Review* (1873), 56. 'One thing I always like to have –

the hatred of the *Saturday Review* and the love of God' (C.H. Spurgeon, quoted *ibid.*, 72).

8. G.M. Young, *Victorian Essays*, ed. W.D. Handcock (1962), 11.

9. 'We take pleasure – or should take pleasure, in architectural construction as the manifestation of an admirable human intelligence . . . in no art is there a closer connection between our delight in the work, and our admiration of the workman's mind, than in architecture' (J. Ruskin, *Stones of Venice* i, ch. ii; *Works* IX, 64).

Chapter 1: George Aitchison

Epigraph: G. Aitchison, *Builder* xliv (1883), 207.

1. G.M. Young, 'The Greatest Victorian', in *Today and Yesterday* (1948), 237–43, reprinted in *Victorian Essays*, ed. W.D. Handcock (1962), 123–8.

2. RIBA Drawings Collection: drawings for interior decoration, including Leighton House, deposited 1910 and later.

3. J.A. Gotch, ed., *The Growth and Work of the RIBA, 1834–1934* (1934), ill. For his lecturing, see *Builder* 29 January and 25 June 1898, 103, 609.

4. I have developed this 'revisionist' thesis at some length in the following publications: intro. J.T. Emmett, *Six Essays* (New York, 1972); intro. R. Kerr, *The Gentleman's House* (New York, 1972); 'Sydney Smirke and the Architecture of Compromise', in *Seven Victorian Architects*, intro. N. Pevsner (1976), 141–4, 152; *William Burges and the High Victorian Dream* (1981); 'Progressive Eclecticism: the case of Beresford Hope', in *Architectural Design* liii (1983), 56–63; 'Architecture and History', in *Architectural History* xxvii (1984), 355–78; 'T.G. Jackson and the Cult of Eclecticism', in *In Search of Modern Architecture*, ed. H. Searing (1982), 102–20; and *The Dilemma of Style: Architectural Ideas from the Picturesque to the Post-Modern* (1987; 1989).

5. *Builder* liv (1888), 61. Not just names and dates: 'it is interesting enough to know who built the Parthenon, or the Pantheon, or King's Cross, but it is no more architecture than playing the fiddle or dancing the polka' (*Builder* lxxiii, 1897, 368). 'Deceased architecture is the architect's lesson-book, as history is the statesman's and poetry the poet's' (*Builder* lxxi, 1896, 382).

6. *Builder* liv (1888), 61, quoting Reynold's *Discourses*.

7. *Ibid.*

8. *Builder* liv (1888), 63 and l (1886), 404.

9. *Builder* lxvi (1894), 169–72, 193.

10. J. Mordaunt Crook, 'Architecture and History', in *Architectural History* xxvii (1984), 356–7.

11. *Builder* lvi (1889), 142.

12. *Builder* lxxi (1896), 382. See W. Coleman, *Georges Cuvier, Zoologist. A Study in the History of Evolutionary Theory* (Cambridge, Mass., 1964).

13. *Builder* lxvi (1894), 193. Architecture will evolve, 'by gradual addition to or suppression from an original type, just as widely-differing wings of the albatross and the apteryx have been derived from a common type' (*Builder* lii, 1887, 346–7). See also 'Darwinism in Architecture', in *Building News* 2 April 1875.

14. *Builder* lxx (1896), 109. We want 'a new vitality [in] architecture, so that it may go on improving till it drives out the antiquarian interloper . . . We want every moulding to tell of its real date by its shape . . . [Let us therefore] set our grand art [back] on its feet again' (*Builder* lxx, 1896, 111). As things stand at present, 'we have not even a moulding we can call our own'. Somehow we must 'put the breath of life [back] into architecture, so that it may again become a progressive art' (*Builder* lxx, 1896, 132).

15. *Builder* lxx (1896), 109. Similarly *Builder* lxvi (1894), 87: the 'art of expression is mainly learned from the past, but the artist must be animated by the spirit of the present'; 'Saracen architecture should be studied not to imitate Saracen architecture, but to help us learn the aesthetic part of architecture itself' (*Builder* lxvi, 1894, 153); 'architectural monuments should express the taste, feeling and skill of the nation at the time of their building' (*Builder* lxvi, 1894, 87); they should embody 'the flavour of the age' (*Builder* lxviii, 1895, 79).

16. 'The [apparently] eccentric shapes [of its] vaults and domes are purely the result of the unimpeachable logic of construction' (*Builder* lx, 1891, 190). For Byzantine architecture Aitchison chiefly relied on: de Vogüé, *Syrie Centrale*, 2 vols (Paris, 1865–97); M. Dieulafoy, *L'Art Antique de la Perse* (Paris, 1884–9); C.E.M. Tessier and R.P. Pullan, *Byzantine Architecture* (1864); A.J. Butler, *The Ancient Coptic Churches of Egypt* (Oxford, 1884); F. de Verneilh, *L'Architecture Byzantin de France* (Paris, 1851); C. Bayet, *L'Art Byzantin* (Paris, 1883); T.G. Jackson, *The Architecture of Dalmatia* (1887); C.E. Isabelle, *Les édifices circulaires et les domes* (Paris, 1855); J. Labarte, *Le Palais Impérial de Constantinople* (Paris, 1861); and of course the work of Auguste Choisy, Engineer-in-Chief of Roads and Bridges, Paris – in Aitchison's eyes 'a genius' (*Builder* lx, 1891, 187, 190) – notably *Histoire de l'Architecture*, 2 vols (Paris, 1898–9; lectures at the École Polytechnique) and 'Voute', in Viollet-le-Duc's *Dictionnaire de l'Architecture*, vol. ix (1868).

17. *Builder* lxx (1896), 159. Aitchison's authorities for Romanesque were: Tessier, Choisy, Gailhabaud, De Caumont (to whom, rather than the Revd W. Gunn, he attributed the stylistic term), Rupricht-Robert, Cataneo, F. De Dartoin (on Lombard architecture), and of course Viollet-le-Duc: 'he is always as interesting as a good novel, and a great deal more interesting than most novels' (*Builder* lxx, 1896, 133, 206).

18. *Builder* lxx (1896), 227.

19. *Builder* lxx (1896), 159.

20. *Builder* lvi (1889), 428.

21. *Builder* lxx (1896), 133.

22. *Builder* lxviii (1895), 139. Even Burges, 'the most original and vigorous of the band of Neo-Goths', could not make Gothic the style of his own day (*Builder* lv, 1888, 3).

23. *Builder* lxxviii (1900), 129. 'The Gothic revival has done excellent service, but it was doomed from the first to be ephemeral' (*Builder* xlviii, 1885, 582).

24. *Builder* lv (1888), 431. Similarly *RIBA Journal* 3rd series (1901–2), 383.

25. *Builder* lv (1888), 431. Unlike Morris, however, Aitchison saw no prospect of a new style emerging out of social revolution (*Builder* lv, 1888, 2).

26. *Builder* l (1886), 404. Similarly *Builder* lxvi (1894), 88.

27. *Builder* lxxiv (1898), 610: on receiving the Royal Gold Medal. See also *Builder* lxxvi (1899), 409: on opening the International Building Trades Exhibition.

28. 'Historicism' in this sense seems first to have been popularised by Pevsner (*Architectural Review* lxxxvi, 1939, 55 and subsequently *passim*). Its philosophical use – teleological and determinist – is more correctly defined in K. Popper, *The Poverty of Historicism* (1957; first expounded in *Economica* 1944–5). See D. Watkin, 'Sir Nikolaus Pevsner: a Study in Historicism', in *Apollo*, Sept. 1992, 169–71.

29. *Builder* lxxii (1897), 267–71.

30. 'We see the art of building first absorbing all useful and constructional inventions, then gradually converting them into aesthetic features, and producing in special buildings . . . grand emotional results. The question we naturally ask ourselves is, why we cannot do the same' (*Builder* lxiv, 1893, 166–9). Similarly *Builder* lxx (1896), 205–6.

31. *Builder* lxviii (1895), 180.

32. *Builder* xiv (1856), 282–4: 21 April 1856; *RIBA Transactions* viii (1857–8), 47: 14 Dec. 1857. In years to come he maintained his enthusiasm for external polychromy, praising the use of mosaics, *sgraffito*, encaustic tiles, glazed bricks and terracotta (*Builder* xliv, 1883, 274).

33. *RIBA Transactions* xiv (1863–4), 97, 103: 29 Feb. 1864. He pressed for the foundation of a Professorship of Construction at the Royal Academy, to stifle criticism that the Academy Schools produced only 'draughtsmen and scene painters' (*Builder* xlviii, 1885, 396). 'Practical geometry, stereotomy and stonecutting are shamefully neglected amongst English architects' (*Builder* lii, 1887, 636). The Architectural Association is 'a mutual improvement society rather than a school' (*Builder* lii, 1887, 699). The contrast with Paris was striking: in Paris there were even prizes for theoretical exploration, e.g., the Bordin prize ('To seek if there be a common aesthetic law, applicable to the monuments of the great epochs of art') and the L.J. Duc prize ('To determine by special studies the style of modern architecture'). See *Builder* lviii (1890), 75.

34. As a member of the Foreign Architectural Book Society (FABS), Aitchison was very much part of the inner circle of the RIBA. See J. Mordaunt Crook, *William Burges and the High Victorian Dream* (1981), 73–4.

35. *RIBA Transactions* xiv (1863–4), 107. For George Aitchison Snr (1792–1861), of 6 Muscovy Court, Trinity Square, Tower Hill, see *Minutes of Proceedings of the Institution of Civil Engineers* xxi (1862), 569–71. He left £800. George Aitchison Jnr of 150 Harley Street – the subject of this lecture – left £13,284 10s. 1d. (Probate Records).

36. *Builder* lxxiv (1898), 609.

37. 'The labours of the field are performed by hideous engines; the commonest household services are being done by machinery. The moors, heaths, commons and forest make way for fields of cabbages, mangel wurzel and pota-

toes – trees and hedges will shortly be extirpated. All splendour in dress is laid aside, and we may expect to see the materials of clothing so improved and cheapened, that the labourer in his best clothes, and the king on his throne, shall be almost indistinguishable. Processions and Civic pomp are doomed, warfare itself is becoming an unpicturesque as civil life . . . Sculpture and painting have ceased to have any marked influence on mankind, and . . . must be clothed in the forms of past ages, or other countries, to make [them] palatable . . . ornament is looked on either as an advertisement, or as a humouring of the prejudices of the vulgar' (*RIBA Transactions* xiv, 1863–4, 105). 'Nearly everyone is dressed alike, to give an appearance of equality, equality being one of the favourite fictions of the day' (*Builder* lxiv, 1893, 209–12).

38. *RIBA Transactions* xiv (1863–4), 105.

39. *Ibid.*

40. *Building News* xi (1864), 134: ill. Aitchison remained proud of this building; as late as 1901 he exhibited a perspective by D. Varey, now in the RIBA Drawings Collection (*Building News* lxxx, 1901, 583).

41. *Buildings of England: London* iii (1991), 481; *Leighton House Guide* (n.d.); Mrs Haweis, *Beautiful Houses* (1882); M.B. Adams, *Artists' Houses* (1883); F.G. Stephens, *Artists at Home* (1884); C.F. Stell, 'Leighton House, Kensington', in *Archaeological Journal* cxiv (1959), 122–5.

42. *Vernon Lee's Letters*, ed. J. Cooper-Willis (privately printed, 1937), 123.

43. Quoted in L. and R. Ormond, *Lord Leighton* (1975), 62.

44. Mrs Haweis, *Beautiful Houses* (1882), 2, 7.

45. Contemporary description quoted in R. Dutton, *London Houses* (1952), 117.

46. *Builder* xliv (1883), 207. Similarly *Builder* lxvi (1894), 153.

47. *Builder* l (1886), 404.

48. *Ibid.* 'We live in a world of words; the foremost men are engaged in unravelling the secrets of nature or the past, or in making machines to apply the forces of nature to common use. The things wanting are a comprehension of the supreme importance of the visual arts and a sense of the beauty of form; this last is one of nature's gifts to man . . . it is withering away from want of use' (*Builder* lxviii, 1895, 180). 'If there is absolutely no desire for anything but bare shelter . . . a plain dog-kennel or rabbit hutch . . . then architecture as a fine art must cease' (*Builder* lxiv, 1893, 209–12).

49. *Builder* lii (1887), 636.

50. *Builder* lxvi (1894), 107. Architects 'create organisms in emulation of Nature' (*Builder* lxi, 1891, 139). Buildings on the Renaissance principle which separate interior and exterior aesthetics, deny their basis in nature: a building which treats a façade independently of its structure 'does not emulate one of Nature's organisms' (*Builder* lxvi, 1894, 108).

51. Whewell, 'Some Analogies between Architecture and the other Fine Arts', RIBA 9 March 1863, reported in *Ecclesiologist* xxiv, N.S. xxi (1863), 124–5.

52. *Builder* lxi (1891), 139.

53. *Builder* lxxii (1897), 221.

54. *Builder* lxviii (1895), 79.

55. *Builder* lxviii (1895), 81.
56. *Builder* lvi (1889), 142.
57. *Builder* lxvi (1894), 194. Similarly *Builder* lxvi (1894), 107.
58. *Builder* lxxiii (1897), 367. 'Architecture became a scholastic exercise in a dead language' (*Builder* lxvi, 1894, 171).
59. *Builder* lxvi (1894), 153, 169. Renaissance architects 'were not architects at all, [they] had no idea what architecture meant' (*Builder* lxxii, 1897, 420). 'They not only left a bitter drop in the cup, but that bitterness was rank poison . . . producing stupor from which we are only now beginning to awaken' (*Builder* lxxiv, 1898, 147–9).
60. *Builder* lxi (1891), 138.
61. Real architecture in England, he believed, had ended with the sixteenth-century staircase at Christ Church, Oxford (*ibid.*).
62. *Builder* lxvi (1894), 88. 'We shall, I think, find out these shapes partly by theory, and partly by experiment' (*Builder* lxiv, 1893, 83–7). 'I suspect that we will have to go back again to the rectilinear form, for that is the form that iron most conveniently . . . takes' (*Builder* lxiv, 1893, 209–12).
63. *Builder* xliv (1883), 207. 'Very ordinary algebra' (Ruskin, *Works* IX, 456).
64. 'Though heavy . . . outside, [it] is wonderful inside and produces strong emotions from the brilliancy of its height, its vastness, lightness and height; and this happens mainly through mere effort to cover a large space economically' (*Builder* lxiv, 1893, 108–10). 'The constructors' of 'the Crystal Palace and . . . large modern railway station roofs are the really modern Medieval architects', the true cathedral builders of the Victorian age (*Builder* xxix, 1871, 417).
65. *Builder* lxviii (1895), 100. Similarly *Builder* lx (1891), 82.
66. *Builder* lx (1891), 95.
67. *Builder* lviii (1890), 109. Similarly *Builder* lxxviii (1900), 129. For the fragmentation of the building professions, see J. Mordaunt Crook, 'The Pre-Victorian Architect: Professionalism and Patronage', in *Architectural History* xii (1969), 62–78.
68. *Builder* lv (1888), 431. 'The engineers have eliminated beauty from their structures' (*Builder* lii, 1887, 636).
69. *Builder* lxviii (1895), 121.
70. *Builder* lii (1887), 700.
71. For Aitchison's criticism of Baltard's Halles Centrales, see *Builder* xliv (1883), 208. He preferred J.I. Hittorf's Gare du Nord (using columns cast in Glasgow in 1862); Henri Labrouste's Bibliothèque Nationale ('as agreeable a room as you could wish to see'); J.F. Duban and Coquart's École des Beaux-Arts; and 'Les Magasins du Printemps', near St Lazare, by Paul Sédille (*ibid.*).
72. É. Zola, *The Belly of Paris* (1873).
73. É. Zola, *The Masterpiece* (1886), trans. T. Walton and R. Pearson (1993).
74. *Builder* lxxiii (1897), 368 and lxvi (1894), 151.
75. *Builder* lxxii (1897), 219 and lxxviii (1900), 129. For a commentary on L. Eidlitz, *The Nature and Function of Art, more especially of architecture* (1881), see *Builder* xli (1881), 593–4, 655–6.

76. *Builder* lxi (1891), 138.
77. *Builder* lxxiii (1897), 767. Even our mouldings are in 'the antiquarian chrysalid state' (*Builder* lxviii, 1895, 181). 'A knowledge of statics gives us a true ratio between every part of a structure, and it gives a real shape each part must take; if we were as clever as Nature, it would in all probability give us a beautiful shape. Unfortunately, we are far from being as clever, and . . . we have to learn by other means how a beautiful shape can be made out of the necessary shape. For this purpose we must study deceased architecture and Nature. Every piece of deceased architecture that we admire can be made to show us the aesthetic laws that govern it and produce its excellence and these laws are as capable of being employed now as then.' For example, 'a Greek Doric column showed the statical knowledge of its day, but it certainly does not now' (*Builder* lxxiv, 1898, 102). Hence the challenge.
78. *Builder* liv (1888), 62. 'The present generation lives wholly in the present, owing to the discoveries in science and to mechanical invention. This age is cut off by a gulf from the past . . . our oldest heroes are Smeaton and Brindley, Trevithick, Watt and George Stephenson, the Brunels, Hodgkinson and Fairbairn, Davy, Dalton, Faraday and Wheatstone' (*RIBA Transactions* N.S. iv, 1887–8, 178). 'In each art nations get the embodiment of what they are' (*Builder* lv, 1888, 432). 'For architecture is a social expression' (*Builder* lv, 1888, 432).
79. *Builder* lxviii (1895), 121. Similarly *Builder* lv (1888), 433. Not until 'new and noble aspirations again lift men from their present [obsessions] with filling their bellies and their pockets, [will] a new iron architecture . . . soar above' (*Builder* liv, 1888, 62). We have painters, sculptors and architects whose skill matches any in the past 'but there is no high ideal in society to be expressed by them' (*Builder* lv, 1888, 432 and lxviii, 1895, 80). Our present ideal would seem to be 'the land of Cocagne, where the little pigs run about ready roasted asking people to eat them' (*Builder* lxviii, 1895, 121). 'Our age is marked by its creed of gain, and its love of banquetting, but it is redeemed by a taste for literature, some love of humanity, and a passion for scientific research' (*Builder* lv, 1888, 432). 'Turtle, whitebait, venison, and stuffed truffles, washed down with punch, champagne, old claret and port, are excellent things occasionally, but if all our happiness is centred on them, what can be expected of us?' (*Builder* lv, 1888, 432).
80. 'An Architect on Architecture', in *Merry England* iv (1884–5), 235–7.
81. *Builder* l (1886), 334, 404. Similarly *Builder* lxxxix (1905), 595 and lxxiv (1898), 180–2.
82. 'The Neglect of Architecture', in *Merry England* vii (1886), 119–30, 169–75.
83. *Builder* lii (1887), 635.
84. *Builder* lx (1891), 85. There is some consolation: 'living architecture' does progress, though 'its progress is not always in a direct line' (*ibid.* 83).
85. *Builder* lxii (1892), 179–83. 'Those who reproach architects with not inventing a new style forget that hundreds of years are required to evolve one' (*ibid.* 75–8).

86. *Builder* lxvi (1894), 88.
87. *Builder* lxiv (1893), 63–6.
88. *Builder* lxviii (1895), 180, 182.
89. *Builder* lxxii (1897), 117.
90. *Builder* lxviii (1895), 81, 99. 'Almost every country has produced a style of its own, [but] this country has yet to take that step' (*Builder* lxvii, 1894, 372: the editor demurred – 'What about English Gothic, the Early English and Tudor Gothic especially?'). 'There are explorers in every direction, [but] the real road has not yet been found' (*Builder* lxxi, 1896, 383).
91. *Builder* lxxii (1897), 117–19.
92. *Builder* lxxiv (1898), 252. 'The thing we all want is the advancement of architecture. But who is to show us the way?' (*Builder* lxxv, 1898, 425). Are mankind's 'powers of invention' doomed to become 'atrophied [like] the wings of the apteryx?' (*ibid.*, 426).
93. *Builder* lxxviii (1900), 130.
94. *Builder* lxxiii (1897), 117–19.
95. *Builder* lxxviii (1900), 130.
96. *RIBA Journal*, 3rd series (1901–2), 199.
97. *Builder* lxxxiv (1903), 186, 214. He cites the iron spire of Rouen Cathedral as an instance of how not to use iron; and a house front in George Street, off the Strand, Westminster, by Halsey Ricardo, as an example worth following. When Aitchison announced in 1905 that he would again lecture on Vitruvius, Statham commented: 'We confess that we should have thought enough had been said of late years about Vitruvius, and that lectures . . . illuminating the art of architecture from a modern standpoint . . . would have been of more value to the Academy students' (*Builder* lxxxviii, 1905, 5). Aitchison had, in fact, already dismissed Vitruvius as treating the 'aesthetic part [of architecture] like a recipe from a cookery book' (*Builder* lxiv, 1893, 209–12).
98. *Builder* lxiv (1893), 209–12.
99. *Builder* lxxiii (1897), 368.
100. *Builder* xlviii (1885), 582.
101. *Builder* lxviii (1895), 121.
102. *Builder* lxvi (1894), 193.
103. *Builder* lxxiv (1898), 251–2.
104. *Builder* v (1847), 492.
105. A. Poynter, *On the effects which should result to architectural taste with regard to arrangement and design from the general introduction of iron in the construction of buildings* (RIBA medal essay, 1842); W. Vose Pickett, *Metallurgic Architecture* (1844; 1845). See *Builder* lxvi (1894), 131–4.
106. 'Statics [should] give us . . . important lessons in aesthetics, for it gives us the proper proportion of each part of a building when we know the height, the weight to be carried, and the strength of material to be used. When these particulars are known and provided for, we may roughly say that we have only to accentuate the important parts by mouldings, or have them advanced by the sculptor, to make it into architecture' (*Builder* lxxiii, 1897, 367).

107. 'Have we got an architecture that does fulfil all the wants, satisfies the taste, and expresses all the emotions of the day? . . . If we cannot affirm this, we must admit we have failed' (*Builder* lxiv, 1893, 63–6).

108. F. Maddox Ford [Hueffer], *Rossetti: a Critical Essay on his Art* (Chicago, 1915), quoted in J. McGann, *Dante Gabriel Rossetti and the Game that Must be Lost* (2000), 144.

109. 'No doubt, a century or two hence, it will be as easy to recognise the architecture of Queen Victoria's reign as it is now to distinguish that of Queen Elizabeth' (*Builder* xvii, 1859, 603). Aitchison rejected this: 'Every modern building . . . has a nineteenth-century air about it . . . but I cannot admit that this flavour amounts to a style', for that would involve 'new forms by reason of new wants or new materials . . . Eclecticism itself would constitute a new style [only] if all pillaged the same things' (*Builder* lviii, 1890, 75).

110. During a discussion in 1887, Aitchison was told this by J.A. Gotch, but failed to respond. Gotch explained: 'people [today] do not go on from step to step in one style . . . as the medievals did'; because Victorian eclecticism was the product of a pluralistic culture (*Builder* lii, 1887, 654).

Chapter 2: Butterfield and Webb

Epigraph: 'Pied Beauty', Hopkins, *Poems*, ed. R. Bridges and C. Williams (1933 edn), no. 13, 30: 1877.

1. E.g., H.-R. Hitchcock, 'Ruskin and Butterfield', in *Architectural Review* cxvi (1954), 285–9 and *Early Victorian Architecture in Britain* ii (1934), 572; G.L. Hersey, *High Victorian Gothic: a study in associationism* (1972); M.W. Brooks, *John Ruskin and Victorian Architecture* (1989).

2. Ruskin, *Works* XI, 230.

3. J.M. Neale and B. Webb, intro. G. Durandus, *The Symbolism of Churches and Church Ornaments* (trans. 1843).

4. H.C.G. Matthew, 'Gladstone, Evangelicalism and "The Engagement"', in *Revival and Religion Since 1700*, ed. J. Garnett and C. Matthew (1993), 125. The Engagement lasted from 1844 to 1852; its members were mostly Tractarian in religion and Liberal in politics, e.g., Gladstone, A.H.D. Acland, J.T. Coleridge and Roundell Palmer. See J.E. Acland, *A Layman's Life* (1904), 171–6.

5. He was, for example, a member of Nobody's Friends, a dining club of High Anglican laymen, named after William ('Nobody') Stevens (1732–1807), a City hosier who was Treasurer of Queen Anne's Bounty. Benjamin Webb was elected in 1878 (Webb, 'Diary', 22 May 1878). See *The Club of Nobody's Friends: a Biographical List of Members . . . 1800 to . . . 1885* (privately published, 1938). Butterfield declined to worship at either All Saints, Margaret St. or St Alban's, Holborn; he preferred a 'lower' level of ritual in Tottenham.

6. Athenaeum Club MSS. Beresford Hope did not support his election.

7. H.S. Goodhart-Rendel, 'Victorian Conservanda', in *Journal of the London Society*, February 1959, 9.

8. N. White, *Hopkins* (Oxford, 1992), 47. In 1866 Hopkins' tutor was Walter

Pater of Brasenose (Hopkins, *Poems and Prose*, ed. W.H. Gardner, 1985 edn, 105, 194).

9. 1862, quoted in *Oxoniensia* iv (1939), 187. As late as 1911, T.G. Jackson would have been happy to rebuild it (Balliol Coll. Archives, D.10.16/B; *ex inf.* Dr William Whyte). Freeman harboured a particular resentment against Balliol: the college had preferred Matthew Arnold as a potential scholar, and he ended up at Trinity.

10. *Note Books and Journals of Gerard Manley Hopkins*, ed. H. House (1937), 7–8.

11. Hopkins, *Poems*, ed. R. Bridges and C. Williams (1933 edn), no. 13, 30: 1877.

12. By August 1849 *The Ecclesiologist* was already becoming uneasy at Butterfield's 'crotchets' and idiosyncracies at West Lavington: 'We trust we may not be now registering the first traces of an excessive reaction from traditionary architectural rules' (ix, N.S. vi, 1849, 68).

13. Hopkins, *Note Books*, 197, 205–7: 12 June and 18 Aug. 1874. Butterfield 'is worth comparing with Gerard Manley Hopkins in his clash of interrupted rhythms, no less than in the indigestibility of his detail' (K. Clark, *Gothic Revival*, 1962 edn, 191, note 1).

14. Ruskin, *Works* VIII, 128 n. The college was founded by Beresford Hope in 1844 and completed in 1848. It was praised in *Ecclesiologist* ix, N.S. vi (1848), 1–8. See also *Builder* vi (1848), 163: ill.; R.J.E. Boggis, *A History of St Augustine's College, Canterbury* (1907); M. Sparks, 'The Recovery and Excavation of the St Augustine's Abbey Site, 1844–1947', in *Archaeologia Cantiana* c (1984), 325–44. Hope spent some £40,000 on the project, say £2 million today.

15. Ruskin, *Works* XI, 36, 229. Building was supported financially by Beresford Hope, Henry Tritton and Sir Stephen Glynne; £70,000 was raised; the foundation stone was laid in 1849 by Dr Pusey.

16. Ruskin thought Woodward's work at Trinity College, Dublin was truly Ruskinian (*Works* XVIII, 149–50). He thought Waterhouse's Assize Courts at Manchester (1859; dem.) an admirable reflection of his *Stones of Venice* (*Works* XVIII, lxxv). He called Teulon's St Stephen, Rosslyn Hill 'the finest specimen of brick building in all the land'. And he was famously proud of his influence on Street (*Works* X, 458–9). He called St Paul's, Herne Hill, 'one of the loveliest churches of its kind in the country . . . a remarkable piece of colouring' (*Works* XVI, 463); indeed, he thought Street's designs 'pure beyond anything he had ever seen in modern architecture' (*Works* XVI, 462). See also D. Dishon, 'Three Men in a Gondola: Ruskin, Webb and Street', in *A Church As It Should Be: The Cambridge Camden Society and its Influence*, ed. C. Webster and J. Elliott (Stamford, 2000), 190–210.

17. C. Hobhouse, *Oxford* (1952 edn), 97.

18. He stated clearly that early English Decorated (e.g., the Angel Choir at Lincoln Cathedral) was intrinsically superior, and preferable as a model for modern work (*Works* VIII, 258). He had intended to write another volume, on thirteenth-century French Gothic, but the current practice of drastic restoration in France had dissuaded him: 'he gave up the undertaking, and . . .

he gave up architecture too' (address by Ruskin to the Ecclesiological Society, 13 June 1861: *Ecclesiologist* xxii, N.S. xix, 1861, 254).

19. *Works* VIII, 48: *Seven Lamps* i, para 12.

20. *Works* VIII, 180–1: *Seven Lamps* iv, para. 39.

21. *Works* VIII, 176, 178: *Seven Lamps* iv, paras. 35–6.

22. *Works* IX, 347: *Stones of Venice* xxvi, para. 1.

23. *Works* VIII, 218–19: *Seven Lamps* v, para. 24. The MS. version reads: 'dead ornament is to my mind the most dismal mourning that a building can wear. I am grieved . . . when I hear of any attempts at the building of florid Gothic; we have it not in us, and it will need severe discipline before we gain it.'

24. E.g., M.G. Bindesboll's design for Copenhagen Zoological Museum (1844) or J.C. von Lassaulx's St Arnulph, Nickenich at Maria Laach, Germany (1844–8). See German, *Gothic Revival* (1972), 114–18 and pl. 85, and N. Pevsner, in *The Listener* xl (1948), 808–9.

25. *Civil Engineer and Architect's Journal* xiii (1850), 128–30, 215–16. Sydney Smirke commented: 'Throughout western Germany bricks are worked with a fantastic ingenuity rarely visible with us: by the use of various coloured bricks intermixed, an ornamental character is given to the commonest build-ings – somewhat whimsical perhaps to our plain English eyes, but yet well deserving observation' (*ibid.*, 130). Interestingly, it was at the second of these meetings that Beresford Hope was elected Honorary Fellow (*Builder* viii, 1850, 293). For a recent survey, see N. Nussbaum, *German Gothic Church Architecture*, trans. S. Kleager (2000), 76 *et seq.*

26. *Ecclesiologist* xi, N.S. viii (1850), 228; *Brick and Marble in the Middle Ages* (1855).

27. Quoted in P. Thompson, *William Butterfield* (1971), 82.

28. To T.F. Bumpus, in *The Architect* lxiii (1900), 226.

29. Thompson, *Butterfield*, 97.

30. S. Hart, *Flint Architecture of East Anglia* (2000), ills.

31. Letter to Coleridge, 30 Sept. 1854, private collection, quoted in *Oxford Dictionary of National Biography*, s.v. Butterfield; letter to Benjamin Starey, quoted in Thompson, *Butterfield*, 92.

32. *Ecclesiologist* xvi, N.S. xiii (1855), 397.

33. 'He is an excellent man, and one who has entirely risen by his merits, his father being a London tradesman . . . and St Paul's School the first nurse of his advancement. He has no worldly means, having just missed a scholarship at Trinity' (Hope to Gladstone, 30 Dec. 1846: B.L. Add. MS. 44213 f. 265).

34. Mostly inherited from his father – Benjamin Webb of Webb and Sons, wheelwrights, London – who sent young Webb to St Paul's and Trinity College, Cambridge. For details, see J. Mordaunt Crook, 'Benjamin Webb and Victorian Ecclesiology', in *Studies in Church History* xxxvi (1997), 423–57. By comparison, Butterfield – who was largely self-made – left £16,369 in 1900 (Probate Office records).

35. Hope to Gladstone, 30 Dec. 1846: B.L. Add. MS. 44213 f. 265.

36. *Ecclesiologist* xxvii, N.S. xxiv (1866), 115.

37. Bodleian Library, Oxford, SC.44750–88. For Webb at Cambridge, see *Romilly's Cambridge Diary, 1842–47*, ed. M.E. Bury and J.D. Pickles (1994), 208–9 and *1848–64* (Cambridge, 2000), 136, 162.

38. *Ecclesiologist* xv, N.S. xii (1854), 4.

39. 'Parliamentary Survey on New Church Building and Restoration between 1840 and 1875', in *Parliamentary Papers* 1876, lviii, 553–658.

40. *The Architect* 22 November 1873, 264 and 19 September 1874, 141. Whether the growth of congregations kept pace with the expansion of accommodation is a nice matter for debate. 'If Anglican churches increased their congregations by only half the Free Church total of 658,543, the total increase [for 1859–65] would be just under a million [for all Christian denominations]' (J.H. Williams, citing E. Orr, *The Second Evangelical Awakening in Britain,* 1949, in *The Times* 29 April 1989, 11).

41. Quoted in P.B. Nockles, *The Oxford Movement in Context: Anglican High Churchmanship, 1760–1857* (Cambridge, 1994), 214.

42. *Ecclesiologist* i (1842), 209–10. Various patent cements were in use. Liardet's cement dates from 1773; Parker's Roman cement from 1796; Dehl's mastic from 1815; Hamelin's mastic from 1817; Portland cement from 1824 (R. Brunskill and A. Clifton-Taylor, *English Brickwork*, 1977, 43).

43. *Ecclesiologist* vi (1846), 98–101.

44. *Ecclesiologist* viii, N.S. v. (1848), 146–7.

45. R. Willis, *Remarks on the Architecture of the Middle Ages, especially of Italy* i (1835), iii. For example, St Mark's, Venice had been condemned for its 'extreme ugliness' and 'bad taste' (J. Woods, *Letters of an Architect, from France, Italy and Greece* i, 1828, 256).

46. He had been sent to Italy in 1844, partly to find precedents for the use of Gothic in hot climates: the Camden Society suggested that Mediterranean Gothic might supply useful prototypes for missionary churches in the tropics (B. Webb, 'On Pointed Architecture as adapted to Tropical Climates', in *Transactions of the Ecclesiological Society*, 1845, 199–218).

47. Some plates were re-drawn from F. von Quast, *Die alt-christlichen Bauwerke von Ravenna* (1842).

48. *Builder* iii (1845), 326–7; iv (1846), 334; v (1847), 468; vi (1848), 577.

49. Wyatt followed this with *Specimens of Geometrical Mosaic manufactured by Maw and Co. . . . from patterns designed and arranged by M.D.W.* (1857), and *On Pictorial Mosaic as an architectural embellishment* (1866). Wyatt travelled the Continent, making nearly a thousand ink and watercolour drawings, in 1844–6.

50. Hope to Gladstone, 9 Oct. 1850: B.L. Add. MS. 44213 f. 294. See also P. Thompson in *Country Life*, 14 Jan. 1965, 61.

51. H.C.G. Matthew in *Revival and Religion Since 1700*, ed. J. Garnett and C. Matthew (1993), 125. In October 1842, it was noted that 'this chapel is about to be rebuilt on nearly the same site . . . with a view to consecration, which the present building does not enjoy, and of course in a more catholic style and design' (*British Critic* xxxii, 1842, 462, note).

52. 'The Irish [estate churches, paid for by Hope] have taken up so much money this year, that we have postponed our new church till next year, and in the interim are planning a refitting of Margaret Chapel which Butterfield is working out. It will really turn out very nice I think. There will be a chancel with four stalls on each side and a sacrarium, and the nave filled with open seats. The galleries make aisles' (Beresford Hope to E.A. Freeman, 15 June 1847: Freeman MSS., Rylands Library, Manchester, FA1/1/41a). See also E. Bourne, 'Old Margaret Street Chapel', in *Merry England* iv (1884–5), 357–63.

53. Hope to Gladstone, 6 Nov. 1847: B.L. Add. MS. 44213 f. 277.

54. PRO, CRES 2/662. Hope bought old Margaret Street chapel for £1,350 and presented some of the fittings to Webb's church at Sheen, Staffordshire (Murray, *Staffordshire*, 1892, 205).

55. Hope to W.E. Gladstone, 9 Dec. 1846: B.L. Add. MS. 44213 f. 259–60.

56. Hope to E.A. Freeman, 14 May [1846?]: Freeman MSS., Rylands Library, Manchester, FA1/1/65.

57. Hope to E.A. Freeman, 8 Jan. 1850: *loc. cit.* FA1/1/46.

58. *Ibid.*, 21 Oct 1852: *loc. cit.* FA1/1/48a.

59. 'Webb is hard at work on his book and hopes to go to press June 1 [*sic*]' (Hope to E.A. Freeman, 15 June 1847: *loc. cit.*, FA1/1/41a).

60. P. Thompson, in *Architectural History* viii (1965), 76; this revises the chronology of H.-R. Hitchcock in *Architectural Review* cxvi (1954), 285–9. See also W.A. Whitworth, *Quam Dilecta: a description of All Saints, Margaret Street* (1891); *All Saints, Margaret Street* (Pitkin Guide, 1950). The tile paintings on the north wall – painted by Alexander Gibbs; manufactured by Henry Poole and Sons – date from as late as 1873, replacing the original geometrical decoration; those below the west window are even later, dating from 1889; and that on the north wall of the tower dates from as late as 1891. All were installed under Butterfield's direction. In the chancel and sanctuary, William Dyce's painted vault and frescoed reredos (1853–9) had to be replaced by Comper in 1909. The decoration in the baptistery was simplified at about the same time.

61. Wyatt lectured to the RIBA on 1 Nov. 1847 (*Builder* v, 1847, 537–7); his book was reviewed a year later (*Builder* vi, 1848, 530).

62. Sale Catalogue: Sotheby, Wilkinson and Hodge (1888), lot 2211.

63. *A Few Words to Church Builders* (Cambridge, 1841), 9.

64. *Ecclesiologist* iii (1844), 86–7; B. of E., *Lancashire, South* (1969), 90.

65. *Ecclesiologist* i (1841), 20. See also [Revd J. Elstob], in *Gentleman's Magazine* xvii (1842), 144.

66. T. James, 'On the Use of Brick in Ecclesiastical Architecture', in *Fourth Report of the Architectural Society of . . . Northampton* (1847), 25–37. For details, see B. of E., *London, South* (1983), 333 and N. Jackson, 'Christ Church, Streatham and the Rise of Constructional Polychromy', in *Architectural History* xliii (2000), 219–52. James died in 1864; a memorial was placed in the round section of St Sepulchre's, Northampton (*Ecclesiologist* xxv, N.S. xxii, 1864, 179). Christ Church, Streatham and the New Cross engine house

were also praised by William Boutcher in a lecture at the Architectural Association, 7 July 1848 (*Builder* vi, 1848, 411–12, 422–4).

67. T. Hope, *Historical Essay on Architecture* (1835); Willis, *op. cit.* n. 44; H. Gally Knight, *Ecclesiastical Architecture of Italy from the time of Constantine to the Fifteenth Century*, 2 vols (1842–4).

68. Willis, *op. cit.*, 12.

69. Knight, *op. cit.*, xxiv.

70. Webb, *op. cit.*, 381.

71. Knight, *op. cit.*, vi, vii.

72. Webb, *op. cit.*, 251.

73. Knight, *op. cit.*, xxxi.

74. Webb, *op. cit.*, 368–9.

75. *Ibid.*, 277–81.

76. *Ibid.*, 225

77. *Ibid.*, 232, 234.

78. *Ibid.*, 242, 299.

79. Lord Lindsay, *Sketches of the History of Christian Art* i (1847), 66; E.A. Freeman, *History of Architecture* (1849), 175.

80. [Benjamin Webb and J.M. Neale,] *A Few Words to Church Builders* (1844), 29.

81. *Ecclesiologist* viii, N.S. v (1848), 118.

82. Webb, in *Ecclesiologist* xxii, N.S. xix (1861), 261.

83. [Webb,] 'A kind of communism which is near akin to despotism' (in *Saturday Review* v, 1858, 90–1); 'A practical socialism, regulated by a paternal despotism' (in *ibid.* x, 1860, 273–5, 310–12).

84. [Webb,] 'Mr Ruskin's Seven Lamps of Architecture', in *Ecclesiologist* x, N.S. vii (1850), 111–20.

85. [Webb,] 'Ruskin's Stones of Venice', in *Ecclesiologist* xii, N.S. ix (1851), 275.

86. [Webb,] reviewing Ferrey's Pugin, in *Saturday Review* xii (1861), 121–3 and in *Ecclesiologist* xxii, N.S. xix (1861), 79–85. 'Pugin's . . . pencil was lightening-like in its manipulation and magical in its accuracy' ([Webb,] reviewing *Pugin's Sketches*, ed. E.W. Pugin, in *Saturday Review* xx, 1865, 589–90). But his 'talent was, in fact, essentially that of an archaeologist rather than of an architect' ([Webb,] in *Saturday Review* xxv, 1868, 276–8).

87. 'Wrote and despatched paper on All Saints for *Ecclesiologist*' (Webb, 'Diary', 25 May 1859); [Webb,] 'All Saints, Margaret Street', in *Ecclesiologist* xx, N.S. xvii (1859), 184–9.

88. Coventry Patmore had compared Butterfield with Rossetti: 'about the most startlingly original living artist' ([Patmore,] in *Saturday Review* iv, 1857, 583–4). Gerente's west window figures at All Saints were considered 'more than Pre-Raphaelite in ugliness' (*The Times* 30 May 1859, 7).

89. [Webb,] in *Ecclesiologist* xx, N.S. xvii (1859), 184–9.

90. These windows are by Michael O'Connor (1853), as in the glass in the east window of the south aisle. Hope had initially given responsibility for all windows to Henri Gerente. After his death in 1849 he was succeeded by his

brother Alfred. It was the latter's west window (1853–8) which caused particular dispute between Hope and Butterfield; it was replaced in 1877, under Butterfield's direction, with glass by Alexander Gibbs. Similarly, Alfred Gerente's glass in the south aisle was replaced in the late 1860s with windows also designed by Gibbs. One window at the west end of the north aisle is perhaps the only surviving piece of Gerente's work at All Saints.

91. H.W. and I. Law, *The Book of the Beresford Hopes* (1925), 175–7: letters of Hope to Webb.

92. [Webb,] 'The Prospects of Art in England', in *Bentley's Quarterly Review* i (1859), 143–82; and [Webb,] 'Beresford Hope on the Modern English Cathedral', in *Christian Remembrancer* xlii (1861), 477–8.

93. *Ecclesiologist* i (1842), 11; *Saturday Review* vii (1859), 680–2. Much of the latter passage was plagiarised by T.F. Bumpus in *London Churches Ancient and Modern* ii (1908), 238 *et seq.* 'The building is not only decorated with extreme richness . . . the decorative work is throughout real' (*British Almanac and Companion*, 1860, 231).

94. Webb, 'Diary', 13 Oct. 1880.

95. 'I will not review further the controversy about Butterfield's merits than to say that *without* seeing his works you cannot judge if his merits be . . . great, for his drawings are confessedly bad . . . St Augustine's [Canterbury] would I think convert you, and so I trust will All Saints, Margaret Street' (Beresford Hope to E.A. Freeman, 26 Dec. 1850: Freeman MSS., Rylands Library, Manchester, FA1/1/47a).

96. 'William Butterfield; or the Glory of Ugliness', in *Architectural Review* xcviii (1945), 165–75, reprinted in *Heavenly Mansions* (1949; 1963), 159–76.

97. C. Brooks, *Signs for The Times* (1984), 168.

98. For climatic conditions, see J.D. Rosenberg, *The Darkening Glass: a portrait of John Ruskin's Genius* (1961), 214 n.7.

99. 8 and 9 Vict. cap. 6. See *Builder* iii (1845), 145.

100. 13 and 14 Vict. cap. 9. See *Builder* viii (1850), 97, 257. Bricks and tiles were first taxed by Pitt in 1784; thereafter the rate, and regulation of sizes, became more stringent until tiles were relieved in 1833 and bricks in 1850 (S. Dowell, *History of Taxation and Taxes in England*, iv, 1888, 376–84; N. Lloyd, *A History of English Brick-work*, 1925, 52).

101. 14 and 15 Vict. cap. 36. See *Civil Engineer and Architect's Journal* xii (1849), 360 and xiv (1851), 543–4. The window duties were first enacted in 1696.

102. R. Brunskill and A. Clifton-Taylor, *English Brickwork* (1977), 46; G. Lynch, *Brickwork: History, Technology and Practice* (1994), 4–15.

103. *Church Builder*, Jan. 1863, 17. It was said to be more expensive than stone.

104. *Civil Engineer and Architect's Journal* xii (1849), 360.

105. *Builder* ix (1851), 733 and x (1852), 37, 168, 180, 197.

106. Hope explained that the increasing polychromy – and rising cost (£10–15,000 to £25,000) – of the designs between June 1849 and August 1850 stemmed from the fact that 'the aesthetic possibilities of different materials have become more and more clear' (letter of 6 Aug. 1850 to Henry

Tritton, quoted in P. Thompson, 'All Saints, Margaret Street, Reconsidered', in *Architectural History* viii, 1965, 76). When George Wightwick described All Saints as the sort of building 'a brickmaker might construct to show off his varied stock in trade' (*The Critic*, 1 March 1853, 130), he was not too far from the truth: it was a triumphant celebration of the repeal of the brick tax.

107. *Builder* viii (1850), 56, 97–8, 121 (*oratio recta*); referring to the Duties on Brick Act (1839), 2 and 3 Vict. cap. 24. In 1839 duties on bricks produced an excise revenue of £459,664; in 1845 the figure was £558,415 (*Civil Engineer and Architect's Journal* ix, 1846, 160). From 1840 bricks were measured, for purposes of duty, dry rather than moist (*ibid*. iii, 1840, 180).

108. *Builder* viii (1850), 121, 257.

109. *Builder* viii (1850), 267.

110. James, *op. cit.* (n. 66), 37.

111. Keble College MSS., Butterfield to E.S. Talbot: 12 Dec. 1872 (Bodleian MS. ENG. LETT. d. 275a). See also *The Guardian*, 14 April 1875, 460.

112. B. of E., *Warwickshire* (1966), 387.

113. *Civil Engineer and Architect's Journal* viii (1845), 7.

114. For statistics, 1845–7, see *ibid*. xi (1848), 333–4 and *Builder* xxxv (1878), 865.

115. *Civil Engineer and Architect's Journal* xiv (1851), 543–4.

116. B. of E., *Lincolnshire* (1989), 343, pl. 126; *Oxford Dictionary of National Biography*, s.v. Wild.

117. *Builder* xiv (1856), 282–4; at the Architectural Museum, 21 April 1856.

118. M. Girouard, *The Victorian Country House* (1979), 179–87 and *Country Life* cxlvi (1969), 1042–6. Butterfield's father, William (d. 1864), is buried in the churchyard.

119. B. of E., *Warwickshire* (1966), 387–90. Many of Butterfield's drawings for Rugby School, formerly in the Starey collection, are now at the Getty Center Library, Santa Monica, California, ref. 850998.

120. *Bricks and Brickmaking* (Wood and Ivery, West Bromwich, n.d.), see *Builder* xxxv (1878), 865.

121. *Builder* x (1852), 385; xiii (1855), 50–1 and xiv (1856), 442–4, 454–7: Chamberlain on 'The Manufacture of Bricks by Machinery', at the Society of Arts. George, 8th Marquess of Tweeddale is credited with the invention of rollers to compress clay into shaped bricks. For the chemistry of coloured brick, and precedents, see *Builder* xiii (1855), 377–9, 419, 421–3, 427.

122. *Builder* xxxv (1878), 865. For machines invented by J.P. Oates, originally of Erdington, near Birmingham, used by Messrs Kirk and Parry at Fort Elsen, near Gosport, Hants., see *Builder* xvi (1858), 235 and xxxv (1878), 865.

123. G. Smith, *Cry of the Children from the Brickyards of England* (4th edn 1871), quoted in A. Hulme, *Bricks for St Pancras* (British Brick Society, 1993). See also 'Brick Children', in *The Graphic* 27 May 1871, ill. For Edward Gripper's patent bricks, see *Building News* xvi (1869), 136, 141 and R. Mellors, *Men of Nottingham and Nottinghamshire* (1924), 232–3.

124. *Builder* xxxv (1878), 865.

125. *Builder* xxv (1867), 6.

126. For the west front of St Augustine's, Queen's Gate, Thompson suggested the Klosterkirche at Chorin; Bumpus the brick churches near Toulouse, e.g., Montgiscard, Villefranche and Villenouvelle (Bumpus, *London Churches* ii, 307).

127. *National Review* v (1857), 64–5.

128. G.G. Scott, *Personal and Professional Recollections* (1879), 228. For Chanter's (originally Heath) House, see [Bernard,] Lord Coleridge, *The Story of a Devonshire House* (1905) and M. Hall in *Country Life* 10 January 1991, 50–5.

129. [Webb,] 'Churches and Schools in London', in *Ecclesiologist* xxii, N.S. xix (1861), 317–18, 321.

130. *Builder* xiv (1856), 282, 453 and xxvi (1868), 869–70; *Building News* iii (1857), 9.

131. G.E. Street, *Brick and Marble in the Middle Ages* (1855; 2nd edn, reprinted 1986), 240; *Ecclesiologist* xxii, N.S. xix (1861), 354; xxiii, N.S. xx (1862), 16.

132. C.E. Mallet, *A History of the University of Oxford* iii (1927), 427, 430.

133. G.H. Fellowes-Prynne, in *Architectural Association Notes* xv (1900), 60.

134. Quoted in W.R.W. Stephens (ed.), *The Life and Letters of Edward A. Freeman* ii (1895), 462–3.

135. Mallet, *op. cit.*, iii, 430. See also *The Guardian*, 26 April 1876, 539.

136. Murray's *Handbook for Oxfordshire* (1894), 54.

137. P. Thompson, *William Butterfield* (1971), 33.

138. Keble College MSS., correspondence concerning mosaics, 1873, 14–15 (Bodleian MS. ENG. LETT. d. 275a/1 [13–14], 20 Jan. 1873). Iconographic details, supplied by Butterfield, are given in *Builder* xlviii (1885), 10, 47.

139. Keble College MSS., correspondence concerning mosaics, 1873, *loc. cit.* Butterfield to Shaw Stewart, 13 May 1873.

140. Quoted in Thompson, *Butterfield*, 485–6.

141. *Ibid.*

142. Butterfield plans, Keble College archives. For collegiate planning, see Basil Champneys in *RIBA Journal* x (1903), 207–10; J.B. Lock, *ibid.* xi (1904), 382–93; and E.W. Warren, *ibid.* xix (1912), 291–5. Also [Committee of Vice-Chancellors and Principals,] *The Planning of University Halls of Residence* (Oxford, 1948).

143. [Unpublished copy] quoted in Thompson, *Butterfield*, 85.

144. Quoted by P. Thompson in *Architectural History* viii (1865), 55.

145. Mallet, *op. cit.*, iii, 429; Murray's *Handbook to Oxfordshire*, 54–5. 'People did not like [Beauchamp's] brusque, straight address, as I did. [He] was a very smart, bright man, and a little chimerical – gaily dressed, and brushed, and beneath a most loving son of the church' (Archbishop Edward Benson, quoted in *Complete Peerage* ii, 43 n.).

146. See W.M. Matthew, *The House of Gibbs and the Peruvian Guano Monopoly* (1981); and J.M. Skaggs, *The Great Guano Rush: Entrepreneurs and American Overseas Expansion* (1994). Lord Aldenham died in 1906 worth over £700,000. For William Gibbs, see *The Guardian*, 7 April 1875, 425–6.

147. *The Guardian* 26 April 1876.

148. *Gladstone Diaries* ix, 287: 31 January 1878; 'One of the most beautiful structures of modern England, and even of the city of Oxford itself' (*The Spectator* 29 April 1876, 547).

149. Mallet, *op. cit.*, iii, 430.

150. Keble College MSS., 1872.

151. *The Times* 26 April 1876, 7.

152. *Illustrated London News* 26 August 1876, 205.

153. Murray's *Handbook for Oxfordshire* (1894), 55.

154. 'In spite of Keble College . . . Oxford still remains the most beautiful thing in England' (Oscar Wilde, in *Dramatic Review*, 23 May 1885, quoted in *Magdalen College Record*, 1999, 104).

155. Mallet, *op. cit.*, iii, 430.

156. C. Hobhouse, *Oxford* (1952 edn), 97–8.

157. B. of E., *Oxfordshire* (1974), 227.

158. Bodleian MS, ENG, LETT. d. 275/1 (13–15), 20 and 22 Jan. 1873.

159. *Works* XXIII, 86: *Val D'Arno* vi, paras. 141–2.

160. 7 Nov. 1873, quoted in *Works* XXIII, lv.

161. G.F. Palgrave, ed., *Francis Turner Palgrave* (1899), 139: 5 June 1875.

162. [Webb,] reviewing Eastlake's *Gothic Revival*, in *Saturday Review* xxxiii (1872), 382–3.

163. [Webb,] 'Classical and Byzantine: St Paul's and Keble College', in *Church Quarterly Review* ii (1876), 449, 460–1.

164. *Building News* xlix (1885), 1023.

165. Beresford Hope's attempt to secure him the RIBA Gold Medal was opposed on collectivist and teleological grounds: Butterfield 'is thought to work mainly for himself; is never heard of as reading papers, labouring on voluntary committees, or aiding in any way the general movement forwards' (*Builder* xxiv, 1866, 165). The medal went to Matthew Digby Wyatt. Henry Woodyer was Butterfield's only major pupil. See J. Elliott and J. Pritchard, eds, *Henry Woodyer* (Reading, 2002).

166. H.S. Goodhart-Rendel, 'Rogue Architects of the Victorian Era', in *Journal of the Royal Institute of British Architects* lxi (1949), 251–9.

167. E.g., Most Holy Trinity, Dockhead, Bermondsey (1951–61). See B. of E., *London Docklands* (1998), pl. 44.

168. 'Pied Beauty', Hopkins, in *Poems*, ed. R. Bridges and C. Williams (1933 edn.), no. 13, 30: 1877.

Chapter 3: Beresford Hope

Epigraph: *Building News* iv (1858), 617.

1. Hope to E.A. Freeman, 5 March 1846: Freeman MSS., Rylands Library, Manchester, FA1/1/38a.

2. *Benjamin Disraeli Letters* iv (1989), no. 1213: 22 Feb. 1842, to Mrs Disraeli.

3. *Gladstone Diaries*, ed. H.C.G. Matthew, xi (1990), 284: 28 Jan. 1885.

4. E.g., his perceptive – if over-lofty – comment on the young Philip Webb: 'This young aspirant indicates promise' (RA exhibit, 1858, no. 1053), in

[Beresford Hope], 'Architecture, 1858', in *Saturday Review* v (1858), 561. Comparing Oxford and Cambridge ecclesiology, he once praised Cambridge's 'priority of onwardness' (*Ecclesiologist* vii, N.S. iv, 1847, 90).

5. H.W. and Irene Law, *The Book of the Beresford Hopes* (1925), 195. He strongly opposed female emanication (*Hansard* ccxxiii, 1875, 467 and 3rd series, cci, 1887, 229). For a kinder appreciation, see *Saturday Review* lxiv (1887), 585–6.

6. *Building News* xlvii (1884), 499.

7. Dod's *Parliamentary Companion*, 1858, 1870, 1881.

8. H. Heathcote Statham, in *Fortnightly Review*, N.S. xx (1876), 484.

9. G. Smith, *Reminiscences* (New York, 1911; ed. A. Haultain), 162.

10. *Builder* liii (1887), 665; *Building News* xlvii (1884), 491, 496–9 and liv (1888), 417. 'An amateur, though not an ordinary one. For there are amateurs, and amateurs' (*Builder* xlvii, 1884, 413). A portrait illustration appeared in *Builder* xxviii (1870), 206. There are portraits at the RIBA and at St Augustine's College, Canterbury.

11. Ritualists – notably J.M. Neale – attacked him as a trimmer: for 'ratting' on his allies by putting politics before religion and aesthetics before faith; for degrading the Ecclesiological Society 'from a pioneer of Church progress into a mere dilettante club for talking about crockets and Munich glass'. See J.M. Neale, *Extreme Men* (1865), and 'A Rat Behind the Arras', in *Church Times* 8 December 1866, 411. For correspondence on church politics with Robert Cranborne, 3rd Marquess of Salisbury, see Hatfield MSS., 3M/E97.

12. Law, *op. cit.*, 126, 232. For his 'sadness', see *Building News* liii (1887), 648. In fact, thanks to his expenditure on churches etc., Hope left only £78,270 (Probate Office Records).

13. *Building News* liii (1887), ii, 675; *The Architect* xxxviii (1887), 259.

14. B. of E., *West Kent and the Weald* (1969), 338–40.

15. Some early writings are listed in M. Bevington, *The Saturday Review, 1855–68* (New York, 1941), 334–5, based on the marked file at Columbia University, New York. The London Library's copy of *Saturday Review*, vol. i, contains MS. attributions. Other attributions mostly stem from Hope's correspondence with Benjamin Webb, W.E. Gladstone and E.A. Freeman (Freeman MSS., Rylands Library, Manchester; Gladstone MSS., British Library; Law, *Book of the Beresford Hopes*, 1925).

16. When Balliol chapel was unveiled in 1858, his only substantial criticism was that the polychromy was too pale (*Ecclesiologist* xix, N.S. xvi, 1858, 241–4). The museum, however, he decided, 'has been beyond the powers of the gentlemen . . . who have been entrusted with the perilous honour of developing the unknown capacities of the new style' (*ibid.* xxii, N.S. xix, 1861, 22–6).

17. [Hope,] 'The Artistic Merit of Mr Pugin', in *Ecclesiologist* v, N.S. ii (1846), 10–16 and 'The Death of Mr Pugin', *Ecclesiologist* xiii, N.S. x (1852), 353–7.

18. [?Hope,] 'J.R. on Political Economy' and 'Mr Ruskin Again', *Saturday Review* x (1860), 136–8, 582–4. These articles are unlikely to be by Benjamin Webb – at least on the evidence of his diary – though he would have

approved of their sentiments. There was certainly no love lost between Beresford Hope and Ruskin. At his death, his library contained numerous volumes by Pugin and Viollet-le-Duc, but scarcely a hint of Ruskin.

19. [Hope,] 'Merton College and Mr Butterfield', in *Ecclesiologist* xxix, N.S. xvii (1861), 218–21.

20. *Builder* xxxv (1877), 550; *Athenaeum* No. 3131 (1887), 571. As early as 1847 he proclaimed himself an eclectic in matters of restoration: 'All arts called out invention and imitation. The early Poems of Tennyson were an example of failure in invention. But this was better than the imitation of [Sir Richard] Blackmore. There was [a similar] danger of excess in imitation in conservative church restoration' (*Ecclesiologist* vii, N.S. iv, 1847, 233). What he favoured was not preservation but 'practical progressive conservatism' (*Ecclesiologist* xxii, N.S. xix, 1861, 218–19).

21. For St Paul's, see J. Mordaunt Crook, 'William Burges and the Completion of St Paul's', in *Antiquaries Journal* lx (1980, ii), 285–307. Webb supported Hope's historical justification in 'Classical and Byzantine: St Paul's and Keble Chapel', in *Church Quarterly Review* ii (1876), 447–64.

22. 'I asked myself the question, what principles of beauty and convenience are there which give a charm to Gothic and yet can be grafted into Italian without detriment to its unity of style? My answer to myself was, high roofs and tower-like chimneys' (Beresford Hope, 'The Skyline in Modern Domestic Buildings', in *RIBA Transactions* xiv, 1863–4, 103–15). See also *The Architect* xxxviii (1887), 265–6; T.H.S. Escott, *Society in the Country House* (1909), 143–6; and S.A. Clark, *A History of Bedgebury* (1949). Robert Willis visited Bedgebury in 1857: 'it is on so princely a scale that an addition lately made contains 100 rooms!!' (*Romilly's Cambridge Diary, 1848–64*, Cambridge, 2000, 270). There are sketches by John Buckler in the Paul Mellon Collection, B.1977, 14.1738–1328. The Piccadilly house of Henry Thomas Hope, MP, by Dusillon and Donaldson, was a notable example of French Classicism. See *Builder* vii (1849), 493–4, 498 (ill.) and 534 (ill.).

23. G.F. Waagen, *Galleries and Cabinets of Art in Great Britain* (1857), 189.

24. Sold by Sotheby, Wilkinson and Hodge (1888). Hope's silver was later presented to the British Embassy at Warsaw.

25. R. O'Donnell, 'The Cambridge Camden Society and A.W. Pugin', in *A Church As It Should Be: The Cambridge Camden Society and its Influence*, ed. C. Webster and J. Elliott (Stamford, 2000), 98–120.

26. P. Thompson, 'All Saints, Margaret Street, Reconsidered', in *Architectural History* viii (1965), 73–94; C. Brooks, 'William Butterfield, Beresford Hope and the Ecclesiological Vanguard', in Webster and Elliott, *op. cit.*, 121–48.

27. [Hope,] 'Progress at Oxford', in *Ecclesiologist* xix, N.S. xvi (1858), 241: despite its 'studied neglect of beauty', it has 'dignity . . . virility and powerful originality'.

28. Hope to E.A. Freeman, 29 Dec. 1858: Freeman MSS., Rylands Library, Manchester, FA1/1/55.

29. [?Hope,] 'Mr Ruskin Again', in *Saturday Review* x (1860), 582–4. Webb

shared Hope's hostility to Socialism (e.g., in *Christian Remembrancer* xlii, 1862, 475); so no doubt this review represents their shared opinion.

30. [Hope,] in *Ecclesiologist* x, N.S. vii (1850), 397–8.
31. Hope to E.A. Freeman, 14 Jan. 1845: Freeman MSS., Rylands Library, Manchester, FA1/1/61a.
32. [Hope,] in *Ecclesiologist* vi, N.S. iii (1846), 132.
33. [Hope,] in *Ecclesiologist* v, N.S. ii (1846), 52.
34. [Hope] reviewing Street's *Brick and Marble in the Middle Ages*, in *Saturday Review* ii (1856), 68.
35. [Hope,] in *Saturday Review* viii (1859), 190.
36. [Hope,] in *Saturday Review* viii (1859), 254. Similarly, T.H. Wyatt's Orchardleigh Park, Somerset 'exhibits that partial combination of [Classical] Italian detail with pointed mass which forms the characteristic of the impure though seductive Jacobean. But the whole effect is Gothic' ([Hope,] in *Saturday Review* v, 1858, 560–1).
37. Hope, in *RIBA Transactions* (1883–4), 231.
38. Hope, in *Saturday Review* viii (1859), 610.
39. [Hope,] in *Ecclesiologist* xxv, N.S. xxii (1864), 209. 'Squire after squire began restoring or building his church in a fashion which would have made his father's hair stand on end' ([Hope,] 'The Church Cause and the Church Party', in *Christian Remembrancer* xxxix, 1860, 85).
40. [Hope,] in *Ecclesiologist* iv, N.S. i (1845), 31.
41. *Ibid.*, 33.
42. Hope to E.A. Freeman, 14 Jan. 1845: Freeman MSS., Rylands Library, Manchester, FA1/1/61a.
43. Hope, 'Essay on the Present State of Ecclesiological Science', in *Ecclesiologist* vii, N.S. iv (1847), 85–91.
44. [J.M. Capes,] in *The Rambler* vii (1851), 325; reviewing [Hope] on 'Oratorianism and Ecclesiology' in *Christian Remembrancer* xxi (1851), 141–64. Hope contended that 'medieval ritual is *anti-Roman*, as Rome *now* is . . . Whatever faults may be found with the Eastern Church, it certainly does not Oratorianise' (*ibid.*, 159–60). *The Guardian* called him 'a progressive Tractarian' (9 Dec. 1874, 1585).
45. [Hope,] 'The Church Cause and the Church Party', *loc. cit.*, 122–3 note.
46. Hope to Gladstone, 7 Feb. 1853: B.L. Add. MS. 44213 f. 298. For Richards's career, see F. Boase, *Modern English Biography* iii (1901), 142–3. He was minister of the Margaret Chapel 1845–9; incumbent of All Saints 1849–68; and vicar of All Saints 1868–73. See P. Galloway and C. Rawll, *Good and Faithful Servants* (1988).
47. *Letters of J.M. Neale* [ed. M.S. Lawson] (1910), 94: 1846. See also J. Mordaunt Crook, 'Benjamin Webb and Victorian Ecclesiology', in *Studies in Church History* xxxiii (1997), 443. For Hope's churchmanship, see his essay 'On the Character of the English People', in *Essays* (1844), 1–68 and Law, *Book of the Beresford Hopes*, 241.
48. Hope, 'On the Common Sense of Art', in *Builder* xvi (1858), 831.

49. 'Christian architecture must be developed to suit present exigencies . . . [hence our support for] the principle of development' (Hope to E.A. Freeman, 5 March 1846: Freeman MSS., Rylands Library, Manchester, FA1/1/38a).

50. [Hope,] in *Ecclesiologist* v, N.S. ii (1846), 236.

51. *Ecclesiologist* xxiii, N.S. xx (1862), 229.

52. Hope, *The Condition and Prospects of Architectural Art* (1863), 13.

53. [Hope] reviewing Fergusson's *Handbook* in *Saturday Review* i (1856), 234–6.

54. Scott, *Secular and Domestic Architecture, present and future* (1858), 263.

55. *Saturday Review* i (1856), 234–6.

56. 'International Exhibition, South Kensington', in *Ecclesiologist* xxiii, N.S. xx (1862), 229.

57. [Hope,] 'Architectural Exhibition', in *Saturday Review* v (1858), 160, re Burges's Sabrina Fountain design for Gloucester.

58. [Hope,] 'History of the Modern Styles of Architecture', in *Saturday Review* xv (1863), 668.

59. *Builder* viii (1850), 169–70.

60. *The Architect* xii (1874), 203.

61. [Hope] reviewing the 1862 Exhibition, in *Quarterly Review* cxiii (1863), 176–207.

62. [Hope] reviewing Fergusson, in *Saturday Review* i (1856), 234–6.

63. *The Common Sense of Art* (1858), 10 (lecture inaugurating the Architectural Museum; reprinted in *oratio obliqua* in *Builder* xvi, 1858, 830–1).

64. *Ibid.*, 21; Hope, *The English Cathedral of the 19th Century*, 45; *Ecclesiologist* iv, N.S. i (1845), 48.

65. Hope was only able to admit this publicly when 'that man had been long enough in the grave for polemic feeling to have vanished away'. See his address to the Ecclesiological Society in *Builder* xvii (1859), 429. By 1856 he was already recalling Pugin 'in his best days . . . eager and indefatigable . . . [bubbling with] boy-like delight and enthusiasm' ([Hope,] in *Saturday Review* ii, 1856, 68). By 1863 he could concede that Pugin's 'reputation and influence was won by sheer merit, in spite of . . . being a Roman Catholic', and that he had even managed 'to teach Church of England men . . . good architecture' ([Hope,] 'History of the Modern Style of Architecture', in *Saturday Review* xv, 1863, 666). By 1878 he was able to place Pugin at the very forefront of the Gothic Revival: 'the man who raised the taste for Gothic into a "principle", and tied it irreversibly to the new appreciation of religious decorum' ([Hope,] 'Sir Gilbert Scott', in *Saturday Review* xlv, 1878, 427).

66. For example, at proof stage Hope changed the title of his 1846 Oxford paper from 'The Present State of Ecclesiological Art' to 'The Present State of Ecclesiological Science' (Hope Collection, Trinity College Cambridge; reprinted in *Ecclesiologist* vii, N.S. iv, 1847, 85–91).

67. Twenty-fifth Anniversary Meeting, *Ecclesiologist* xxv, N.S. xxii (1864), 225–7. Formally, Whewell was tutor to Hope, Thorp to Neale and Webb (*Admissions to Trinity College, Cambridge* iv, 1911, 424, 442, 454).

68. 'Present State of Ecclesiological Science', in *Ecclesiologist* vii, N.S. iv (1847), 85–91.
69. *Ibid.*, 89–90. 'We must become the confidants of Arnolfo, and Walsingham, and Steinbach.'
70. [Hope,] 'Past and Future Developments of Architecture', in *Ecclesiologist* v, N.S. ii (1846), 48–53.
71. 'Church Restoration', in *Ecclesiologist* vii, N.S. iv (1847), 238, 239 and viii, N.S. v (1848), 82.
72. *Common Sense of Art*, 13.
73. [Hope,] reviewing Fergusson, in *Saturday Review* i (1856), 234–6.
74. *Common Sense of Art*, 14.
75. *Ibid.*, 21.
76. [Hope,] reviewing Fergusson, in *Saturday Review* i (1856), 234–6; *Ecclesiologist* xxv, N.S. xxii (1864), 209.
77. *Common Sense of Art*, 14; *Builder* xvi (1858), 831; *Public Offices and Metropolitan Improvements* (1857), 24.
78. 'An iron church of the greatest simplicity' had been designed by Slater 'under Mr Beresford Hope's advice', for the Irish estate of Sir Augustus Stafford-Jerningham, 9th Bt, later 10th Baron Stafford. In 1862 he had been officially declared insane, so the estate was presumably managed by trustees (*Complete Peerage*, s.v. Stafford; *Ecclesiologist* xix, N.S. xvi, 1868, 268).
79. [Hope,] 'Architecture at the RA', in *Saturday Review* ii (1856), 172.
80. *Building News* xxiii (1872), 35.
81. [Hope,] reviewing designs for the Oxford Museum competition, in *Saturday Review* i (1856), 208–9.
82. *The Architect* xxxviii (1887), 265–6. For the Malebolge, see Dante's *Inferno* xviii, 19 *et seq.*
83. *Public Offices and Metropolitan Improvements*, 34.
84. *The English Cathedral of the Nineteenth Century* (1861), 31–2. For [Webb's] review, see *Saturday Review* xi (1861), 643–4.
85. *Builder* xxxiv (1876), 18.
86. [Webb,] reviewing *Common Sense of Art*, in *Saturday Review* vii (1859), 96–7.
87. E.E. Viollet-le-Duc, *Discourses*, trans. B. Bucknell (1889), i, 455.
88. 'The Plague of Art' was his motto in the Lille Cathedral competition. Lassus was a dogmatic anti-latitudinarian: 'The situation is grave . . . in the state of anarchy into which art is now reduced . . . there remains . . . only one anchor of safety, unity of style; and, as we have no art belonging to our own time – everyone is convinced of it and deplores it – there is only one thing for us to do: . . . choose one [style] . . . not . . . to copy . . . but . . . to compose' (*Ecclesiologist* xvii, N.S. xiv, 1856, 284–7, 322–3, 414–31; xviii, N.S. xv, 1857, 46–9, 89–91). For Lassus, see J.-M. Leniaud, *Jean-Baptiste Lassus* (Paris, 1980).
89. *Land and Building News* ii (1856), 775–6.
90. *Building News* iv (1858), 617.
91. 'Our architecture must embrance within its pale, the semi-circular, the semi-ellipse, the segmental and the pointed arches, but would reserve a

strong preference for the pointed' (*Secular and Domestic Architecture*, 267–8). This book was dedicated to Beresford Hope, 'who has . . . taken a leading position among those who, in different countries of Europe, are labouring in the revival of their indigenous architecture, as the nucleus on which to develop that of the future.' As early as 1850 Scott had lamented the fact that architects 'were in shackles . . . the shackles of knowing too many styles and developing none' (*Builder* viii, 1850, 253–4).

92. J. Mordaunt Crook, *Burges*, 103–5, 110–11.

93. 'The present period is one of architectural anarchy'; a combination of Classic and Gothic might 'lead to the formation of an original style, fitted to . . . our present high state of civilisation' (*Architectural Magazine* v, 1838–9, 658).

94. 'The Anglo-Classic style . . . awaits . . . an infusion . . . of . . . the fire and energy . . . [of] Gothic' (*Builder* xi, 1853, 573).

95. 'Our . . . architecture is . . . a confused assemblage of many styles . . . a ship entangled amidst unknown shoals'; evolutiionary eclecticism might supply a solution to 'the difficulties which beset this transitional period' (*RIBA Papers*, 1866–7, 152).

96. P. Metcalf, *James Knowles* (1980), 218–19, citing Knowles's Neo-Hegelian view of 'Science and Art in History', in *Contemporary Review* (1869).

97. 'Cosmos, we hope, will presently come out of . . . CHAOS' (*The Architect* iv, 1870, 1).

98. J.T. Emmett, *Six Essays*, intro. J. Mordaunt Crook (New York, 1972).

99. R. Kerr, *The Gentleman's House*, intro. J. Mordaunt Crook (New York, 1972).

100. T. Hope, *An Historical Essay on Architecture*, 2 vols (1835), 561.

101. *Builder* xvi (1858), 830.

102. [Hope,] in *Saturday Review* i (1856), 208–9 and ii (1856), 172–3; *Ecclesiologist* xxii, N.S. xix (1861), 25–6. He thought Smirke's 'prodigious cupola . . . a monument at once of the skill of its architect and of [the Trustees'] want of forethought'. He thought Woodward's colouring 'atrocious' and Skidmore's iron roof too imitative of masonry rib-vaults: better to have followed the domical principle of Smirke's Reading Room or else to have created a stone ceiling pierced with 'transparent vaulting cells'.

103. Hope, *Builder* xxi (1863), 219.

104. *Macmillan's Magazine* xxv (1871–2), 250–6. Fergusson was speaking of Fowke's unexecuted design, in similar style, for the Natural History Museum.

105. *Quarterly Review* cxiii (1863), 176–207.

106. [Hope,] 'The International Exhibition', in *Quarterly Review* cxiii (1862), 179–219; [Hope,] 'The New Exhibition Buildings', in *Saturday Review* xi (1861), 340.

107. [Hope,] 'The Exhibition Buildings', in *Saturday Review* xiii (1862), 99.

108. *Idem.*, *Saturday Review* xiii (1862), 472; *Quarterly Review* cxiii (1862), 213, 218.

109. *The Condition and Prospects of Architectural Art* (1863), 16.

110. *Ecclesiologist* xxiii, N.S. xx (1862), 228–34; *Gentleman's Magazine* cxxxiii, N.S. xiv (1863), 602; *Builder* xxi (1863), 219.

111. Hope, 'Ceramic Art in Architecture', in *Builder* xxi (1863), 185; *Ecclesiologist* xxiv, N.S. xxi (1863), 135–6.
112. Hope acted as referee with M. Digby Wyatt and J.C. Robinson, and contributed to the cost of ceramic decoration. See *Civil Engineer and Architect's Journal* xxvi (1863), 313; *Companion to the Almanac*, 1865, 119 and *Builder* xxi (1863), 185. For later extensions, see *Building News* lxvii (1894), 678: ill.
113. B. of E., *London, North West* (1991), 649–50.
114. *The Condition and Prospects of Architectural Art* (1863), reported in *Builder* xxi (1863), 220.
115. *Ibid.*
116. *Gentleman's Magazine* N.S. xiv (1863), 600–6; *Quarterly Review* cxii (1862), 179–219; *RIBA Papers* xiv (1863–4), 103–15; *Builder* xxi (1863), 220.
117. [Webb,] 'The New Exhibition Building', in *Saturday Review* xii (1861), 351.
118. [Webb,] 'Classical and Byzantine: St Paul's and Keble Chapel', in *Church Quarterly Review* ii (1876), 460.
119. [Webb,] in *Christian Remembrancer* xlii (1861), 477.
120. 'Hope to [RIBA], where [Sir William] Tite selected over his head as President' (Webb, 'Diary', 13 May 1861).
121. T.L. Donaldson was elected.
122. *Builder* xxiii (1865), 795–8. James Knowles repeated this call a decade later (*Builder* xxxii, 1874, 1080).
123. *Builder* xxiv (1866), 831; *RIBA Reports* (1866–7), 9.
124. *Builder* xxv (1867), 334.
125. [Hope,] 'The Queen Anne Craze', in *Saturday Review* xl (1875), 142–3.
126. 'The World's Debt to Art', in *Builder* xxi (1863), 191.
127. *The Condition and Prospects of Architectural Art*, reported in *Builder* xxi (1863), 219–20. Similarly [Webb,] 'Architecture in 1864', in *Saturday Review* xvii (1964), 782–3.
128. [Hope,] 'The Style and Site of the Law Courts', in *Saturday Review* xxv (1866), 751–2.
129. *The Condition and Prospects of Architectural Art* (1863), 17, 33.
130. 'The Position of the Art-Workman', in *Builder* xxii (1864), 204–5; *Gentleman's Magazine* cxxxiii, i, N.S. xiv (1863), 605.
131. Evidence before the Royal Academy Commission, *Ecclesiologist* xxv, N.S. xxii (1864), 243.
132. [Hope,] 'The Queen Anne Craze', in *Saturday Review* xl (1875), 142.
133. [Hope,] 'Architecture at the RA', in *Saturday Review* xlv (1878), 824.
134. *The Condition and Prospects of Architectural Art* (1863), 14.
135. [Hope,] in *Saturday Review* l (1880), 371–2.
136. [Hope,] 'Architecture in 1884', in *Saturday Review* lvii (1884), 813. Interestingly, in 1937 H.-R. Hitchcock still held much the same opinion: the style of Charing Cross Hotel was 'an extremely corrupt version of French Late Renaissance architecture – proportionless, confused, excessively ugly in materials'; it was a style favoured by 'City men' which 'tended to complete

the destruction of all stylistic sense in the lay mind' (*RIBA Journal*, 3rd series, xliv, 1937, 1033–4).

137. [Hope,] in *Saturday Review* l (1880), 557.

138. *Builder* liii (1887), 589–90: 'He stuck to his guns to the last.'

139. H. Hucks Gibbs in *RIBA Transactions* N.S. iv (1888), 58.

140. *Building News* liv (1888), 417. At Hope's death there were still 141 unsold copies of The *Common Sense of Art* (1858) at Arklow House. See *The Library of the Rt Hon A.J.B. Beresford Hope*, sold by Sotheby, Wilkinson and Hodge, June 1888.

141. This argument was popularised by H. Heathcote Statham and R. Phené Spiers, in *Encyclopaedia Britannica*, 11th edn, ii (1910), 435–6.

142. *Building News* xxix (1875), 10–13; *The Architect* 10 May 1873. Beresford Hope called this a parody of the Haarlem Butter Market (*Saturday Review* xl, 1875, 142–3), but it was equally a parody of the Hôtel d'Écoville, Caen.

143. J. Mordaunt Crook, 'T.G. Jackson and the Cult of Eclecticism', in *In Search of Modern Architecture: a tribute to Henry-Russell Hitchcock*, ed. H. Searing (New York, 1982), 102–20.

144. [Hope,] 'Architecture in 1882', in *Saturday Review* liii (1882), 800–1.

145. [Hope,] 'Architecture at the RA', in *Saturday Review* xliv (1877), 18.

146. *Art Journal* (1887), 209.

147. D. Bassett, '"Queen Anne" and France', in *Architectural History* xxiv (1981), 83–91.

148. E.g., T. Hayter Lewis and R. Langton Cole, *Companion to the Almanac*, 1887, 129; 1891, 289–90.

149. R. Langton Cole, *Companion to the Almanac*, 1893, 290 and 1894, 289. See also *The Times* 11 May 1893; *Builder* 2 July 1887; *Building News* 1 July 1887; *RIBA Journal* January 1956; C. Hussey, in *Country Life* cxix (1956), 329–30.

150. [Hope,] 'Architecture in 1885', in *Saturday Review* lix (1885), 855–6.

151. Hope, in *Hansard's Parliamentary Debates* ccxcvi (9 april 1885), 1170; [Hope,] in *Saturday Review* lix (1885), 855–6.

152. R. Kerr, *The Gentleman's House*, intro. J. Mordaunt Crook (1972), 342.

153. *The Architect* xxxviii (1887), frontispiece: epigraph from Hope's inaugural address as PRIBA 1865 (*Builder* xxiii, 1865, 795–8); *Ecclesiologist* xxvi, N.S. xxiii (1865), 354–61.

154. H.S. Goodhart-Rendel, 'Architecture since 1834', in *The Growth and Work of the RIBA*, ed. J.A. Gotch (1934), 168.

Chapter 4: Coventry Patmore

Epigraph: A. Reichensperger, 'Aphorisms Respecting Christian Art', in *Ecclesiologist* xxii, N.S. xix (1861), 402.

1. W.J. Fredeman, *The PRB Journal* (Oxford, 1975), 106–7, listing additional names.

2. B. Champneys, *Memoirs and Correspondence of Coventry Patmore* (1900), i, 84: ill. 'A man of dreams, a man of business, and a man of vehement physical determination' (E. Gosse, *Coventry Patmore*, 1905, 202). 'We were little more

than boys together,' Patmore recalled of the Pre-Raphaelites; 'simple, pure-minded, ignorant and confident' (Champneys, *Patmore*, i, 83). Ruskin was godfather to one of Patmore's sons, Tennyson to another. On at least one memorable occasion Browning, Ruskin, Tennyson and Patmore dined *à quatre* at Patmore's table (J. Ruskin, *Works*, ed. Cook and Wedderburn, XXXVI, xxxii, 305).

3. By his death, the *Angel* had sold 250,000 copies (Gosse, *Patmore*, 105).

4. Champneys, *Patmore*, ii, frontis: ill.; Gosse, *Patmore*, 201–2.

5. Gosse, *Patmore*, 200; Champneys, *Patmore*, ii, 58: ill.

6. Champneys, *Patmore*, i, 100: 22 March 1847.

7. *Ibid.*, 92: 21 March 1850. One possible competitor was Lord Lindsay, another was E.A. Freeman. In 1847 Beresford Hope wrote to Freeman as follows: 'If you look at the extracts from Lord Lindsay's book [on the *History of Christian Art*] in the new *Quarterly* [*Review* lxxxi, 1847, 16], you will find he has got hold of your theory or something very like it, touching Romanesque as the architecture of rest ["Lombard . . . Architecture . . . symbolises an infinity of Rest . . . [Gothic] of Action"]. You should look at the book. I have not yet had courage to read it' (Beresford Hope to E.A. Freeman, 9 July 1847: Freeman MSS., Rylands Library, Manchester, FA1/1/42). On 5 December 1849 Freeman spoke to the Oxford Architectural Society on 'The Constructive Systems of the Entablature and the Arch' (*Builder* vii, 1849, 622). In 1854 T.M. Rickman spoke at the Architectural Association 'On the Contrast between Classic and Gothic Architecture as evidenced in the treatment of apparent weight' (*Builder* xii, 1854, 39–40).

8. E. Moxon (Princeton Univ. MSS., cited by J.C. Reid, *The Mind and Art of Coventry Patmore*, 1957, 204 n.).

9. A further selection appeared as *Courage in Politics and Other Essays, 1885–96*, ed. F. Page (1921). Page added an appendix containing a bibliography of Patmore's writings, as did J.C. Reid in *The Mind and Art of Coventry Patmore* (1957). Since then the *Wellesley index of Victorian Periodicals*, ed. W.E. Houghton, 5 vols (1966–89) has again added to the list.

10. He was recommended by Monckton Milnes, with whom he worked on Keats's letters (Champneys, *Patmore*, i, 64–5). He retired on 1 January 1866, with a pension of £126 18s. 4d. p.a. (F. Boase, *Modern Biography*, vi, 1921, 363–4). For Patmore's account of the library and its Round Reading Room – 'one of the most marvellous triumphs ever attained by system and order' – see [Patmore,] 'Library of the British Museum', in *Edinburgh Review* cix (1859), 201–26.

11. Champneys, *Patmore*, i, 60, 62.

12. E.g., Percy Street, Tottenham Court Road; or Brecknock Crescent, Camden Town. In 1852 Ruskin was invited by Patmore to meet Browning at The Grove, Highgate. 'Patmore lives in a small enough house', he told his father, 'but in a pretty part of the world . . . I had no idea there were such nice, old-fashioned, quiet houses and avenues in that direction' (Ruskin, *Works*, XXXVI, 141).

13. Previously Old Lands, later Temple Grove Preparatory School; since altered. Patmore chose Bentley because he was 'the only architect who knew more of architecture than I did myself' (Champneys, *Patmore*, i, 226–8, 230). For ills. see *Country Life* xiii (1903), 638–42 and advertisement, June 2001; also *Architectural History* xxiii (1980), 106–7, 115. 'His green lawns were designed on principles taken from the Parthenon, for he had discovered that there are no true horizontals in architecture' (S. Leslie, *Studies in Sublime Failure*, 1932, 143). In 1874 Patmore first let, then sold it to the Duke of Norfolk for £27,000 – a considerable profit, which he explained in *How I Managed and Improved my Estate* (1886). In effect, Heron's Ghyll became a dower house for the Dowager Duchess of Norfolk: 'I understand she will have her own chaplain with her wherever she may settle. Heron's Ghyll has the rare privilege of being allowed the reservation of the Blessed Sacrament in it. I am told the Duchess requires eighteen bedrooms. There are only fifteen at [present] . . . but it would be easy to add three or four rooms' (Patmore to Aubrey de Vere, 28 May 1874(?), transcript by Shane Leslie, Berg Collection, New York Public Library). Oldlands Hall was built nearby, on part of the estate sold by Patmore in 1875 (*Country Life* 29 March 2001, 109: ill.). At his death Patmore left only £9,861 16s. 4d., minus debts of £1,084 8s. 5d. (Inland Revenue, 59/175: *ex inf.* Professor C. Harvey).

14. Ills. and plan: *Builder* liii (1887), 311. Patmore thought it 'the only Catholic church in England without any bad taste in it'. He contributed *c.* £5,300 to its cost (Champneys, *Patmore*, i, 336). See Patmore's letter to *The Tablet*, 18 May 1883.

15. 'A bluish building, standing coyly and askew among the trees, very retired and dowdy-looking, on a muddy point of land opposite the Isle of Wight . . . but with enchanting views of the bright, tidal expanses' (Gosse, *Patmore*, 173, ill.). See also *Times Literary Supplement* 9 June 1932, 427. For Patmore's tomb, designed by Champneys, see Champneys, *Patmore*, i, 348: ill.; *Athenaeum* 5 May 1897 and *Times Literary Supplement* 19 May 1932, 368. For recollections of Patmore at Hastings and Lymington, see M. Bethan-Edwards, *Mid-Victorian Memories* (1919), 1–15.

16. See Gosse, *Patmore*, 119–20.

17. [Patmore,] 'Sources of Expression in Architecture', in *Edinburgh Review* xciv (1851), 367–8. Echoing Karl Schnaase: 'Beauty in architecture lies not in function; it begins in the assertion of art over function' (K. Schnaase, *Geschichte der bildenden Kunste*, 7 vols, 1843–64, intro.). See also Schnaase, *Uber das Organische in der Baukunst* (1844), a reply to Franz Kugler's notions of organic expression.

18. [Patmore,] 'Expression', in *Edinburgh Review* xciv (1851), 382.

19. *Ibid.*, 370.

20. *Ibid.*, 385.

21. *Ibid.*, 390.

22. Patmore, 'Architectural Styles', in *Principle in Art* (1898), 194.

23. [Patmore,] 'Expression', in *Edinburgh Review* xciv (1851), 390.

24. [Patmore,] 'Character in Architecture', in *North British Review* xv (1851), 461.
25. *Ibid.*, 463, 467, 470.
26. *Ibid.*, 464.
27. *Ibid.*, 479.
28. *Ibid.*, 470, as illustrated by Flaxman.
29. [Patmore,] 'Character', in *North British Review* xv (1851), 462.
30. 'A bald Doric, totally without distinctive character, save that of baldness. The omission of triglyphs makes the separation of architrave and frieze unnerving; the astragal, on the neck of the shaft, . . . suggests weakness; the fillet above the abacus and the filletless ovolo that crowns the cornice, are sheer nonsense, the fillet being a separate member where there is no separation operated, the ovolo being a supporting member when there is nothing to support' (*ibid.*, 479).
31. [Patmore,] 'Expression', in *Edinburgh Review* xciv (1851), 401.
32. E.g., Palazzo Thiene, Vicenza or Palazzo Renuccini, Florence. See [Patmore,] 'Character', in *North British Review* xv (1851), 476.
33. *Ibid.*, 492.
34. *Ibid.*, 473.
35. *Ibid.*, 478; [Patmore,] 'Expression', in *Edinburgh Review* xciv (1851), 379.
36. [Patmore,] 'Character', in *North British Review* xv (1851), 473.
37. [Patmore,] 'Expression', in *Edinburgh Review* xciv (1851), 385.
38. *Ibid.*, 388–9.
39. *Ibid.*, 390.
40. Patmore, 'Styles', in *Principle in Art*, 161.
41. [Patmore,] 'Ruskin's *Seven Lamps of Architecture*', in *North British Review* xii (1849–50), 324.
42. [Patmore,] 'Expression', in *Edinburgh Review* xciv (1851) 373.
43. *Ibid.*, 369; [Patmore,] 'London Street Architecture', in *National Review* v (1857), 61; [Patmore,] 'Gothic Architecture – Present and Future', in *North British Review* xxviii (1858), 350.
44. [Patmore,] 'Expression', in *Edinburgh Review* xciv (1851), 391.
45. Patmore, 'Styles', in *Principle in Art*, 194–6.
46. *Ibid.*, 166.
47. *Ibid.*, 198.
48. Like 'a spark of fire introduced into a pile of timber, converting it into a heaven-aspiring flame' (Patmore, 'Architecture and Architectural Criticism', in *Courage in Politics*, ed.F. Page, 1921, 179).
49. [Patmore,] 'Expression', in *Edinburgh Review* xciv (1851), 385.
50. Patmore, 'Criticism', in *Courage in Politics*, 182.
51. Patmore, 'Styles', in *Principle in Art*, 197.
52. [Patmore,] 'Expression', in *Edinburgh Review* xciv (1851), 369.
53. *Ibid.*, 386, 388.
54. Patmore, 'Styles', in *Principle in Art*, 166.
55. *Ibid.*, 200.
56. [Patmore,] 'Ruskin's *Seven Lamps*', in *North British Review* xii (1849–50), 324.

57. [Patmore,] 'Expression', in *Edinburgh Review* xciv (1851), 391; 'Styles', in *Principle in Art*, 163. For a repetition of Patmore's views, see J. Taddy, 'On the Moral and Intellectual Expression of Architecture', in *Associated Architectural Societies Reports and Papers* ii (1852), 182–90.

58. Patmore, 'Churches and Preaching Halls', in *Courage in Politics*, 191–2.

59. [Patmore,] 'Street Architecture', in *National Review* v (1857), 62; [Patmore,] 'Present and Future', in *North British Review* xxviii (1858), 350.

60. 'Suspension bridges are generally pleasing objects, but their beauty is precisely that of a well proved geometrical theorem, and it is the very reverse of architecture as a *fine* art. All fine art appeals primarily to the imagination, but a suspension bridge . . . has [only the] low merit of mechanical beauty. Perhaps the ugliest thing in or out of nature is a great tubular bridge' (*ibid.*, 367–8).

61. *Ibid.*

62. *Ibid.*

63. J. Mordaunt Crook, *The Dilemma of Style: Architectural Ideas from the Picturesque to the Post-Modern* (1987), 111–12; M. Brooks, 'John Ruskin, Coventry Patmore and the Nature of Gothic', in *Victorian Periodicals Review* xii (1979), 130–40.

64. 'There will never be an architecture in iron, every improvement in machinery being uglier and uglier, until they reach the supremest specimen of all ugliness – the Forth Bridge.' His chief designer, Benjamin Baker, replied with a statement of the bridge's expressive function: 'the compression members [had been made as] strong tubes, and the tension members light lattice work, so that to any intelligent eye the nature of the stresses and the sufficiency of the structure to resist them were emphasised at all points . . . The object had been so to arrange the leading lines of the structure as to convey an idea of strength and stability. This, in such a structure, seemed to be at once the truest and highest art' (quoted in M. Baxendall, *Patterns of Intention*, 1985, 24–5).

65. [Patmore,] 'American Poetry', in *North British Review* xvii (1852), 224.

66. [Patmore,] 'Street Architecture', in *National Review* v (1857), 71–2. Similarly, [Patmore,] 'Character', in *North British Review* xv (1851), 495.

67. Patmore suggests Roberts's view of the temple of Dekkeh, in Nubia: [Patmore,] 'Expression', in *Edinburgh Review* xciv (1851), 374; D. Roberts, *Egypt and Nubia*, 3 vols (1846–50); D.V. Baron Denon, *Voyage dans le basse et la haute Egypte* (Paris, 1802).

68. [Patmore,] 'Architects and Architecture', in *Fraser's Magazine* xlvi (1852), 655.

69. [Patmore,] 'Ruskin's *Seven Lamps*', in *North British Review* xii (1849–50), 324.

70. [Patmore,] 'Present and Future', in *North British Review* xxviii (1858), 349.

71. [Patmore,] 'Street Architecture', in *National Review* v (1857), 50. Gwilt failed to 'enter into the spirit' of Egyptian architecture, complaining that 'solidity is abused . . . the means employed seem always greater than the ends' ([Patmore,] 'Expression', in *Edinburgh Review* xciv, 1851, 375).

72. B. Champneys, 'Architectural Styles: Old and New', in *Building News* lii (1887), 110.
73. Patmore, 'Styles', in *Principle in Art*, 164.
74. [Patmore,] 'Expression', in *Edinburgh Review* xciv (1851), 377.
75. *Ibid.*, 374; [Patmore,] 'Ruskin's *Seven Lamps*', in *North British Review* xii (1849–50), 325. 'All these are forms in which the simplest idea of power and duration is expressed either by passive ponderosity, or by slight contradictions and oppositions, juxtaposed, as foils, to its more direct and predominant expression' ([Patmore,] 'Street Architecture', in *National Review* v, 1857, 50).
76. [Patmore,] 'Expression', in *Edinburgh Review* xciv (1851), 373.
77. [Patmore,] 'Architects', in *Fraser's Magazine* xlvi (1852), 657–8. 'This fact of mechanical science no doubt expresses itself to the eye, and is one of the reasons why the Doric shaft is such a noble object to look upon' (*ibid.*, 656). 'A fact of which the eye probably becomes sensible before the principle is comprehended by the understanding' ([Patmore,] 'Ruskin's *Seven Lamps*', in *North British Review* xii, 1849–50, 331). Did Patmore know the Giant's Causeway, Co. Antrim? Its primeval rocks – irregular hexagons of columnar basalt, formed under titanic pressure – echo the shape of Doric drums.
78. [Patmore,] 'Present and Future', in *North British Review* xxviii (1858), 349; Patmore, *Principle in Art*, 177.
79. [Patmore,] 'Street Architecture', in *National Review* v (1857), 51.
80. [Patmore,] 'Athenian Architecture', in *Edinburgh Review* xcv (1852), 397.
81. [Patmore,] 'Present and Future', in *North British Review* xcviii (1858), 347.
82. [Patmore,] 'Ruskin's *Seven Lamps*', in *North British Review* xii (1849–50), 340.
83. 'An additional expression of the general idea' (*ibid.*, 338).
84. [Patmore,] 'Expression', in *Edinburgh Review* xciv (1851), 378, 380.
85. [Patmore,] 'Present and Future', in *North British Review* xxviii (1858), 349.
86. [Patmore,] 'Street Architecture', in *National Review* v (1857), 51.
87. [Patmore,] 'Ruskin's *Seven Lamps*', in *North British Review* xii (1849–50), 344: 'to aid the expression of weight and of active supporting energy'.
88. *Ibid.*, 347.
89. *Ibid.*, 345–7; *Principle in Art*, 178–9.
90. [Patmore,] 'Street Architecture', in *National Review* v (1857), 51.
91. [Patmore,] 'Expression', in *Edinburgh Review* xciv (1851), 382.
92. [Patmore,] 'Ruskin's *Seven Lamps*', in *North British Review* xii (1849–50), 337.
93. [Patmore,] 'Architects', in *Fraser's Magazine* xlvi (1852), 657.
94. Hence 'the hundred-times repeated, and never yet . . . comprehended, law of architectural unity, which, to use the words of Milizia, "requires that all the parts of an edifice, and all its ornaments, should have reference to the principal object"' ([Patmore,] 'Ruskin's *Seven Lamps*', in *North British Review* xii, 1849–50, 320).
95. *Ibid.*, 349. Similarly, near Waterloo Station, Patmore noticed a Commissioners' Church (Francis Bedford's St John, Waterloo Road) whose portico looked curiously 'light-headed': the details of the entablature were incomplete; 'there seems to be no meaning in the vast amount of upward

force in the fluted shafts, if that is all they have to carry' (*ibid.*, 336 n.; *Principle in Art*, 174–5). In other words, it no longer made sense to the eye.

96. [Patmore,] 'Ruskin's *Seven Lamps*', in *North British Review* xii (1849–50), 329.

97. [Patmore,] 'Architects', in *Fraser's Magazine* xlvi (1852), 656. On the other hand, he considered St Pancras Church 'the finest restoration of Greek architecture in the world' ([Patmore,] 'Ruskin's *Seven Lamps*', in *North British Review* xii, 1849–50, 341 n.). He considered Schinkel's use, in Berlin, of angels in place of triglyphs, as 'the grossest architectural blunder we have ever met with' (*ibid.*, 336 n.).

98. [Patmore,] 'Expression', in *Edinburgh Review* xciv (1851), 394.

99. [Patmore,] 'Street Architecture', in *National Review* v (1857), 61.

100. Patmore, 'Architectural Criticism', in *Courage in Politics*, 180.

101. Patmore, 'Styles', in *Principle in Art*, 189.

102. [Patmore,] 'Expression', in *Edinburgh Review* xciv (1851), 396.

103. [Patmore,] 'Street Architecture', in *National Review* v (1857), 53.

104. Patmore, 'Architectural Criticism', in *Courage in Politics*, 180.

105. [Patmore,] 'Expression', in *Edinburgh Review* xciv (1851), 369.

106. Patmore, 'Styles', in *Principle in Art*, 187.

107. *Ibid.*, 189.

108. Patmore, 'Liverpool Cathedral', in *Courage in Politics*, 186.

109. Patmore, 'Styles', in *Principle in Art*, 186.

110. [Patmore,] 'The Aesthetics of Gothic Architecture', in *British Quarterly Review* x (1849), 58–9.

111. [Patmore,] 'Present and Future', in *North British Review* xxviii (1858), 361.

112. Contradicting E.A. Freeman, who held foliation to be of only secondary significance compared with verticality. See [Patmore,] 'Aesthetics', in *British Quarterly Review* x (1849), 62–3. 'The generally more beautiful forms of Decorated foliage show a considerably more subtle union of natural growth and superadded geometrical form, than is exhibited either in the rigid and stringy vegetation of the Early English, or the angularly-bounded foliage of the Perpendicular style' (*ibid.*, 65).

113. *Ibid.*, 66. There is a hint of this in Ruskin: 'truly fine Gothic work . . . unites fantasy and law' (*Stones of Venice, Works*, VIII, 89).

114. [Patmore,] 'Present and Future', in *North British Review* xxviii (1858), 361.

115. Patmore, 'Styles', in *Principle in Art*, 192–3.

116. *Ibid.*

117. *Ibid.*

118. [Patmore,] 'Ruskin's *Stones of Venice*', in *British Quarterly Review* xiii (1851), 495.

119. [Patmore,] 'Street Architecture', in *National Review* v (1857), 52.

120. For Patmore and 'the Christian celebration of the paradox of the Infinite enclosed', see Sister M.A. Weinig, *Coventry Patmore* (Boston, 1981), reviewed by P.M. Ball in *Modern Language Review* lxxx (1985), 916. See also P.W. Platt, 'The Spiritual Vision of Coventry Patmore' (Ph.D., Toronto, 1976).

121. Patmore, 'Styles', in *Principle in Art*, 198.

122. [Patmore,] 'Expression', in *Edinburgh Review* xciv (1851), 396.

123. *Ibid.*, 397; [Patmore,] 'Aesthetics', in *British Quarterly Review* x (1849), 49–50. Patmore also instances the sculptured screen at St Albans: 'with magic vividness [it] represented the glorious ascension of a company of saints' (*ibid.*, 62).

124. Patmore, 'Styles', in *Principle in Art*, 184.

125. [Patmore,] 'Ruskin's *Seven Lamps*', in *North British Review* xii (1849–50), 324.

126. [Patmore,] 'Character', in *North British Review* xv (1851), 462.

127. R. Willis, 'The Introduction and Criticial Reception of Hegelian Thought in Britain, 1830–1900', in *Victorian Studies* xxxii (1988), 87–111.

128. [G.H. Lewes,] 'Hegel's Aesthetics', in *British and Foreign Review* xiii (1842), 3 n.

129. Carlyle admired Patmore's poetry, but felt unqualified to comment on his architectural criticism: 'To myself, as to everyone, the spiritual qualities manifest in what you say are very welcome. Unhappily, I have next to no knowledge of architecture; and in late years (must I blush to own?) absolutely no care whatever about it – except to keep well out of the way of it, and of the twaddle too commonly uttered upon it!' See A. M[eynell], ed., *A Catalogue of the Library of Coventry Patmore*, published by E. Meynell, Serendipity Shop, 1921, 44: 22 July 1860. Carlyle seems to have preferred Ruskin's moralistic approach: he called *Stones of Venice*, Vol. i, Ruskin's 'best piece of schoolmastering in Architectonics' (Ruskin, *Works*, IX, xlvi: 1851).

130. He studied French in Paris in 1839, but 'learned more German than French' (Champneys, *Patmore*, i, 36). In youth he claimed credit for the invention of a new chloride of bromine (Gosse, *Patmore*, 9).

131. G.E. Lessing, *Laocoon* (Berlin 1766), trans. W. Ross (1836), E.C. Beaseley (1853). Lessing's enthusiasm for Shakespeare – taken up by Herder – no doubt attracted Patmore: his own projected book on Shakespeare, however, was anticipated – and, according to Robert Browning, plagiarised – by H. Ulrici, *Shakespeare's Dramatic Art* (1846). See Meynell, *Library of Coventry Patmore*, 33.

132. Patmore named Lessing, Goethe and Coleridge as supreme critics: they went beyond aesthetics ('a science deserving a better name') in pursuit of objective principle – 'a science in which truth stands first and feeling second, and of which the conclusions are demonstrable and irreversible' (Patmore, *Principle in Art*, 4). His library included an annotated copy of Goethe's *Conversations with Eckermann and Soret* (1875). In 1871 he presented Goethe's *Werke*, 4 vols (Leipzig, n.d.) to his future third wife (Meynell, *Library of Coventry Patmore*, 17).

133. J.G. Fichte, *Characteristics of the Present Age*, etc., trans W. Smith (1848).

134. F. Schiller, *Philosophical and Aesthetic Letters and Essays* (1795; trans. J. Weiss, 1845), reviewed by Patmore in *Douglas Jerrold's Shilling Magazine* ii (1845), 277–9: 'Schiller . . . perceived . . . that aesthetics were a portion of morals, and that their foundation was consistent with nature and the human soul.' One of the *Essays* appeared in translation in *Monthly Chronicle*, February

1841. Patmore's library included a copy of Schiller's *Gedichte* (Stuttgart, 1859). See Meynell, *Library of Coventry Patmore*, 33. He considered 'magnificent' Schiller's notion of the universe as 'a thought of the Deity . . . [Each] new acquaintance in this kingdom of truth, gravitation [, for instance, enables me to] converse with the Infinite through the instrument of Nature' (*The Critic*, ii, N.S., 1845, 189).

135. F.W. Schelling, *The Philosophy of Art* [lectures, 1802–3], trans. A. Johnson (1845), reviewed by Patmore in *The Critic*, May 1845. He considered it 'admirable' ([Patmore,] in *Douglas Jerrold's Shilling Magazine* ii, 1845, 278).

136. Patmore, *Principle in Art*, 207; Patmore, *Courage in Politics*, 105–6.

137. Patmore, *Principle in Art*, 49. Patmore's library contained annotated copies of Aristotle's *Ethics, Rhetoric and Poetic*, 2 vols (1850–1) and of Hegel's *Cours d'Esthétique*, 5 vols (Paris, 1840) and *Lectures on the Philosophy of History* (1878). See Meynell, *Library of Coventry Patmore*, 5, 19.

138. Champneys, *Patmore*, i, 68, 78.

139. 'Coleridge's philosophical standpoint was . . . entirely Hegelian' (Patmore, *Courage in Politics*, 92, 106). Patmore was annotating Coleridge's *Table-Talk* (2nd edn, 1836) at the age of sixteen (Meynell, *Library of Coventry Patmore*, 11). He admired A. Brandl's *Coleridge and the Romantic School*, trans. Lady Eastlake (1887).

140. Lord Lindsay, *Progression by Antagonism* (1846); *Sketches of the History of Christian Art*, 3 vols (1847), reviewed by [Patmore] in *The Critic* N.S. v (1847), 177–80. See J. Steegman, 'Lord Lindsay's *History of Christian Art*', in *Journal of the Warburg and Courtauld Institutes* x (1947), 123–33; H. Brigstocke, 'Lord Lindsay and the *Sketches of the History of Christian Art*', in *Bulletin of the John Rylands Library* lxiv (1981), 27–60. Compare Schiller's sequence of physical, aesthetical and moral (*The Critic* ii, N.S., 1845, 189).

141. E.A. Freeman, *History of Architecture* (1849), xviii, 11: 'Where there is no strife there is no victory; the vertical line cannot be called predominant unless the horizontal exists in a visible condition of subjection and inferiority.' Freeman in turn admitted that Lindsay's views had anticipated his, though he was not at the time aware of them.

142. A. Reichensperger, *Fingerzeige auf dem Gebiete der kirklichen Kunst* (Leipzig, 1854). Reichensperger was editor of *Kölner Domblatt*. See bibliographical studies by L. Pastor (Freiburg, 1899) and M.J. Lewis (New York, 1993).

143. J. Pennethorne, *The Elements and Mathematical Principles of the Greek Architects and Artists* (1844); F.C. Penrose, *Two Letters from Athens* (1847) and *An Investigation of the Principles of Athenian Architecture* (1852; 1888).

144. See B.D. MacGregor, 'Victorian Concepts of Form' (D.Phil., Oxon, 1979). For the application of such ideas to Patmore's poetry, see F.W. Piderit, 'The Odes of Coventry Patmore: a Study of Architectural Criticism and Poetic Practice' (Ph.D., Fordham University, 1979).

145. E.g., Strasbourg and Cologne. See J.W. Goethe, *Literary Essays*, ed. J.E. Spingaen (1921; 1967). Patmore instanced a 'striking passage' on Strasbourg's 'intricate simplicity' in 'Dichtung und Warhreit' ([Patmore,] 'Aesthetics', in

British Quarterly Review x, 1849, 51–2). Kugler similarly called Gothic the Germanic style (*ibid.*).

146. Patmore was familiar with Hegel's *Encyclopaedia* of 1817 ([Patmore,] in *Douglas Jerrold's Shilling Magazine* iii, 1845, 206–9). He recommended C. Bernard's French translation of Hegel's *Aesthetics* (Paris, 1840–52) and W. Hastie's English translation of its introduction (Edinburgh, 1886). H.G. Hotho's revised edition of the *Aesthetics* (1835) appeared in 1842 as vols xii–xiv in H. Glockner's collected edition. This text became the basis of T.M. Knox's translation of 1975. See also P.M. Locke, 'Hegel on Architecture' (Ph.D., Boston, 1984).

147. I. Kant, *Critique of Aesthetic Judgement* (*Critique of Judgement* pt. i), trans. J.C. Meredith (Oxford, 1911). Kant, in fact, says little directly about architecture (e.g., *Critique of Judgement* i, 16).

148. A.W. Schlegel, *A Course of Lectures on Dramatic Art and Literature* (1817, trans. J. Black and A.J.W. Morrison, 1840; 1846). See D. Stempel, 'Coleridge and Organic Form; the English Tradition', in *Studies in Literature* vi (1962), 93–104. F. Schlegel, *Aesthetic and Miscellaneous Works*, trans. E.J. Millington (1849), was reviewed by [Patmore] in 'The Ethics of Art', in *British Quarterly Review* x (1849), 441–62; and he retained a copy in his library (Meynell, *Library of Coventry Patmore*, 33).

149. G.W.F. Hegel, *Aesthetics*, trans. T.M. Knox (Oxford, 1975), II, iii, 689–90, 693: '. . . to the last detail . . . aspiring sublimely and illimitably'; Hegel, *The Philosophy of Fine Art*, trans. F.P.B. Osmaston, i (1920), 112–13; W. Whewell, *Architectural Notes on German Churches* (Cambridge, 1842); A.W.N. Pugin, *The True Principles of Pointed or Christian Architecture* (1841), 7, n. 1: '*Height* or the vertical principle, emblematic of the resurrection, is the very essence of Christian architecture'. See also a letter of 1843 from Pugin concerning verticality, printed in *Architectural Review* xxiii (1908), 3.

150. Hegel's distinction between 'masses that support' and 'masses that are supported' formed the basis of Schopenhauer's architectural theory. Hegel noted that a Doric column has 'the look of being there for a purpose . . . [it displays] firmness and solidity, dominated by the law of gravity . . . its sole purpose is to serve as support . . . the peculiarity of Greek architecture is . . . that it gives shape to this supporting [role, for] . . . art must . . . give shape to . . . the mechanical determinant of load-bearing' (Hegel, *Aesthetics*, trans. Knox, ii, 666–9 and xiv, 310–12). Schopenhauer sees the aim of architecture as 'bringing to greater distinctness' the 'universal qualities of matter . . . the bass notes of nature' – gravity, cohesion, rigidity, hardness. 'Properly speaking, the conflict between gravity and rigidity is the sole aesthetic material of architecture; its problem is to make this conflict appear with perfect distinction in a multitude of different ways . . . Architecture does not affect us merely mathematically, but also dynamically, and . . . what speaks to us through it, is not mere form and symmetry, but rather those fundamental forces of nature, those first Ideas, those lowest grades of the objectivity of will.' He saw all this in Greek architecture, but not in Gothic. See A.

Schopenhauer, *The World as Will and Idea* (1819–1844, trans. Haldane and Kemp, 1888, i, 277–9). Something of this can be seen in K. Schnaase, *Geschichte der bildenden Kunste*, 7 vols (1843–64); 8 vols (1869–79); extracts, translated into French, appeared in *Annales Archéologiques* xi (1851), 167–73, 325–34 and xii (1852), 320–5.

151. F.T. Kugler, *Handbuch der Kunstgeschichte* (Stuttgart, 1842).

152. R. and J.A. Brandon, *An Analysis of Gothic Architecture* (1847).

153. Willis distinguished between 'mechanical' and 'decorative' structure (R. Willis, *Remarks on the Architecture of the Middle Ages, especially of Italy*, 1835).

154. Popular taste was 'revolutionised . . . at a blow' when 'Strawberry Hill Gothic vanished like a nightmare' at the application of Pugin's principle: decorate your construction, do not construct your decoration (Patmore, *Principle in Art*, 2–3).

155. [Patmore,] 'Ruskin's *Seven Lamps*', in *North British Review* xii (1849–50), 309, 311.

156. Hegel, *Aesthetics*, trans. Knox, II, iii, 638.

157. For a rather more sympathetic view, see J. Summerson, *The Classical Language of Architecture* (1963; 1980).

158. [Patmore,] 'Ruskin's *Seven Lamps*', *North British Review* xii (1849–50), 314. Quatremère de Quincey, *Essays on the Nature, the End, and the Means of Imitation in the Fine Arts*, trans. J.C. Kent (1827) and *Essai sur l'Idéal dans ses applications pratiques aux arts du Dessein* (Paris, 1837); L. Batissier, *Histoire de l'Art Monumental dans l'Antiquité et au Moyen Age* (1845). There was a marked copy of Batissier's *Éléments d'Archéologie Nationale* (Paris, 1843) in Patmore's library (Meynell, *Library of Coventry Patmore*, 7).

159. [Patmore,] 'Ruskin's *Seven Lamps*', in *North British Review* xii (1849–50), 314.

160. See J. Harris [with E. Harris and J. Mordaunt Crook], *Sir William Chambers* (1970).

161. Gwilt, 'though by no means a clever man', recognised in his *Encyclopaedia* the significance of formal 'fitness' in heightening effect; then contradicted himself by categorising 'mouldings' as stemming from 'the love of variety' ([Patmore,] 'Ruskin's *Seven Lamps*', in *North British Review* xii,1849–50, 322, 338 n.).

162. Alison correctly ascribed our perception of beauty in architectural proportion to a sense of fitness hallowed by association; but he failed to follow this insight with any explanation of ornamental expression: 'What constitutes an Order is its Proportions, not its ornaments' (A. Alison, *Essays on the nature and Principles of Taste* ii, 1825, 141, 167–8).

163. [Patmore,] 'Ruskin's *Seven Lamps*', in *North British Review* xii (1849–50), 312, 345.

164. [Patmore,] 'Letters and Essays of Schiller', in *Douglas Jerrold's Shilling Magazine* ii (1845), 277–9. Patmore could be a merciless reviewer of philosophical pretension: he found Prof. J.S. Blackie's *On Beauty* 'as arrant nonsense as was ever drivelled in a lunatic asylum' ([Patmore,] '*On Beauty: Three Discourses* by John Stuart Blackie', in *Literary Gazette*, 20 March 1858, 274–5).

165. Patmore, 'Coleridge', in *Courage in Politics*, 92, 106.

166. [Patmore,] 'Athenian Architecture', in *Edinburgh Review* xcv (1852), 404.

167. In reviewing the 1842 edition of the *Handbuch der Kunstgeschichte*, Patmore called him 'the highest German authority on architectural aesthetics' ([Patmore,] 'Ruskin's *Seven Lamps*', in *North British Review* xii, 1849–50, 310).

168. Kugler thought Semper a 'red' revolutionary; Semper called Kugler a 'German *hofrat*' (G. Semper, *Die vier Elemente der Baukunst*, 1851). For further criticisms of Kugler, see Semper, *Uber Baustile* (1869).

169. [Patmore,] 'Ruskin's *Seven Lamps*', in *North British Review* xii (1849–50), 314–15.

170. 'A book which ought to be translated into English' ([Patmore,] 'Expression', in *Edinburgh Review* xciv, 1851, 372). This work, as Kugler explained, was quite 'distinct' from his better-known *Handbuch der Geschichte der Malerei* (Berlin, 1837 and 1847; trans. [M. Hutton], ed. C.L. Eastlake, 1842 and 1851; revised Lady Eastlake 1874; 5th edn, revised A.H. Layard, 1887). Kugler's *Geschichte der Baukunst*, 3 vols (Stuttgart, 1856–9), continued by J. Burckhardt and W. Lübke, was translated into Spanish by J. Caveda (1858), but not into English.

171. [Patmore,] 'Ruskin's *Seven Lamps*', in *North British Review* xii (1849–50), 314–15. Patmore praised him for one sentence: 'Though Grecian is by no means the only style constructed on the mechanical principle of the entablature, it is the only one which thoroughly carries out the aesthetical notion suggested by that principle' (E.A. Freeman, *History of Architecture*, 1849, 124).

172. E.g., C.O. Mueller, *Handbuch der Archaeology der Kunst* (Breslau, 1835, 1848), trans. J. Leitch (1847) and F.D. Welecker (1850). Mueller was Semper's teacher at Gottingen.

173. Patmore doubtless knew H. Hubsch's *In Welchem Style Sollen Wier Bauen?* (Karlsruhe, 1828), which anticipates his own view of Roman architecture. But he found more to interest him in the Hegelian sections of Hubsch's *Die Architektur und Ihr Verhaltnis zur heutigen Malerie und Skulptur* (Stuttgart, 1847): he translates a brief section – 'the essence of Greek art is a serene rest', etc. – in *North British Review* xii (1849–50), 320. Hubsch was a pupil of F. Wienbrenner.

174. [Patmore,] 'Ruskin's *Seven Lamps*', in *North British Review* xii (1849–50), 315.

175. 'Kugler rejects this plausible absurdity, without . . . proving the justice of that rejection, as he might easily have done, by instancing the Ionic details, and Corinthian *modillions*, or consoles, as examples of members which *force* the attention upon the construction, and ought, therefore, according to the "Hut theory", to be the most conspicuous beauties, instead of being eye-sores . . . They are . . . essentially constructive features, and, in this, differ from the triglyphs, mutules, and other members, which, though no doubt they had an equally constructive origin, do not refer to that origin for their only or chief significance . . . Every member . . . ought to have a strict constructive propriety: but this constitutes not the artistical significance, but only its condition' (*ibid.*, 320).

176. 'Alison and Lord Aberdeen . . . have attributed all the vast surplus beauty for

which they could not account [in constructional terms] to the force of "classical associations"' (*ibid.*, 322–3).

177. [Patmore,] 'Expression', in *Edinburgh Review* xciv (1851), 372.

178. [Patmore,] 'Ruskin's *Seven Lamps*', in *North British Review* xii (1849–50), 323.

179. Ruskin called Patmore 'one of my severest models and tutors in use of English' (Ruskin, *Works*, XXXIV, 488–90: 27 October 1860). Patmore ranked Ruskin with Jeremy Taylor for the glory of his prose ([Patmore,] 'Aesthetics', in *British Quarterly Review* x, 1849, 75).

180. Not initially: it was Patmore who persuaded Ruskin to write his famous letter to *The Times* in 1851 in defence of the Pre-Raphaelites (Ruskin, *Works*, XII, xlvi). And not finally: Patmore's initial optimism as regards cast iron soon gave way to Ruskinian pessimism (see note 60).

181. When Patmore went over to Rome, Ruskin told him: 'It is a great nuisance that you have turned Roman Catholic, for it makes all your fine thinking so ineffectual to us English' (Ruskin, *Works*, XXXVI, 478–9: 23 December 1864). Patmore – at Aubrey de Vere's suggestion – tried to persuade Ruskin to follow him (Champneys, *Patmore*, ii, 342).

182. [Patmore,] 'Ruskin's Lectures', in *The Critic* N.S. xiii (1854), 288.

183. F. Grose, *Antiquities of England and Wales*, 8 vols (1783–97); *Scotland*, 2 vols (1789–91); *Ireland*, 2 vols (1791–5).

184. J. Milner, *A Dissertation on the Modern Style of Altering Ancient Cathedrals* (1798); *A Treatise on the ecclesiastical architecture of England during the Middle Ages* (1811). Milner did, however, come nearer to unravelling the secret of Gothic when he remarked that it 'produces an artificial infinite in the mind of the spectator' (Milner, *et al.*, *Essays in Gothic Architecture*, 1802, xvi–xviii). Similarly Coleridge: 'the principle of . . . Gothic . . . is Infinity made imaginable' (Coleridge, *Complete Works*, ed. W.G.T. Shedd, 1954, vi, 461: *Table Talk*, 29 June 1833).

185. J. Carter, *Ancient Architecture of England*, 2 vols (1795–1814; 1837); *Specimens of Ancient Sculpture and Painting*, 2 vols (1780–94). See J. Mordaunt Crook, *John Carter and the Mind of the Gothic Revival* (Society of Antiquaries, 1995).

186. Of Pugin's *True Principles* (1841) he noted: 'We believe there is some peculiar propriety in Gothic decoration which lies far deeper than Mr Pugin supposes and is of far more substantial significance than could result from any such negative virtue as that of never getting in the way of constructive necessities' ([Patmore,] 'Aesthetics', in *British Quarterly Review* x, 1849, 51).

187. T. Rickman, *An Attempt to Discriminate the Styles of English Architecture* (1819; 5th edn 1848).

188. R. and J.A. Brandon, *An Analysis of Gothic Architecture* (1849).

189. M.H. Bloxham, *Principles of Gothic Architecture* (11 edns, 1829–82).

190. F.A. Paley, *A Manual of Gothic Mouldings* (1845; 1877, etc.)

191. For Schnaase on harmonic integration, see M. Podro, *The Critical Historians of Art* (1982), 35–41.

192. For Semper on optical effect, see *ibid.*, 47–52.

193. S. Boisserée, *Histoire et Description de la Cathédral de Cologne* (Munich, 1843).

194. J. Michelet, *Histoire de France* (1833–65), ii.

195. *The Symbolism of Churches and Church Ornaments*, by W. Durandus; trans. and ed. J.M. Neale and B. Webb (Oxford, 1845).

196. [Patmore,] 'Aesthetics', in *British Quarterly Review* x (1849), 52.

197. W. Whewell, *The Philosophy of the Inductive Sciences* i (1840), intro., 113.

198. Hegel, *Aesthetics*, trans. Knox, II, iii, 674, 687.

199. [Patmore,] 'Aesthetics', in *British Quarterly Review* x (1849), 52, citing W. Whewell, *Architectural Notes on German Churches* (1842). E.A. Freeman – like Pugin before him – had been an enthusiast for the inspirational qualities of altitude in churches (*Ecclesiologist* v, N.S. iii, 1846, 181). But that is not quite the same thing as aspiration in the form of a counterpoint to gravitational thrust. Freeman lectured 'On the Constructive Principles of the Principal Styles of Architecture' at the Royal Institution in 1853; a report, together with a letter by Freeman to the *Evening Journal* 7 March 1853, is preserved among the Freeman MSS. (2/2/9), John Rylands Library, Manchester.

200. E.g., Hegel, *Aesthetics*, trans, Knox, II, iii, 687–9: 'romantic architecture constructs a building which exists as an enclosure for the spirit, and . . . so far as is architecturally possible [makes] spiritual convictions shine through the shape and arrangement of the building and so determines the form of its interior and exterior . . . from the terrestial to the infinite . . . [it is as if] the strict difference between load and support has disappeared . . . [Indeed,] the way the building strives upwards . . . converts load carrying to free ascending . . . [and in] the eye . . . the worshipping heart . . . rises above the territory of finitude and finds rest in God alone.'

201. [Patmore,] 'Expression', in *Edinburgh Review* xciv (1851), 395.

202. *Ibid.*, 376.

203. *Ibid.*, 392–3, 398; [Patmore,] 'Character' in *North British Review* xv (1851), 481 *et seq.* See Hegel, *Aesthetics*, trans. Knox, II, iii, 698: 'In secular architecture . . . there is no room for beauty except as decoration.' Hence Patmore's comparative contempt for Italian Gothic. It is 'not a real style at all', he contended, 'but the wreck of several preceding and imperfect styles, grown over with a mass of parasitical and incidental decoration' (Patmore, 'Architectural Criticism', in *Courage in Politics*, 179). Indeed, it 'has about it as much relation to a true style as a curiosity shop has to a well-ordered living room' (Patmore, 'Styles', in *Principle in Art*, 160). 'Shafts and mouldings . . . maimed in their upward flight by horizontal bands of colour'; arch mouldings interrupted by voussoirs carved, jointed and separately marked; pointed arches deprived of their 'natural expression' by enclosure within a semicircle; decoration through rich materials rather than 'pure form' – all these were essentially 'anti-Gothic' devices which, by comparison with classicism, deprived Gothic of its 'expressional powers' ([Patmore,] 'Expression', in *Edinburgh Review* xciv, 1851, 398). This 'securalisation' of the style, however, made it eminently suitable for Italian *palazzi* and modern civic buildings ([Patmore,] 'Character', in *North British Review* xv, 1851, 482, 484–5).

204. [Patmore,] 'Ruskin's *Stones of Venice*', in *British Quarterly Review* xiii (1851), 490.

205. [Patmore,] 'Expression', in *Edinburgh Review* xciv (1851), 397, 400. Ruskin seemed to Patmore to think of Gothic details 'as if they might be plucked from the building, like flowers from the stalk, without any loss of significance' (*ibid.*, 379).

206. *Ibid*, 390. Patmore approved of Tudor building as vernacularised Gothic: 'The broad window, divided vertically into equal compartments by mullions, and horizontally into unequal portions by transomes, and surmounted by a dripstone . . . is the only window that ought to be seen in a northern house. [Unlike the Georgian sash – a mere hole in the wall –] it is unsurpassable in the expression as well as in the reality of convenience and safe construction; and upon the display of those qualities the beauties of private house architecture must always depend' ([Patmore,] 'Character', in *North British Review* xv, 1851, 486). Perhaps one day, 'by a combination of . . . Italian Gothic decoration [and] . . . Tudor masses, we shall be able to boast of a domestic architecture surpassing any that has yet existed' (*ibid.*, 488). Meanwhile, let buildings grow organicially: 'the most beautiful examples of British and foreign house architecture – not public or palatial – are those in which all care of . . . symmetry and order is cast away . . . [so that] the house seems to grow . . . from its root in the hearth, as wildly as the trees that surround it' (*ibid.*, 493). In all building, the best effect comes from a 'modest *ostentation* of . . . extreme substantiality': the fifteenth-century inn at Aldfriston, Sussex, for example. Patmore admired its rustic grandeur: 'a fit abode for a duke in difficulties' (Patmore, 'Ideal and Material Greatness in Art', in *Principle in Art*, 149–53). 'If the devil were an architect, his "favourite sin" would be [a sham Pictureque] . . . "cottage of gentility"' (Patmore, 'Old English Archtecture, Ancient and Modern', in *Principle in Art*, 157).

207. In a letter to Robert Bridges, quoted in *Times Literary Supplement*, 24 May 1957, 320, reviewing J.C. Reid, *The Mind and Art of Coventry Patmore* (1957). 'The most devout, subtle, and sublimated love-poetry of our century' (A. Symons, *New Review*, xvi, 1897, 71–7). 'A fund of inspired poetry' worth 'the whole baggage of the Victorian legacy in general' (H. Read, 'Coventry Patmore', in *The Great Victorians*, ed. H.J. and H. Massingham, 1952, 394–410). Gosse compared the odes of *The Unknown Eros* (1877–8) to 'Rosicrucian symbols, wholly unintelligible to the multitude, but discovered with a panic of delight by a few elect souls in every generation' (Gosse, *Patmore*, 151). They certainly confirm Patmore's enthusiasm for the ideas of Emanuel Swedenborg. See Meynell, *Library of Coventry Patmore*, 35. For a critical view, see J.J. Dunn, 'Love and Eroticism: Coventry Patmore's Mystical Imagery', in *Victorian Poetry* vii (1969), 203–19. For a sympathetic explanation by a close friend, Frank Harris, see Harris, *Contemporary Portraits* iii (1920), 199–200.

208. R. Chambers, *Vestiges of the Natural History of Creation* (2nd edn 1844), 362. For the debate caused by this book, see W.F. Poole, *Index to Periodical Literature*, ed. W.I. Fletcher (1891).

209. *Dictionary of National Biography* xxii (supp. 1901), 1124.
210. Patmore, *Religio Poetae* (1898 edn), 66–7.
211. [Patmore,] 'Athenian Architecture', in *Edinburgh Review* xcv (1852), 402.
212. [Patmore,] 'Ethics', *British Quarterly Review* x (1849), 441. 'Who but a "scientist" values greatly or is greatly moved by anything he can understand?' (Patmore, *Religio Poetae*, 140).
213. *RIBA Journal*, 3rd series viii (1901), 49–51.

Appendix

*Selected writings on art and architecture
by George Aitchison, Benjamin Webb,
Beresford Hope and Coventry Patmore*

NOTE. No bibliography is ever complete, least of all a bibliography largely consisting of anonymous writings. This list of work, therefore, aims to be representative rather than comprehensive. Attributions, wherever possible, have been made on direct rather than indirect evidence.

I. George Aitchison

[Brickwork and polychromy,] *Builder* xiv (1856), 282–4: 21 April 1856 [Architectural Museum]

'On Colour as applied to Architecture', *RIBA Transactions* viii (1857–8), 47–54: 14 December 1857 [RIBA]

'On Iron as a Building Material', *RIBA Transactions* xiv (1863–4), 97–103: 29 February 1864 [RIBA]

'Progressive Use of Iron in Building', *RIBA Transactions* xxi (1871), 81–2; *Builder* xxix (1871), 417 [RIBA conference]

'What principles should govern the restoration of ancient buildings or their preservation as memorials?', *Transactions of the National Association for the Promotion of Social Sciences* (1877), 712–20

'Iron'; 'Colour', *Builder* xliv(1883), 207–8, 273–4 [Royal Academy]

[Obit.,] 'The Late William Burges, ARA', in *RIBA Transactions* 1883–4, 204–9; reprinted in *Merry England* iii (1884), 72–84

'On Marble and Marble Mosaic', *Builder* xlvi (1884), 281–2 [Royal Academy]

'On Coloured Glass', *Builder* xlvi (1884), 382–3 [Royal Academy]

'On Staircases', *Builder* xlviii (1885), 395–6, 396–7 [Royal Academy]

'An Architect on Architecture', *Merry England* iv (1884–5), 235–7 [Architectural Association]

'Architecture in the 19th century', *Builder* xlviii (1885), 581–2, 637 [Society for the Encouragement of Fine Arts]

'The Neglect of Architecture', *Merry England* vii (1886), 119–23, 169–75 [Leeds and Yorkshire Architectural Society]

'Architectural Education', *Builder* l (1886), 331–5 [Royal Academy]

'Mouldings', *Builder* l (1886), 365–6, 402–4 [Royal Academy]

'Paul Sédille', *RIBA Journal* 1886–7, 89–91 [RIBA]

'On Doorways; Windows; Balustrades', *Builder* lii (1887), 346–7, 380–2 [Royal Academy]

'Stray Thoughts on Education', *Builder* lii (1887), 635–6, 654 [Architectural Association]

'On Architectural Education', *Builder* lii (1887), 690–700 [General Conference, RIBA]

'Sculpture and its relation to architecture', *RIBA Transactions* 1887–8, 176–80 [RIBA]

'The History of Architecture', *Builder* liv (1888), 61–3 [Royal Academy]

'Greek Architecture', *Builder* liv (1888), 118 [Royal Academy]

'Utilitarian Ugliness in Towns', *Builder* lv (1888), 430–3 [National Art Congress, Liverpool]

'The Revival of Architecture', *Builder* lv (1888), 2–3 [reply to William Morris]

'The Roman Thermae', *RIBA Transactions* N.S. v (1888–9), 105–22 [RIBA]

'The Origin of Roman Imperial Architecture', *RIBA Transactions* N.S. v (1888–9), 158–61 [reply to G. Baldwin Brown, RIBA]

[Obit.,] 'The Late Mr Pullan', *RIBA Transactions* N.S. vi (1888–9), 249–54

[Memoir,] 'Charles Robert Cockerell', *RIBA Transactions* N.S. vi (1888–9), 255–61

'Roman Architecture', *Builder* lvi (1889), 85–8, 103–6, 121–4, 142–5, 162–5, 181–3, 194–201, 204, 224 [Royal Academy]

'Roman Architecture', *Builder* lviii (1890), 75–8, 94–7, 109, 113–16, 130–3, 135, 137, 152–5, 169–72 [Royal Academy]

[Review,] L. Eidlitz, *The Nature and Function of Art; more specifically of Architecture* (1881), *RIBA Journal* N.S. vii (1890–1), 389–90

'Byzantine Architecture', *Builder* lx (1891), 82–6, 103–7, 123–6, 144–7, 164–7, 187–90 [Royal Academy]

'The Advancement of Architecture', *Builder* lxi (1891), 138–9 [Architectural Association]

'Byzantine Architecture', *RIBA Transactions* viii (1892), 221–46 [RIBA]

'Saracenic Architecture', *Builder* lxii (1892), 75–8, 95–9, 116–19, 136–40, 156–9, 179–83 [Royal Academy]

'What is Architecture, and how can it be advanced?', *Builder* lxiv (1893), 63–6, 83–7, 108–10, 146–50, 166–9, 209–12 [Royal Academy]

'The Advancement of Architecture', *Builder* lxvi (1894), 86–9, 107–11, 131–4, 151–3, 169–72, 192–4 and *RIBA Journal* 3rd series, i (1893–4), 243–4, 279–80, 320–3, 363 [Royal Academy]

'The Use and Abuse of Marble for Decorative Purposes', *RIBA Journal* 3rd series, ii (1894–5), 401–7: 22 April 1895 [RIBA]

'The Advancement of Architecture', *Builder* lxviii (1895), 79–81, 99–101, 119–22, 137–40, 159–62, 179–82 [Royal Academy]

'Lord Leighton: some reminiscences', *RIBA Journal* 3rd series, iii (1896), 264–5
'Romanesque Architecture', *Builder* lxx (1896), 109–11, 132–4, 158–60, 180–2, 204–6, 227–9 [Royal Academy]
Presidential Address, RIBA, 1896, *Builder* lxxi (1896), 381–3
'The Advancement of Architecture', *Builder* lxxii (1897), 117–19, 141–3, 165–6, 191–4, 217–19, 296–71, 316 [Royal Academy]
'Speeches at the Festival Dinner', *RIBA Journal* 3rd series, v (1897–8), 102–3, 105 [Whitehall Rooms]
'Speech at the Architectural Association Jubilee Banquet', *Builder* lxxii (1897), 420
Presidential Address, RIBA, 1897, *Builder* lxxiii (1897), 366–9 and *RIBA Journal* 3rd series, v (1897–8), 1–8: 1 November 1897
'Address to the Central Association of Master Builders', *Builder* lxxiv (1898), 104–5 [Trocadero Restaurant, Piccadilly]
'Address on receiving the Royal Gold Medal', *Builder* lxxiv (1898), 610 and *RIBA Journal* 3rd series, v (1897–8), 412–13 [RIBA]
'Address to Students', *Builder* lxxiv (1898), 102–3 and *RIBA Journal* 3rd series, vi (1898–9), 1–8 [RIBA]
'The Renaissance', *Builder* lxxiv (1898), 124–6, 147–9, 180–2, 200–1, 226–7, 251–2 [Royal Academy]
Presidential Address, RIBA, 1898, *Builder* lxxv (1898), 424–6 and *RIBA Journal* 3rd series, vi (1898–9), 1–8: 7 November 1898
'Address to Students', *Builder* lxxvi (1899), 83–4 and *RIBA Journal* 3rd series, vi (1898–9), 137–41: 23 January 1899 [RIBA]
'Address at the International Building Trades Exhibition', *Builder* lxxvi (1899), 409–10 [Agricultural Hall, Islington]
'Greek Architecture', *Builder* lxxvi (1899), 109–11, 136–9, 163–6, 187–90, 216–19, 241–4 [Royal Academy]
'Progress in Architecture', *Builder* lxxviii (1900), 128–30 [Royal Academy]
'St Peter's, Rome', *Builder* lxxx (1901), 105–8, 130–2 and *RIBA Journal* 3rd series, viii (1900–1), 245–55, 453–63; ix (1901–2), 49–61, 77–89 [Royal Academy]
'The Learning of Architecture', *RIBA Journal* 3rd series (1901–2), 193–200, 321–6, 381–91, 401–13, 449–58 [Royal Academy]
'Coloured Buildings'; 'Coloured Terra-Cotta'; 'Marble', *RIBA Journal* 3rd series, x (1902–3), 493–503, 513–22, 529–38.
'Metallic Architecture', *Builder* lxxxiv (1903), 186, 214, 246, 272; *RIBA Journal* 3rd series, x (1902–3), 433–40, 469–77 [Royal Academy]
'Coloured Glass', *RIBA Journal* 3rd series, xi (1903–4), 53–65
'Vitruvius'; 'Excellence in Architecture', *RIBA Journal* 3rd series, xiii (1905–6), 21–8, 61–7, 341–6, 451–6

2. Benjamin Webb

[Anon. review,] J.L. Petit, *Remarks on Church Architecture* (1842), *Ecclesiologist* i (1842), 91–105
[Anon., with J.M. Neale,] *A Few Words to Church Builders* (Cambridge Camden Society, 1841; 3rd edn, 1844)

[Anon., with J.M. Neale,] *A Few Words to Churchwardens II, suited to Town and Manufacturing Parishes* (Cambridge Camden Society, 1841; 7th edn, 1851)

[With J.M. Neale,] trans. and intro., G. Durandus, *The Symbolism of Churches and Church Ornaments: a translation of the first book of the Rationale Divinorum Officiorum* (Leeds, 1843; re-issued 1893)

[Anon. review,] A.W. Pugin, *Glossary of Ecclesiastical Ornament and Costume* (1844), *Ecclesiologist* iii (1843–4), 141–3

'On Pointed Architecture as adapted to tropical climates', *Transactions of the Ecclesiological Society* 1845, 199–218

[Anon.,] 'The Cambridge Camden Society and the Round Church', *Ecclesiologist* iv, N.S. i (1845), 84–6, 249–51

[Ed.,] Hope, 'Ecclesiological Science', *Ecclesiologist* vii, N.S. iv (1847), 85–91

Sketches of Continental Ecclesiology; or Church Notes in Belgium, Germany and Italy (1848)

[Ed., with J. Fuller Russell,] ed., *Hierurgia Anglicana* (Ecclesiological Society, 1848; ed. V. Staley, 2 vols, 1902)

[Anon.,] 'Colonial Church Architecture', *Ecclesiologist* viii, N.S. v (1848), 141–7, 265–79

[Anon. review,] J. Ruskin, *The Seven Lamps of Architecture* (1849), *Ecclesiologist* x, N.S. vii (1850), 111–20

[Anon.,] 'St Matthias, Stoke Newington', *Ecclesiologist* xi, N.S. viii (1850), 142–3

[Anon. review,] A.W. Pugin, *An Earnest Appeal on the Establishment of the Hierarchy* (1851), *Morning Chronicle*, 4 March 1851, 6

[Anon.,] 'Great Exhibition: history and construction of the building'; 'Fine Arts of the Exhibition', *Morning Chronicle*, 12 May 1851, 2, 2–3

[Anon.,] 'St Ninian's Cathedral, Perth', *Ecclesiologist* xii, N.S. ix (1851), 24–9

[Anon. review,] J. Ruskin, *The Stones of Venice*; (1851), *Ecclesiologist* xii, N.S. ix (1851), 275–84, 341–50

[Anon.,] 'Archaeological Itinerary of Paris', *Saturday Review* i (1855), 36

[Anon. review,] J. Labarte, *Arts of the Middle Ages* (1855), *Saturday Review* i (1855), 304

[Anon.,] 'The Competition for the Proposed Cathedral at Lille', *Ecclesiologist* xvii, N.S. xiv (1856), 78–105

[Anon.,] 'Architectural Exhibition', i and ii, *Saturday Review* iii (1857), 9–11, 32–3

[Anon. review,] A.F. Rio, *De l'art chrétien* (1856), *Saturday Review* iii (1857), 109–10

[Anon. review,] E. Young, *Pre-Raffaelitism* (1857), *Saturday Review* iii (1857), 332–4

[Anon. review,] Exhibition of Art Treasures, Manchester, *Saturday Review* iii (1857), 426–7

[Anon.,] 'Competition for the Memorial Church at Constantinople', *Ecclesiologist* xviii, N.S. xiv (1857), 98–116

[Anon.,] 'The Manchester Exhibition of Art Treasures', *Ecclesiologist* xviii, N.S. xiv (1857), 295–304

[Anon.,] 'An Ecclesiological Day in Manchester', *Ecclesiologist* xviii, N.S. xiv (1857), 304–12

[Anon. review,] J. Coleman Hart, *Designs for Parish Churches, in the Three Styles of*

English Church Architecture (New York, 1857), *Ecclesiologist* xvii, N.S. xiv (1857), 367–8

[Anon. review,] Exhibition of Art Treasures, Manchester, *Saturday Review* iv (1857), 370–1

[Anon. review,] J. Ruskin, *Elements of Drawing* (1857), *Saturday Review* iv (1857), 374–5

[Anon. review,] 'Recent Literature of Art', *Christian Remembrancer* xxxiv (1857), 267–99

[Anon. review,] J. Ruskin, *The Political Economy of Art* (1857), *Saturday Review* v (1858), 90–1

[Anon.,] 'Proposed Memorial of the Great Exhibition of 1851', *Saturday Review* v (1858), 238–9.

[Anon.,] 'The Question of Architectural Style for the New Public Offices', *Saturday Review* vi (1858), 303–5

[Anon. review,] G.F. Waagen, *Galleries and Cabinets of Art in Great Britain* (1857), *Saturday Review* v (1858), 195–6

[Anon. review,] 'Proposed Memorial of the Great Exhibition of 1851', *Saturday Review* v (1858), 238–9

[Anon.,] 'The Photographic Exhibition, 1858', *Saturday Review* v (1858), 344–5

[Anon. review,] G.G. Scott, *Secular and Domestic Architecture* (1858), *Saturday Review* v (1858), 447–9

[Anon. review,] 'The First Exhibition of Modern Art Manufactures at South Kensington', *Saturday Review* vi (1858), 279–80

[Anon.,] 'The Question of Style for the New Public Offices', *Saturday Review* vi (1858), 303–5

[Anon. review,] G.G. Scott, *Remarks on Secular and Domestic Architecture, Present and Future* (1857), *Ecclesiologist* xix, N.S. xvi (1858), 16–23

[Anon.,] 'Blenheim Palace Chapel', *Ecclesiologist* xix, N.S. xvi (1858), 71–3

[As 'E.E.',] 'On Anker-Windows or Lychnoscopes', *Ecclesiologist* xix, N.S. xvi (1858), 86–8

[Anon. review,] A.J.B. Beresford Hope, *The Common Sense of Art* (1858), *Saturday Review* vii (1859), 96–7

[Anon. review,] J. Ruskin, *The Two Paths* (1859), *Saturday Review* viii (1859), 260–1

[Anon. review,] *The Fabric Rolls of York Minster* (Surtees Society vol. xxxv, 1859), *Saturday Review* viii (1859), 427–8.

[Anon. review,] *Facsimile of the Sketchbook of Wilars d'Honnecourt*, ed. Darcell, Lassus, Quicherat and Willis (1859) *Saturday Review* viii (1859), 518–20

[Anon. review,] T. Hudson Turner, *Domestic Architecture in England from the Conquest to the end of the 13th century* (1851); J.H. Parker, *Domestic Architecture in England from Edward I to Richard II* (1853) and *Domestic Architecture in England from Richard II to Henry VIII* (1859), *Saturday Review* viii (1859), 647–8

[Anon.,] 'The Prospects of Art in England', *Bentley's Quarterly Review* i (1859), 143–82

[Anon.,] 'The Art Exhibitions of 1859', *Bentley's Quarterly Review* i (1859), 582–628

[Anon.,] 'All Saints, Margaret Street', *Ecclesiologist* xx, N.S. xvii (1859), 184–9

Appendix

[Anon.,] 'All Saints, Margaret Street', *Saturday Review* vii (1859), 680–2

[Anon. review,] *Directorium Anglicanum*, ed. J. Purchas (1858), *Ecclesiologist* xx, N.S. xviii (1859), 31–4

[Anon. review,] J.B. Waring, *The Arts connected with Architecture, illustrated by Examples, in Central Italy, from the 13th to the 15th century* (1858), *Ecclesiologist* xx, N.S. xviii (1859), 412–14

[Anon. review,] J.M. Neale, *A Commentary on the Psalms* i (1860), *Christian Remembrancer* xxxix (1860), 264–82

[Anon.,] 'Domestic Architecture', *Bentley's Quarterly Review* ii (1860), 474–517

[Anon. review,] M. Walcott, *The Cathedrals of the United Kingdom* (1860); *The Minsters and Abbey Ruins of the United Kingdom* (1860), *Saturday Review* ix (1860), 250–1

[Anon. review,] T.L. Donaldson, *Architectura Numismatica* (1859), *Saturday Review* ix (1860), 376–7

[Anon. review,] 'Exhibited Architecture', *Saturday Review* ix (1860), 743–4

[Anon.,] 'The New Foreign Office and Lord Palmerston', *Saturday Review* x (1860), 110–11

[Anon.,] 'Archaeological Meetings', *Saturday Review* x (1860), 266–8

[Anon. review,] J. Ruskin, *Modern Painters* v (1860), *Saturday Review* x (1860), 273–5, 310–12.

[Anon. review,] 'Additions to the South Kensington Museum', *Saturday Review* x (1860), 304–5.

[Anon. review,] G.E. Waagen, ed., Kügler's *Handbook of Painting* (1860), *Saturday Review* x (1860), 457–9

[Anon. review,] W.S. Okely, *Development of Christian Architecture in Italy* (1860), *Saturday Review* x (1860), 528–9

[Anon.,] 'Halifax and Doncaster', *Ecclesiologist* xxi, N.S. xviii (1860), 145–52

[Anon.,] 'Protestant Ecclesiology in Germany', *Ecclesiologist* xxi, N.S. xviii (1860), 283–5

[Anon. review,] E.E. Viollet-le-Duc, *Military Architecture of the Middle Ages*, trans. M. Macdermott (1860), *Saturday Review* xi (1861), 345–6

[Anon. review,] A.J.B. Beresford Hope, *The English Cathedral of the 19th century* (1861), *Saturday Review* xi (1861), 643–4

[Anon. review,] 'Sculpture and Architecture', 1861, *Saturday Review* xii (1861), 15–16

[Anon. review,] B. Ferrey, *Recollections of A.W. Pugin and his father Augustus Pugin* (1861), *Saturday Review* xii (1861), 121–3

[Anon.,] 'The New Exhibition Building', *Saturday Review* xii (1861), 351–2

[Anon. review,] J.H. and J. Parker, *Our English Home* (1861), *Saturday Review* xii (1861), 413–14

[Anon. review,] L. Jewitt, ed., *The Reliquary* (1861), *Saturday Review* xii (1861), 490–92

[Anon. review,] G.G. Scott, ed., *Gleanings from Westminster Abbey* (1861), *Saturday Review* xii (1861), 567–8

[Anon. review,] A.J.B Beresford Hope, *The English Cathedral of the 19th century* (1861), *Christian Remembrancer* xlii (1861), 466–95

[Anon. review,] W.S. Okely, *Development of Christian Architecture in Italy* (1860), *Ecclesiologist* xxii, N.S. xix (1861), 5–8

[Anon. review,] Murray's *Handbook to the Cathedrals of England: Southern Division*, 2 vols (1861), *Ecclesiologist* xxii, N.S. xix (1861), 79–85

[Anon. review,] J.M. Neale, *Notes Ecclesiological and Picturesque on Dalmatia, Croatia, Istria, Syria, with a visit to Montenegro* (1861), *Ecclesiologist* xxii, N.S. xix (1861), 289–96

[Anon. review,] B. Ferrey, *Recollections of A.W. Pugin and . . . Augustus Pugin* (1861), *Ecclesiologist* xxii, N.S. xix (1861), 305–10, 367–9

[Anon.,] 'Churches and Schools in London', *Ecclesiologist* xxii, N.S. xix (1861), 317–30

[Anon.,] 'Pugin Redivivus', *Saturday Review* xiii (1862), 441–2

[Anon.,] 'Art Criticism', *Saturday Review* xiii (1862), 612–13

[Anon.,] 'The International Exhibition', *Ecclesiologist* xxiii, N.S. xx (1862), 168–76

[Anon.,] 'Ceramic Art and Glass in the International Exhibition', *Saturday Review* xiv (1862), 137–8

[Anon.,] 'Metalwork in the International Exhibition', *Saturday Review* xiv (1862), 280–1

[Anon. review,] C. Dresser, *The Art of Decorative Design* (1862), *Saturday Review* xiv (1862), 318–19

[Anon.,] 'Furniture and Decorative Carving in the International Exhibition', *Saturday Review* xiv (1862), 344–5

[Anon.,] 'Textile Art in the International Exhibition', *Saturday Review* xiv (1862), 409–11

[Anon. review,] 'Painted Glass in the International Exhibition', *Saturday Review* xiv (1862), 476–7

[Anon.,] 'British Architecture in the International Exhibition', *Saturday Review* xiv (1862), 509–10

[Anon.,] 'Foreign Architecture in the International Exhibition', *Saturday Review* xiv (1862), 538–9

[Anon. review,] J.C. Robinson, Catalogue of the Loan Exhibition at South Kensington, *Saturday Review* xiv (1862), 720–1

[Anon. review,] Murray's *Handbook to the Cathedrals of England: Eastern Division* (1862), *Saturday Review* xv (1863), 250–1

[Anon.,] 'The Prince Consort's Memorial', *Saturday Review* xv (1863), 432–3

[Anon. review,] *The Sculptures of . . . Wells Cathedral* (Architectural Photographic Association, 1862), *Saturday Review* xv (1863), 479–80

[Anon. review,] J.C. Robinson, *The Art Wealth of England . . . Photographs . . . of Works of Art on loan to the . . . South Kensington Museum* (1863), *Saturday Review* xv (1863), 737–8

[Anon.,] 'Church Restoration in France', *Saturday Review* xvi (1863), 582–3

[Anon. review,] 'Architecture in 1864', *Saturday Review* xvii (1864), 782–4

[Anon. review,] *Photographs from Churches and other Ecclesiastical Buildings in France* (Architectural Photographic Association, 1863), *Saturday Review* xviii (1864), 31–2

Appendix

[Anon.,] 'Church Architecture Spoilt and Mimicked', *Saturday Review* xviii (1864), 270–1

[Anon.,] 'Church Restoration and Destruction', *Saturday Review* xviii (1864), 326–8

[Anon. review,] R.J. Johnson, *Specimens of Early French Architecture, selected chiefly from the Churches of the Île de France, and illustrated in Geometrical Drawings and Perspective Views* (Newcastle-upon-Tyne, 1864), *Saturday Review* xviii (1864), 732–3

[Anon. review,] C. Texier and R. Popplewell Pullan, *Byzantine Architecture* (1864), *Saturday Review* xix (1865), 181–2

[Anon. review,] G.E. Street, *Some Account of Gothic Architecture in Spain* (1865), *Saturday Review* xix (1865), 353–4

[Anon. review,] R. Kerr, *The Gentleman's House* (1865), *Saturday Review* xix (1865), 706–7

[Anon. review,] C. Texier and R. Popplewell Pullan, *The Principal Ruins of Asia Minor* (1865), *Saturday Review* xx (1865), 524–5

[Anon. review,] *Photographs from sketches by A.W. Pugin* [taken by] S. Ayling, ed. E.W. Pugin (1865), *Saturday Review* xx (1865), 589–90

[Anon. review,] J. Ruskin, *The Ethics of the Dust* (1865), *Saturday Review* xx (1865), 819–20

[Letter,] 'St Andrew's, Wells Street', *The Times*, 16 Oct. 1865, 9

[Anon. review,] C. Winston, *Memoirs Illustrative of the Art of Glass Painting* (1865), *Saturday Review* xxi (1866), 365–6

[Anon. obit.,] J.M. Neale, *Ecclesiologist* xxviii (1866), 265

[Anon. review,] J.C. Buckler, *The Restoration of Lincoln Cathedral* (1866), *Saturday Review* xxii (1866), 281–2

[Anon. review,] J. Fergusson, *History of Architecture*, 3 vols. (1866), *Saturday Review* xxiii (1867), 415

[Anon. review,] A. Barry, *The Life and Works of Sir Charles Barry* (1867), *Saturday Review* xxiv (1867), 733–5

[Anon.,] 'The Report on the Commission of Ritual', *Saturday Review* xxiv (1867), 281–2

[Anon.,] 'The New Law Courts', *Ecclesiologist* xxviii, N.S. xxv (1867), 113–21, 291–3

[Anon.,] 'Sir Charles Barry and Mr Pugin', *Saturday Review* xxv (1868), 276–8

[Anon.,] 'The Government Architects', *Saturday Review* xxv (1868), 785

[Anon. review,] C.L. Eastlake, *Hints on Household Taste* (1872 edn), *Saturday Review* xxxv (1873), 255–6

[Anon. review,] C.L. Eastlake, *A History of the Gothic Revival* (1872), *Saturday Review* xxxv (1873), 315–16, 382–3

[Anon. review,] A.J.B. Beresford Hope, *Worship in the Church of England* (1874), *Saturday Review* xxxviii (1874), 803–4, 830–2

[Anon.,] 'Classical and Byzantine: St Paul's and Keble Chapel', *Church Quarterly Review* ii (1876), 447–64

[Anon.,] 'The Hatcham Case', *Saturday Review* xliii (1877), 39–41 and 66–7

3. Beresford Hope

'The Nomenclature of the Different Styles', *Ecclesiologist* i (1842), 192–3

[Anon.,] 'Parsonage Houses', *Ecclesiologist* ii (1842–3), 145–7

'Bayham Abbey', *Ecclesiologist* ii (1842–3), 163–4

Essays (1844)

[Anon. review,] W. Dyce, *The Theory of Fine Arts* (King's College, London, 1844), *Ecclesiologist* iii (1844), 185–7

[Anon. review,] J.W. Bowden, *Holy Trinity, Roehampton* (1844); H.J. Underwood, *Littlemore Church* (Oxford, 1840), *Ecclesiologist* iv, N.S. i (1845), 30–4

[Anon.,] 'The Artistic Merit of Mr Pugin', *Ecclesiologist* v, N.S. ii (1846), 10–16

[Anon.,] 'Past and Future Developments of Architecture', *Ecclesiologist* v, N.S. ii (1846), 48–53

[Anon. review,] E.A. Freeman, *Development of Roman and Gothic Architecture and their Moral and Symbolical Teaching* (Oxford Architectural Society, 1845), *Ecclesiologist* v, N.S. ii (1846), 53–5

[Anon.,] 'Reply to Mr E.A. Freeman', *Ecclesiologist* v, N.S. ii (1846), 217–49

[Anon. review,] J.L. Petit, *Remarks on Architectural Character* (Oxford, 1846), *Ecclesiologist* vi, N.S. iii (1846), 126–33

'The Present State of Ecclesiological Science in England', *Ecclesiologist* vii, N.S. iv (1847), 85–91 [Oxford Architectural Society, 23 June 1846]

[With J.M. Neale,] 'Church Restoration', reviewing E.A. Freeman, *Principles of Church Restoration* (1846), *Ecclesiologist* vii, N.S. iv (1847), 161–8

[Discussion,] Church Restoration, *Ecclesiologist* vii, N.S. iv (1847), 237–8 [Ecclesiological Society]

[Anon.,] 'On the Restoration of Churches', *Ecclesiologist* viii, N.S. v (1848), 83–5

[Anon.,] 'Ecclesiological Movement in Scotland', *Ecclesiologist* viii, N.S. v (1848), 137–40

[Anon.,] St George's, Lambeth [Southwark Cathedral], *Ecclesiologist* ix, N.S. vi (1848), 151–64

[Anon. review,] E.A. Freeman, *Remarks on the Architecture of Llandaff Cathedral* (1850), *Ecclesiologist* xii, N.S. ix (1851), 106–10

[Anon. review,] *The Address of the Irish Ecclesiological Society* (Dublin, 1849), *Ecclesiologist* x, N.S. vii (1850), 322–3

[Anon review,] A. W. Pugin, *Some Remarks on the Articles which have recently appeared in The Rambler* (1850), *Ecclesiologist* x, N.S. vii (1850), 393–9

[As 'D.C.L.',] *Letters on Church Matters*, 3 vols (1851) [Reprinted from the *Morning Chronicle*]

[Anon.], 'Oratorianism and Ecclesiology', *Christian Remembrancer* xxi (1851), 141–65 [reprinted in Hope, *Worship and Order*, 1883]

[Anon. review,] A.W. Pugin, *A Treatise on Chancel Screens and Rood-lofts* (1851), *Ecclesiologist* xii, N.S. ix (1851), 205–11

[Anon. review,] E.A. Freeman, *A History of Architecture* (1849), *Ecclesiologist* xii, N.S. ix (1851), 377–8

'L'Art Religieux en Angleterre' [London Churches], *Annales Archéologiques* xiii (Paris, 1853), 332–5

Appendix

[Anon. obit.,] 'The Death of Mr A.W. Pugin', *Ecclesiologist* xiii, N.S. x (1852), 353–7 [reprinted, with additions, from the *Morning Chronicle* 1852]
[As 'A Committeeman',] 'Moveable Benches or Chairs?', *Ecclesiologist* xv, N.S. xii (1854), 89–93, 250–5
[Anon.,] 'The Completion of the Palace of Westminster', *Saturday Review* i (1855), 7
[Anon.,] 'The Rebuilding of the Public Offices', *Saturday Review* i (1855), 48–9
[Anon.,] 'A Public Works Department Wanted', *Saturday Review* i (1855), 64–5
[Anon. obit.,] 'The Late Mr Carpenter', *Ecclesiologist* xvi, N.S. xiii (1855), 138–41; *Builder* xiii(1855), 165
[Anon.,] 'The London of the Future', *Saturday Review* i (1855), 132–3
[Anon.,] 'The Architectural Diploma', *Saturday Review* i (1856), 171–2
[Anon.,] 'The Architectural Exhibition', *Saturday Review* i (1856), 208–10
[Anon.,] 'A Revolution in a Corner', *Saturday Review* i (1856), 210
[Anon.,] 'A Commissioner of Public Works Painted by Himself', *Saturday Review* i (1856), 230–1
[Anon.,] 'Fergusson's Handbook of Architecture', *Saturday Review* i (1856), 234–6
[Anon.,] 'London and Paris Improvements', *Saturday Review* i (1856), 295–6, 366
[Anon.,] 'The Public Offices and St James's Park', *Saturday Review* i (1856), 412–13
[Anon.,] 'Public Offices by European Competition', *Saturday Review* i (1856), 473–4
[Anon.,] 'The Proposed Cathedral at Lille and European Competition', *Saturday Review* i (1856), 494–5
[Anon.,] 'The Architectural Museum and its Prizes for Workmen', *Saturday Review* i (1856), 496
[Anon.,] 'The Memorial Church at Constantinople', *Saturday Review* ii (1856), 11
[Anon. review,] G.E. Street, *Brick and Marble in the Middle Ages: Notes on a Tour in the North of Italy* (1855), *Saturday Review* ii (1856), 68–9
[Anon.,] 'Parks and Galleries', *Saturday Review* ii (1856), 151–2,
[Anon.,] 'The Lille Cathedral Job', *Saturday Review* ii (1856), 152
[Anon.,] 'Architecture at the Royal Academy', *Saturday Review* ii (1856), 172–3
[Anon.,] 'The Palace of Administration and the Westminster Bridge', *Saturday Review* ii (1856), 295–6
[Anon.,] 'Public Offices by Universal Competition', *Saturday Review* ii (1856), 416
[Anon.,] 'Shall We Save London', *Saturday Review* ii (1856), 500–1
[Anon.,] 'The Metropolitan Board of Talk', *Saturday Review* ii (1856), 542–4
[Anon.,] 'President Thwaites or Minister of Works', *Saturday Review* ii (1856), 637–8
Public Offices and Metropolitan Improvements (1857; 3rd edn 1857)
The Expense of the Government and of Mr Beresford Hope's Plan of public offices compared (1857)
[Anon.,] 'Memorial Church at Constantinople', *Saturday Review* iii (1857), 217–20, 330–1
[Anon.,] 'Public Office Competition', *Saturday Review* iii (1857), 427

[Anon.,] 'The Judges of the Public Offices' Competition', *Saturday Review* iii (1857), 451

[Anon.,] 'The Competition for the Public Offices', *Saturday Review* iii (1857), 474–5, 496–7

[Anon.,] 'Parks, Palaces and Picture Galleries', *Saturday Review* iii (1857), 593

[Anon.,] 'The Wellington Monument Exhibition', *Saturday Review* iv (1857), 80

[Anon.,] 'The Prizes for the Public Offices', *Saturday Review* iv (1857), 105

'The Wellington Monument and the Report of the Judges', *Saturday Review* iv (1857), 177

The Common Sense of Art (1858) [Architectural Museum; reported in *Civil Engineer and Architect's Journal* xxii, 1859, 50–3]

[Anon.,] 'Architectural Exhibition', *Saturday Review* v (1858), 160–1

[Anon.,] 'The Treasury and the Public Works', *Saturday Review* v (1858), 314–15

[Anon.,] 'Architecture, 1858', *Saturday Review* v (1858), 560–1

[Anon.,] 'The decoration of St Paul's and the Wellington Monument', *Saturday Review* v (1858), 661.

[Anon.,] 'The Memorial Church at Constantinople', *Saturday Review* vi (1858), 208

[Anon.,] 'The Department of Works', *Saturday Review* vi (1858), 586

[Anon.,] 'Progress at Oxford', *Ecclesiologist* xix, N.S. xvi (1858), 241–4

[Letter,] 'Agricultural Cottages', *The Times,* 13 Dec. 1858, 10

[Speech,] 'Model Barracks and Public Offices', *Hansard's Parliamentary Debates* cxlix (1858), 781–2

Address, Ecclesiological Society, *Ecclesiologist* xx, N.S. xvii (1859), 267–9; reprinted in *Builder* xvii (1859), 427–8

Address, Architectural Museum, *Builder* xvii (1859), 468–9

[Anon.,] 'The Architectural Exhibitions', *Saturday Review* vii (1859), 778–9

[Anon.,] 'Palmerston on Art', *Saturday Review* viii (1859), 189–90

[Anon.,] 'The Classicists on the Foreign Office', *Saturday Review* viii (1859), 253–4

[Anon.,] 'Mr Tite on Architecture', *Saturday Review* viii (1859), 609–10

The Church Cause and the Church Party (1860); reprinted from *Christian Remembrancer* xxxix (1860), 80–134

[Anon. obit.,] 'Sir Charles Barry', *Saturday Review* ix (1860), 637–8; reprinted in *Ecclesiologist* xxi, N.S. xviii (1860), 166–8

[Anon.,] [?] 'J.R. on Political Economy' and 'Mr Ruskin Again', *Saturday Review* x (1860), 136–8, 582–4

'Preraffaellitism, and . . . the Gothic Movement', *Ecclesiologist* xxi, N.S. xviii (1860), 237, 246–9, 251 [Ecclesiological Society]

[Anon.,] 'Progress in Oxford', *Ecclesiologist* xxii, N.S. xix (1861), 22–6

[Anon.,] 'Merton College, and Mr Butterfield', *Ecclesiologist* xxii, N.S. xix (1861), 218–21

[Letter to RIBA,] 'Church Restoration in France', *Ecclesiologist* xxii, N.S. xix (1861), 185–6

[Address, Ecclesiological Society,] 'Church Restoration in France', *Ecclesiologist* xxii, N.S. xix (1861), 250–1, 261–3

Appendix

The English Cathedral of the Nineteenth Century (1861) [Cambridge Architectural Society: abstract in *Ecclesiologist* xxi, N.S. xviii, 1860, 219–20]

[Anon.,] '*The Times* on "Gothic" and "Classic"', *Saturday Review* xi (1861), 159–60

[Anon.,] 'The New Exhibition Buildings', *Saturday Review* xi (1861), 340–1

[Anon.,] 'Architecture and the Exhibition of 1862', *Saturday Review* xi (1861), 474–5

[Anon.,] 'The Metropolitan Parliament', *Saturday Review* xii (1861), 345–6

'Architectural Notes on St Augustine's College, Canterbury', *Archaeologia Cantiana* iv (1861), 57–66

'International Exhibition, South Kensington', *Ecclesiologist* xxiii, N.S. xx (1862), 220, 228–34 [Ecclesiological Society]

[Anon.,] 'Two Years of Church Progress', *Christian Remembrancer* xliii (1862), 222–45

[Anon.,] 'The Exhibition Buildings', *Saturday Review* xiii (1862), 98–9, 472

[Anon.,] 'A Minister of Public Works', *Saturday Review* xiii (1862), 326–7

[Anon.,] 'The Brompton Exhibition', *Saturday Review* xiii (1862), 588–9

[Anon.,] 'The Board of Works', *Saturday Review* xiii (1862), 740–1

[Anon.,] 'The Board of Works', *Saturday Review* xiv (1862), 537–8

[Anon. review,] The International Exhibition, 1862; J. Hollingshead, *History of the International Exhibition* (1862), *Quarterly Review* cxii (1862), 174–219

'Ceramic Art in Architecture', *Builder* xxi (1863), 185; *Ecclesiologist* xxiv, N.S. xxi (1863), 135–6 [Wedgwood Memorial Institute]

'St John's Chapel, Tower of London', *Ecclesiologist* xxiv, N.S. xxi (1863), 224–5 [Ecclesiological Society]

The Condition and Prospects of Architectural Art (1863) [Architectural Museum; reported in *Gentleman's Magazine* cxxxiii, I, N.S. xiv, 1863, 600–6 and *Builder* xxi, 1863, 219–20]

'Notes on the College of St Augustine, Canterbury', *Gentleman's Magazine* cxxxiii, I, N.S. xiv (1863), 684–5

The World's Debt to Art (1863) [Town Hall, Hanley: Albert Memorial Fund]

[Evidence,] Commission to Inquire into the Royal Academy (1863–4), reported in *Ecclesiologist* xxv, N.S. xxii (1864), 242–4: 8 May 1863

[Anon.,] 'The Future of the Exhibition Buildings', *Saturday Review* xv (1863), 81–2

[Anon.,] 'Brompton Revisited', *Saturday Review* xv (1863), 623–4

[Anon. review,] J. Fergusson, *History of the Modern Styles of Architecture* (1862), *Saturday Review* xv (1863), 667–8

[Anon.,] 'The Exhibition Buildings', *Saturday Review* xv (1863), 712–13, 743–4, 777–8

[Anon.,] 'The Architectural Exhibitions of 1863', *Saturday Review* xv (1863), 792–3

[Anon.,] 'South Kensington Museum and loan exhibition', *Quarterly Review* cxiii (1863), 176–207

[Anon.,] 'The Doom of the Dish Covers', *Saturday Review* xvi (1863), 2–3

[Anon.,] 'The Board of Works', *Saturday Review* xvi (1863), 44–5

[Anon. review,] S. Huggins, *The Course and Current of Architecture* (1863), *Saturday Review* xvi (1863), 532–3

'The Skyline in Modern Domestic Buildings', *RIBA Papers* xiv (1863–4), 103–15

[Anon.,] 'A Satisfactory New Church in Holland', *Ecclesiologist* xxv, N.S. xxii (1864), 85–8

'Town Churches', etc., *Ecclesiologist* xxv, N.S. xxi (1864), 209, 218, 221, 222, 223–6

'The Architectural Museum' [letter to the Department of Science and Art], *Ecclesiologist* xxv, N.S. xxii (1864), 112–14

The Art Workman's Position (1864) [Architectural Museum; South Kensington Museum]

Church Politics and Church Prospects (1865); reprinted from *Christian Remembrancer*, Jan. 1865.

[As 'A Committeeman',] 'Town Churches', *Ecclesiologist* xxvi, N.S. xxiii (1865), 289–90

Presidential Address, RIBA, 1865, *Builder* xxiii (1865), 795–8; *Ecclesiologist* xxvi, N.S. xxiii (1865), 354–61

[Obit.], 'Dr Whewell', *Ecclesiologist* xxvii, N.S. xxiv (1866), 115–16 [RIBA]

Presidential Address, RIBA, 1866, *Builder* xxiv (1866), 829–31; *RIBA Reports* 1866–7, 1–15; *Ecclesiologist* xxvii, N.S. xxiv (1866), 371–4

'Prize-giving Address, Architectural Museum', *Ecclesiologist* xxvii, N.S. xxiv (1866), 150–5

[Anon.,] 'Government and Art', *Saturday Review* xxi (1866), 409–10

Presidential Address, RIBA, 1867, *Builder* xxv (1867), 334.

'On Mr Cowper's Motion for the Appointment of a Royal Commission on the National Art Collections', *Hansard's Parliamentary Debates* clxxxix, 1 Aug. 1867; *Ecclesiologist* xxviii, N.S. xxv (1867), 345–8

'On Cathedrals and their Arrangements', *Ecclesiologist* xxix, N.S. xxvi (1868), 119–22 [Worcester Architectural Society]

[Anon. review,] J. Ruskin, *Time and Tide, by Weare and Tyne* (1867), *Saturday Review* xxv (1868), 354–5.

[Anon.,] 'Mr Disraeli and the Ritualists', *Saturday Review* xxv (1868), 513–14

[Anon.,] 'The Style and Site of the Law Courts', *Saturday Review* xxv (1868), 751–2

'The Completion of St Paul's', *Saturday Review* xxxiii (1872), 335–6

'Cathedrals in their Missionary Aspect', in J.S. Howson, ed., *Essays on Cathedrals* (1872), 75–105

[Letter,] 'St Paul's Cathedral', *The Times*, 12 March 1872, 11

Hints towards Peace in Ceremonial Matters (1874)

[Speech,] 'The Established Church', *The Times*, 21 Nov. 1874, 7

'The Adaptation of the Fabrics and Services of the Church to the Wants of the Times', *The Architect* xii (1874), 203–6 [Church Congress, Brighton]

[Letter,] 'The Artistic Completion of St Paul's', *The Times*, 1 Dec.1874, 10

'The Completion of St Paul's', *Saturday Review* xxxvii (1874), 586–7

Worship in the Church of England (1874; 1875)

'The Queen Anne Craze', *Saturday Review* xl (1875), 142–3

[Anon.,] 'Keble College Chapel', *Saturday Review* xli (1876), 546–7

[Speech,] 'Fine Arts', *Hansard's Parliamentary Debates*, 3rd ser. ccxxix, 291–4: 9 May 1876

[Anon.,] 'Another South Kensington Bubble', *Saturday Review* xliii (1877), 385–6
[Anon.,] 'Architecture at the Royal Academy', *Saturday Review* xliv (1877), 17–18
[Anon. obit.,] 'Sir Gilbert Scott', *Saturday Review* xlv (1878), 427–9
[Anon.,] 'Architecture at the Royal Academy', *Saturday Review* xlv (1878), 823–5
[Anon.,] 'The Decoration of St Paul's', *Saturday Review* xlvi (1878), 140–1
[Speech,] 'Ritualism', *Hansard's Parliamentary Debates*, 3rd ser. ccxli, 927: 5 July 1878
[Inaugural address, St Paul's Ecclesiological Society,] 'Ecclesiology', *The Architect* xxi (1879), 201–2; *Transactions of the St Paul's Ecclesiological Society* i (1881–5), i-iii
[Anon.,] 'Architecture in 1880', *Saturday Review* l (1880), 18–19
[Anon. review,] R.P. Pullan, *Elementary Lectures on Christian Architecture* (1879), *Saturday Review* l (1880), 371–2
[Anon. review,] J.J. Stevenson, *House Architecture*, 2 vols (1880), *Saturday Review* l (1880), 557–8
[Anon. obit.,] 'Mr Burges', *Saturday Review* li (1881), 554–5
[Anon.,] 'Architecture in 1881', *Saturday Review* li (1881), 816
[Anon. obit.,] 'Mr Street', *Saturday Review* lii (1881), 782–4
[Anon.,] 'Architecture in 1882', *Saturday Review* liii (1882), 800–1
Worship and Order (1883)
[Anon., obit.,] George Edmund Street, *RIBA Transactions* 1883–4, 199–203
[Anon.,] 'Architecture in 1883', *Saturday Review* lvi (1883), 18
'English Architecture Thirty Years Hence' [reply to R. Kerr], *RIBA Transactions* 1883–4, 231–3; *Builder* xlvi (1884), 713
[Anon.,] 'Architecture in 1884', *Saturday Review* lvii (1884), 813–14.
'The Strength and Weakness of Art', *Building News* xlvii (1884), 491, 496–9; *The Architect* xxxii (1884), 209 [Social Science Congress, Birmingham, 20 Sept. 1884]
[Anon.,] 'Architecture in 1885', *Saturday Review* lix (1885), 855–6
[Anon. obit.,] 'The Rev. Benjamin Webb', *The Guardian* lx (1885), 772; reprinted in *Church Quarterly Review* xxi (1885–6), 461–4
[Anon. obit.,] 'The Rev. Benjamin Webb', *Saturday Review* lx (1885), 772
'Whewell as a Writer on Architecture', *The Architect* xxxiii (1885), 264
[Speech,] 'Admiralty and War Office Buildings', *Hansard's Parliamentary Debates*, 3rd ser. ccxcvi, 1170: 9 April 1885
[Discussion,] 'Architectural Restoration', *Builder* xxxv (1887), 550–1; *Athenaeum* no. 3131 (1887), 571 [RIBA]

4. Coventry Patmore

[Anon.,] 'The Philosophical and Aesthetic Letters and Essays of Schiller', *Douglas Jerrold's Shilling Magazine* ii (September 1845), 277–9
[Anon.,] '*Modern Painters*, vol. ii', *Douglas Jerrold's Shilling Magazine* iv (July 1846), 11–16
[Anon.,] 'Lord Lindsay's *Sketches of Christian Art*', *The Critic* N.S. v (March 1847), 177–80
[Anon.,] 'Aesthetics of Gothic Architecture', *British Quarterly Review* x (August 1849), 46–75

[Anon.,] 'Ethics of Art', *British Quarterly Review* x (November 1849), 441–62

[Anon,] 'Ruskin's *Seven Lamps of Architecture*', *North British Review* xii (February 1850), 309–53

[Anon.,] 'British Museum Commission', *Edinburgh Review* xcii (October 1850), 371–98

[Anon.,] 'Ruskin's *Stones of Venice*, vol. i', *British Quarterly Review* xiii (May 1851), 476–96

[Anon.,] 'Character in architecture', *North British Review* xv (August 1851), 461–96

[Anon.,] 'Sources of Expression in Architecture', *Edinburgh Review* xciv (October 1851), 365–403

[Anon.,] 'Athenian Architecture', *Edinburgh Review* xcv (April 1852), 395–405

[Anon.,] 'Architects and Architecture', *Fraser's Magazine* xlvi (December 1852), 653–9

[Anon.,] 'Ruskin and Architecture', *North British Review* xxi (May 1854), 172–200

[Anon.,] 'Ruskin's Lectures on Architecture and Painting', *The Critic* N.S. xiii (June 1854), 283–9

[Anon.,] 'London Street Architecture', *National Review* v (July 1857), 42–72

[Anon.,] 'A Pre-Raphaelite Exhibition', *Saturday Review* iv (4 July 1857), 11–12

[Anon.,] 'Walls and Wall Paintings at Oxford', *Saturday Review* iv (26 December 1857), 583–4

[Anon.,] '*Remarks on Secular and Domestic Architecture*, by G.G. Scott', *Literary Gazette* (9 January 1858), 32–4

[Anon.,] '*On Beauty: Three Discourses*, by J.S. Blackie', *Literary Gazette* (20 March 1858), 274–5

[Anon.,] 'Gothic Architecture: Present and Future', *North British Review* xxviii (May 1858), 346–75

[Anon.,] 'Library of the British Museum', *Edinburgh Review* cix (January 1859), 201–26.

[Anon.,] 'The Gothic Revival', *Pall Mall Gazette* (14 March 1872)

[Anon.,] 'The Point of Rest in Art', *St James's Gazette* (5 March 1886) [reprinted in *Principle in Art*, 1889, 37–42]

[Anon.,] 'Goethe', *St James's Gazette* (20 March 1886) [reprinted in *Courage in Politics*, 1921, 74–9]

[Anon.,] 'Hegel', *St James's Gazette* (22 March 1886) [reprinted in *Courage in Politics*, 1921, 105–9]

[Anon.,] 'Architecture and Architectural Criticism', *St James's Gazette* (30 April 1886) [reprinted in *Courage in Politics*, 1921, 178–83]

[Anon.,] 'Old English Architecture, Ancient and Modern', *St James's Gazette* (12 October 1886) [reprinted in *Principle in Art*, 1889, 154–9]

[Anon.,] 'Ideal and Material Greatness in Architecture', *St James's Gazette* (16 October 1886) [reprinted in *Principle in Art*, 1889, 146–53]

[Anon.,] 'Expression in Architecture', *St James's Gazette* (30 October 1886) [reprinted in *Courage in Politics*, 1921, 174–8]

[Anon.,] 'Architectural Styles', *St James's Gazette* (26 Nov. 1886; 18 Dec. 1886) [reprinted in *Principle in Art*, 1889, 160–201]

Appendix

[Anon.,] 'Liverpool Cathedral', *St James's Gazette* (3 March 1887) [reprinted in *Courage in Politics*, 1921, 183–91]

[Anon.,] 'Churches and Preaching-Halls', *St James's Gazette* (10 March 1887) [reprinted in *Courage in Politics*, 1921, 189–93]

[Anon.,] 'Coleridge', *St James's Gazette* (13 March 1886; 16 March, 13 June, 6 December 1887)

[Anon.,] 'Japanese Houses', *St James's Gazette* (13 April 1887) [reprinted in *Courage in Politics*, 1921, 194–9]

[Anon.,] 'Principle in Art', *St James's Gazette* (20 July 1887) [reprinted in *Principle in Art*, 1889, 1–5]

[Anon.,] 'Real Apprehension', *St James's Gazette* (20 January 1888) [reprinted in *Principle in Art*, 1889, 6–13 and *Religio Poetae*, 1898, 77–84]

[Anon.,] 'Imagination', *St James's Gazette* (18 February 1888) [reprinted in *Principle in Art*, 1889, 43–8 and *Religio Poetae*, 1898, 102–7]

Principle in Art (1889; 1890; 1898; 1913; reprint, 1969)

[Anon.,] 'Distinction', *Fortnightly Review* (June 1890) [reprinted in *Principle in Art*, 2nd edn 1898, 54–74]

[Anon.,] 'Impressionist Art', *Anti-Jacobin* (31 January 1891) [reprinted as 'Emotional Art' in *Religio Poetae*, 1st edn 1893, 85–91]

[Anon.,] 'Bad Morality is Bad Art', *Anti-Jacobin* (7 February 1891) [reprinted in *Religio Poetae*, 1st edn 1893, 79–84]

[Anon.,] 'Simplicity', *Anti-Jacobin* (18 April 1891) [reprinted in *Religio Poetae*, 1st edn 1893, 64–7]

[Anon.,] 'Peace in Life and Art', *Merry England* (September 1892) [reprinted in *Religio Poetae*, 1st edn 1893, 92–7]

Religio Poetae (1893; 1898; 1913)

The Rod, the Root and the Flower (1895; ed. D. Patmore, 1950; reprint New York, 1968)

Courage in Politics and Other Essays, 1885–96, ed. F. Page (Oxford, 1921; reprint New York, 1968)

The Bow Set in the Cloud: Selected Writings of Coventry Patmore, ed. A. Matthew (Fisher Press, 1999)

Note

Preliminary versions of these four studies were delivered as lectures at Norwich Cathedral, at Keble College Oxford, and at four venues in London: the Society of Antiquaries, the Architectural Association, the Art Workers' Guild and the British Academy. Much of Chapter 1 originally appeared in *The Study of the Past in the Victorian Age*, ed. V. Brand (British Archaeological Association and Royal Archaeological Institute, 1998), 77–92. A fuller but unrevised version of the appendix to Chapter 2 appeared in *Studies in Church History*, xxxiii (Ecclesiastical History Society, 1997), 423–57. Parts of Chapter 3 appeared, without appendix, in *Architectural Design* liii (1983), 56–62. Earlier versions of Chapter 4 appeared in *Proceedings of the British Academy* lxxvi (1990), 171–201; *Victorian Poetry* xxxiv (West Virginia U., 1996), 519–43; and *Prince Albert Studies* xv (Munich, 1998), 145–68.

Index

Index

Index

Index